"In what amounts to a carefully guided tour of biblical theology for the church, Gladd and Harmon offer a biblically thick description of Scripture's redemptive narrative. Writing in careful scholarly detail yet in an accessible manner that never loses sight of the big picture, Gladd and Harmon exhort the church and its pastoral leadership to be the end-time people of God, encouraging them to recognize their place within Scripture's redemptive storyline. A very helpful combination of scholarly precision and pastoral sensitivity."

—**Darian Lockett**, Talbot School of Theology, Biola University

"*Making All Things New* is a clear and helpful guide that will enable all Christians to understand why inaugurated eschatology is not just something for the seminary classroom but a doctrine to be lived out and rejoiced in. Gladd and Harmon have done us a great service by demonstrating in a compelling way why eschatology matters in the life of the church. Anyone who is serious about understanding one of the most important aspects of the New Testament ought to read and apply this book."

—**Chris Bruno**, author of *The Whole Story of the Bible in 16 Verses*

"Gladd and Harmon apply to pastoral ministry the inaugurated eschatology they learned from Greg Beale. The book repeatedly moves from sound exegesis to theology to application."

—**Andy Naselli**, Bethlehem College and Seminary, Minneapolis

"What a marvelous book! Gladd and Harmon team up to explore the interface between inaugurated eschatology and pastoral ministry. This book will serve as an excellent resource not only for those training for ministry but for those slogging it out in ministry and looking to reinvigorate their understanding of ministry as an end-time event among God's people. Gladd and Harmon have achieved the rare feat of writing a book that is both substantive and useful, insightful and practical, scholarly and churchly—a model of what I would call 'ecclesial theology.' I recommend it highly!"

—**Todd Wilson**, senior pastor, Calvary Memorial Church

MAKING
ALL THINGS NEW

MAKING
ALL THINGS NEW

Inaugurated Eschatology *for the* Life of the Church

BENJAMIN L. GLADD AND MATTHEW S. HARMON

With an Introductory Chapter by G. K. BEALE

Baker Academic

a division of Baker Publishing Group
Grand Rapids, Michigan

Published by Baker Academic
a division of Baker Publishing Group
P.O. Box 6287, Grand Rapids, MI 49516-6287
www.bakeracademic.com

Printed in the United States of America

Library of Congress Cataloging-in-Publication Data
Names: Gladd, Benjamin L.
Title: Making all things new : inaugurated eschatology for the life of the church / Benjamin L.
    Gladd and Matthew S. Harmon ; with an introductory chapter by G. K. Beale.
Description: Grand Rapids, MI : Baker Academic, 2016. | Includes index.
Identifiers: LCCN 2015037626 | ISBN 9780801049606 (pbk.)
Subjects: LCSH: Eschatology. | Eschatology—Biblical teaching. | Pastoral theology. | Christian
    leadership. | Church. | Kingdom of God. | Jesus Christ—Kingdom.
Classification: LCC BT821.3 .G54 2016 | DDC 236—dc23
LC record available at http://lccn.loc.gov/2015037626

16   17   18   19   20   21   22   7   6   5   4   3   2   1

To our students
—past, present, and future—
who are called to lead God's people
in the latter days

Contents

Preface

This is not your ordinary book on eschatology. Usually when people hear that term, they think of the events connected to the future return of Jesus Christ and the very end of history. As a result, topics such as the rapture, the tribulation, and the millennium take center stage. Such an approach is often reinforced by systematic theology textbooks, which usually treat eschatology as a separate chapter focusing on these issues. But we believe that this understanding of eschatology is too narrow when it comes to what the Bible teaches.

Our English term "eschatology" comes from two Greek words: *eschatos* ("last") and *logos* ("word"). So, eschatology is the study of the "last things." But as we will try to demonstrate, eschatology is not limited to the events connected to the return of Jesus Christ. According to the NT, the life, ministry, death, resurrection, and ascension of Jesus have ushered in the "latter days," as promised in the OT. Therefore, the "latter days" encompass the entire time period between the first and second comings of Christ. As a result, eschatology is not limited to the "last chapter" of what God will do in this world but rather frames all that God has done and will do in Jesus Christ.

Among biblical scholars and theologians this understanding has come to be known as "inaugurated eschatology." The word "inaugurated" reflects the observation that while the latter-day new-creational kingdom has begun with the work of Jesus, it has not yet been consummated in all its fullness. Another way of referring to this phenomenon is to use the expression "already–not yet." God's kingdom has already found its initial fulfillment in and through Jesus Christ, the outpouring of the Spirit, and the formation of the eschatological people of God. But the kingdom has not yet been realized in all its fullness. Stated differently, God's promises have found their initial fulfillment while still awaiting their complete and final consummation.

This understanding of eschatology has been widely recognized and embraced within the academic study of the NT, but it has yet to make a significant and widespread impact on the life of the church. In the pages that follow, we attempt to explain how the already–not yet framework informs our understanding of the life and ministry of the church. While we believe that all Christians can benefit from this book, our focus is on pastors and those aspiring to be in the pastorate. As leaders of the church, they set the tone for how the congregation should live as the people of God. We have not tried to provide a complete picture of pastoral ministry or interact with the many helpful books on the subject. Instead, our goal is to explain how understanding and applying the already–not yet perspective significantly enriches several key aspects of the life and ministry of the church. It is not our intention to provide all the answers (not that we have them!) but to start a conversation about how inaugurated eschatology enhances pastoral ministry.

This project builds on the work of several scholars who have gone before and sketched the already–not yet framework of the NT. We are not seeking to lay this foundation again but to build on it. We will therefore interact only with those portions of Scripture that we deem relevant to the topic at hand. In order to make this project more accessible to the church, particularly its leaders, we have limited our interaction with secondary sources (commentaries, monographs, journals, etc.).

While a number of scholars have done important work in the area of inaugurated eschatology, few have so thoroughly integrated it into their approach to biblical theology and interpretation as G. K. Beale. Every page from his prolific pen flows out of this conviction.[1] Both of us had the privilege of studying under Dr. Beale while earning our doctoral degrees at Wheaton College. Ben wrote his dissertation under Beale's supervision, while Matt frequently consulted with Dr. Beale on his own dissertation. Not only were Beale's passion for the Lord and his knowledge of the Scriptures infectious, but also his explanation of the already–not yet nature of God's new-creational kingdom

1. Beale's work in this area has come to full fruition with the publication of the following: G. K. Beale, "The Eschatological Conception of New Testament Theology," in *"The Reader Must Understand": Eschatology in the Bible and Theology*, ed. K. E. Brower and M. W. Elliott (Leicester, UK: Apollos, 1997), 11–52; G. K. Beale, *The Temple and the Church's Mission: A Biblical Theology of the Dwelling Place of God*, NSBT 17 (Downers Grove, IL: InterVarsity, 2004); G. K. Beale and D. A. Carson, eds., *Commentary on the New Testament Use of the Old Testament* (Grand Rapids: Baker Academic, 2007); G. K. Beale, *We Become What We Worship: A Biblical Theology of Idolatry* (Downers Grove, IL: InterVarsity, 2008); G. K. Beale, *A New Testament Biblical Theology: The Unfolding of the Old Testament in the New* (Grand Rapids: Baker Academic, 2011); G. K. Beale, *Handbook on the New Testament Use of the Old Testament: Exegesis and Interpretation* (Grand Rapids: Baker Academic, 2012).

was compelling. Therefore, in many respects this book is an extension of Beale's project, an attempt to flesh out in practical terms how inaugurated eschatology should shape pastoral ministry and the life of the church. Thus we are especially grateful that Dr. Beale agreed to set the stage for this book by writing chapter 1, which summarizes his understanding of the already–not yet viewpoint.

Of course, whenever the subject of eschatology comes up, division is usually not far behind. Debates between dispensationalism and covenant theology show no sign of ending anytime soon, although the past thirty years have seen an increasing number of scholars searching for a middle ground.[2] As authors, we come from different ends of this spectrum: Matt teaches at a dispensational school (Grace Theological Seminary), and Ben teaches at a covenantal school (Reformed Theological Seminary). So naturally we still differ on how specific details will work themselves out![3] But we are convinced that the perspective on eschatology that we are arguing for in this book is able to transcend the traditional divide between dispensationalism and covenantalism and to provide not only a framework for understanding the NT but also a foundation for the life and ministry of the church.[4]

A word about how to read this book: part 1 lays the theological foundation for the project. The lead chapter by G. K. Beale ("The End Starts at the Beginning") serves as the theological framework for the entire project; it is a thumbnail sketch of key portions of his *New Testament Biblical Theology*. We strongly recommend that those unfamiliar with Beale's book read his introduction to our project carefully. If more discussion is desired, please consult his larger work. Chapter 2 focuses on the corporate nature of the church as the end-time people of God, and chapter 3 describes how individual believers

2. From one end of the spectrum, this has led to what has come to be known as progressive dispensationalism; see, e.g., Darrell L. Bock, Walter C. Kaiser, and Craig A. Blaising, *Dispensationalism, Israel and the Church: The Search for Definition* (Grand Rapids: Zondervan, 1992); and Craig A. Blaising and Darrell L. Bock, *Progressive Dispensationalism* (Wheaton: BridgePoint, 1993; repr., Grand Rapids: Baker Books, 2000). From the other end, the result has been what is sometimes called new-covenant theology or progressive covenantalism; see, e.g., Peter J. Gentry and Stephen J. Wellum, *Kingdom through Covenant: A Biblical-Theological Understanding of the Covenants* (Wheaton: Crossway, 2012).

3. Although the book expresses our shared vision, and we interacted with each other in the writing of each chapter, the primary writing responsibilities were divided as follows: Matt wrote chaps. 2, 4, and 7–9, and Ben wrote chaps. 3, 5–6, and the conclusion.

4. It is true that inaugurated eschatology has traditionally been associated with covenant theology, but in a panel discussion of his book *A New Testament Biblical Theology* at the annual meeting of the Evangelical Theological Society (2012), Beale himself indicated that he believes the already–not yet framework of biblical theology can work within both progressive dispensationalism and the various forms of covenant theology. It is, however, difficult to see how it could fit within either classical or traditional dispensationalism.

live within the overlap of the ages. A good grasp of the contents of part 1 is essential for getting the most out of the remainder of the book.

Although the entire book is oriented toward pastors and those preparing for church ministry, part 2 is specifically focused on pastoral leadership. Because the ministry of the Word is central to pastoral ministry, chapter 4 centers on feeding God's people through preaching and teaching. Chapter 5 addresses guarding the flock from false teaching. Concluding part 2, chapter 6 focuses on guiding the eschatological people of God as they live in the tension of the already–not yet.

In part 3, we turn our attention to other key areas of the life of the church as the temple of God, specifically worship (chap. 7), prayer (chap. 8), and missions (chap. 9). The concluding chapter summarizes the main themes of the book and urges pastors to lead the church in embracing its identity as the end-time people of God.

As seminary professors, we have the privilege of training people for service in God's kingdom. We long for the day when God will consummate his kingdom in a new heavens and new earth, bringing final fulfillment to every single one of his promises. As we wait for that great day, we want to see the church experience all that God has already done for us through his Son, Jesus Christ. It is our prayer that God will use this book to explain what that looks like as we await the day when "the earth will be filled with the knowledge of the glory of the LORD as the waters cover the sea" (Hab. 2:14).

Benjamin L. Gladd
Matthew S. Harmon

Acknowledgments

This project is the fruit of countless conversations with friends, students, and pastors. I stand in their debt. I am also grateful for Reformed Theological Seminary, who graciously provided a grant to finish this book. Nikki, my wife, is a well of encouragement and grace. Above all, I thank Christ for equipping me and energizing me to complete this task.

> To the only God, our Savior, through Jesus Christ our Lord, be glory, majesty, dominion, and authority, before all time and now and forever. Amen. (Jude 25)
>
> BLG

A number of people have helped make this book a reality. Grace Theological Seminary granted me a reduced course load that enabled me to finish this project. A number of students, pastors, and colleagues read through parts or all of the manuscript and provided helpful feedback. I am especially grateful for my pastors at Christ's Covenant Church for striving to embody what this book teaches. My wife, Kate, and our two sons, Jon and Jake, are not only a source of great joy in my life, but they also enthusiastically embrace God's call on my life to help people see the beauty of Christ in Scripture and follow him faithfully. But most of all, I am grateful for God's eschatological Spirit opening my eyes to see the beauty of Jesus Christ, "who loved me and gave himself for me" (Gal 2:20).

> To him be the glory both now and to the day of eternity. Amen. (2 Pet. 3:18)
>
> MSH

Abbreviations

General and Bibliographic

AB	Anchor Bible
ABD	*Anchor Bible Dictionary*. Edited by David Noel Freedman. 6 vols. New York: Doubleday, 1992.
AD	anno Domini
AT	author's translation
BC	before Christ
BDAG	Danker, Frederick W., Walter Bauer, William F. Arndt, and F. Wilbur Gingrich. *A Greek-English Lexicon of the New Testament and Other Early Christian Literature*. 3rd ed. Chicago: University of Chicago Press, 2000.
BDB	Brown, Francis, S. R. Driver, and Charles A. Briggs. *A Hebrew and English Lexicon of the Old Testament*. Oxford: Clarendon, [1907].
BECNT	Baker Exegetical Commentary on the New Testament
Bib	*Biblica*
BZNW	Beihefte zur Zeitschrift für die neutestamentliche Wissenschaft
CahT	Cahiers Théologiques
CBQ	*Catholic Biblical Quarterly*
cf.	*confer*, compare
chap(s).	chapter(s)
DJG	*Dictionary of Jesus and the Gospels*. Edited by Joel B. Green, Scot McKnight, and I. Howard Marshall. Downers Grove, IL: InterVarsity, 1992.
DLNT	*Dictionary of the Later New Testament and Its Developments*. Edited by Ralph P. Martin and Peter H. Davids. Downers Grove, IL: InterVarsity, 1997.
DPL	*Dictionary of Paul and His Letters*. Edited by Gerald F. Hawthorne and Ralph P. Martin. Downers Grove, IL: InterVarsity, 1993.
ed.	editor(s); edited by; edition
e.g.	*exempli gratia*, for example
esp.	especially
ESV	English Standard Version

ET	English translation
EvQ	*Evangelical Quarterly*
exp.	expanded
Gk.	Greek
i.e.	*id est*, that is
Int	*Interpretation*
IVPNT	IVP New Testament Commentary Series
JBL	*Journal of Biblical Literature*
JETS	*Journal of the Evangelical Theological Society*
JSJSup	Supplements to the Journal for the Study of Judaism
JSNT	*Journal for the Study of the New Testament*
JSPL	*Journal for the Study of Paul and His Letters*
lit.	literally
LNTS	Library of New Testament Studies
LXX	Septuagint
marg.	marginal reading
NASB	New American Standard Bible
NCBC	New Century Bible Commentary
NETS	*A New English Translation of the Septuagint*. Edited by Albert Pietersma and Benjamin G. Wright. New York: Oxford University Press, 2007.
NICNT	New International Commentary on the New Testament
NICOT	New International Commentary on the Old Testament
NIGTC	New International Greek Testament Commentary
NIV	New International Version
NIVAC	NIV Application Commentary
NovT	*Novum Testamentum*
NovTSup	Novum Testamentum Supplement Series
NSBT	New Studies in Biblical Theology
NT	New Testament
NTS	*New Testament Studies*
NTT	New Testament Theology
OT	Old Testament
par(s).	parallel(s)
PNTC	Pillar New Testament Commentary
repr.	reprint
ResQ	*Restoration Quarterly*
SBT	Studies in Biblical Theology
SJTOP	Scottish Journal of Theology: Occasional Papers
SP	Sacra Pagina
TDNT	*Theological Dictionary of the New Testament*. Edited by Gerhard Kittel and Gerhard Friedrich. Translated by Geoffrey W. Bromiley. 10 vols. Grand Rapids: Eerdmans, 1964–76.
TDOT	*Theological Dictionary of the Old Testament*. Edited by G. Johannes Botterweck, Helmer Ringgren, and Heinz-Josef Fabry. Translated by John T. Willis et al. 15 vols. Grand Rapids: Eerdmans, 1974–2006.
TynBul	*Tyndale Bulletin*
WBC	Word Biblical Commentary

WTJ   *Westminster Theological Journal*
WUNT   Wissenschaftliche Untersuchungen zum Neuen Testament
ZECNT   Zondervan Exegetical Commentary on the New Testament

Old Testament

Gen.	Genesis	Song	Song of Songs
Exod.	Exodus	Isa.	Isaiah
Lev.	Leviticus	Jer.	Jeremiah
Num.	Numbers	Lam.	Lamentations
Deut.	Deuteronomy	Ezek.	Ezekiel
Josh.	Joshua	Dan.	Daniel
Judg.	Judges	Hosea	Hosea
Ruth	Ruth	Joel	Joel
1–2 Sam.	1–2 Samuel	Amos	Amos
1–2 Kings	1–2 Kings	Obad.	Obadiah
1–2 Chron.	1–2 Chronicles	Jon.	Jonah
Ezra	Ezra	Mic.	Micah
Neh.	Nehemiah	Nah.	Nahum
Esther	Esther	Hab.	Habakkuk
Job	Job	Zeph.	Zephaniah
Ps(s).	Psalm(s)	Hag.	Haggai
Prov.	Proverbs	Zech.	Zechariah
Eccles.	Ecclesiastes	Mal.	Malachi

New Testament

Matt.	Matthew	1–2 Thess.	1–2 Thessalonians
Mark	Mark	1–2 Tim.	1–2 Timothy
Luke	Luke	Titus	Titus
John	John	Philem.	Philemon
Acts	Acts	Heb.	Hebrews
Rom.	Romans	James	James
1–2 Cor.	1–2 Corinthians	1–2 Pet.	1–2 Peter
Gal.	Galatians	1–3 John	1–3 John
Eph.	Ephesians	Jude	Jude
Phil.	Philippians	Rev.	Revelation
Col.	Colossians		

Part 1

Theological Foundation

Grasping the Already–Not Yet

In the first part of this project, we articulate the theological framework for ministering within the NT's conception of the already–not yet. Professor Beale paints the general landscape of the already–not yet in chapter 1 ("The End Starts at the Beginning"), and chapters 2 and 3 develop his work on two levels. Chapter 2 ("The Nature of the End-Time Church") explains how the people of God span the two Testaments, with special emphasis on how the already–not yet informs our view of the identity of the church. Moving from the corporate to the individual, chapter 3 ("Life in the Overlap of the Ages") drills down into some of the specifics of living in the inauguration of the overlap of the ages.

For those wishing to read only select chapters of the book, we ask that you first become familiar with the theological foundation articulated in the first three chapters. These early chapters serve as the backbone of the project, and the remaining chapters assume a firm grasp of their content.

One of humanity's strongest desires is to determine identity. Who are we? The Bible addresses the issue of identity by connecting it to the people of God, especially in the inauguration of the "latter days." Christian identity is forged within the furnace of eschatology, but identity produces action. As the end-time people of God in the inaugurated new creation, Christians are required to live in light of their identity and renewed existence.

1

The End Starts at the Beginning

G. K. BEALE

Theologians generally define "eschatology" as the study of "last things," an investigation and systematization of events that take place at the very end of history. This general definition is often understood on a popular level to mean that eschatology refers *only* to the future end of the world directly preceding Christ's final coming. This popular notion, which some scholars still hold to, needs radical adjustment. On a scholarly level, NT research over the past decades has made great strides in increasing our understanding that the beginning of Christian history was perceived by the first Christians as the *beginning* of the end times but not their *consummation*.[1] New Testament scholarship has still been atomistic enough to prevent serious broad theological reflection on the already–not yet eschatological[2] perspective of the entire NT corpus (though there are significant exceptions, such as N. T. Wright's work).

This chapter is adapted from "The Eschatological Conception of New Testament Theology," in *"The Reader Must Understand": Eschatology in the Bible and Theology*, ed. K. E. Brower and M. W. Elliott (Leicester, UK: Apollos, 1997), 11–52; and *A New Testament Biblical Theology: The Transformation of the Old Testament in the New* (Grand Rapids: Baker Academic, 2011).

1. For articles and relevant bibliography on the eschatology of the Gospels, Paul, and the remainder of the NT, see respectively Dale C. Allison Jr., "Eschatology," *DJG* 206–9; Larry J. Kreitzer, "Eschatology," *DPL* 253–69; G. K. Beale, "Eschatology," *DLNT* 330–45. See also David E. Aune, "Early Christian Eschatology," *ABD* 2:594–609.

2. I use the adjective "eschatological" to refer to events that were prophesied to occur in a discrete period known as the "latter days" (see below).

The apostles understood eschatology not merely as futurology but as a mind-set for understanding the present within the climaxing context of redemptive history. That is, the apostles understood that they were already living in the end times, and that they were to understand their present salvation in Christ to be already an end-time reality. William Manson has well said,

> When we turn to the New Testament, we pass from the climate of prediction to that of fulfillment. The things which God had foreshadowed by the lips of His holy prophets He has now, in part at least, brought to accomplishment. . . . The supreme sign of the Eschaton is the Resurrection of Jesus and the descent of the Holy Spirit on the Church. The Resurrection of Jesus is not simply a sign which God has granted in favour of His son, but is the inauguration, the entrance into history, *of the times of the End.*
>
> Christians, therefore, have entered through the Christ into the new age. . . . What had been predicted in Holy Scripture as to happen to Israel or to man in the Eschaton, has happened to and in Jesus. *The foundation-stone of the New Creation has come into position.*[3]

Every aspect of salvation was to be conceived of as eschatological in nature. To put this another way, the major doctrines of the Christian faith are charged with eschatological electricity. Just as when you put on green sunglasses, everything you see is green, so Christ through the Spirit had placed eschatological sunglasses on his disciples so that everything they looked at in the Christian faith had an end-time tint. This means that the doctrine of eschatology in textbooks should not merely be one among many doctrines that are addressed but should be the lens through which all the major doctrines are best understood. Furthermore, eschatology should not be placed at the end of NT theology textbooks or at the end of chapters dealing with the different NT corpora because it purportedly describes only the very end of the world as we know it. Rather, the doctrine of eschatology could be part of the title of such a textbook because every major theological concept breathes the air of a latter-day atmosphere. For the same reason, books on pastoral ministry must integrate eschatology into their discussions. It is important to say that our understanding of most of the traditional doctrines is not so much changed as radically enriched by seeing them through end-time lenses. For us to appreciate the NT understanding of eschatology, we must first discuss the basic story line of the OT and its conception of a discrete period of time known as the "latter days."

3. William Manson, "Eschatology in the New Testament," in *Eschatology: Four Papers Read to the Society for the Study of Theology*, SJTOP 2 (Edinburgh: Oliver & Boyd, 1953), 6, italics added. Although this sounds like "overrealized eschatology," Manson qualifies it by saying, "The End has come! The End has not come!" (ibid., 7).

The Basic Story Line of the Old Testament

Grasping the OT's view of the very end of history rests squarely on its basic plotline. That is, the events that are to occur at the end of history are deeply related to the OT's larger plotline. Succinctly, the story line of the OT is *the story of God, who progressively reestablishes his eschatological new-creational kingdom out of chaos over a sinful people by his word and Spirit through promise, covenant, and redemption, resulting in worldwide commission to the faithful to advance this kingdom and judgment (defeat or exile) for the unfaithful, unto his glory.*

Genesis 1–3 lays out the basic themes for the rest of the OT, which are essentially end-time or "eschatological" themes. We can speak of Genesis 1:28 as the first "Great Commission," which was repeatedly applied to humanity. The commission was to bless the earth, and part of the essence of this blessing was God's salvific presence. Before the fall, Adam and Eve were to produce progeny who would fill the earth with God's glory being reflected from each of them in the image of God (1:26–28). After the fall, a remnant, created by God in his restored image, was to go out and spread God's glorious presence among the rest of darkened humanity. This witness was to continue until the entire world would be filled with divine glory. Thus Israel's witness was reflective of its role as a corporate Adam, which highlights the notion of missions in the OT.[4]

Without exception, the reapplications of the Adamic commission are stated positively in terms of what Noah, the patriarchs, Israel, and eschatological Israel or its king should do or were promised to do. Always the expression is that of conquering the land, increasing and multiplying population, and filling the promised land and the earth with people who will reflect God's glory. Never is there a hint that this commission is to be carried out by what we might call a negative act—that is, by death. Of course, Isaiah 53, Daniel 9, and Zechariah 12 (and a handful of typological Davidic texts such as Ps. 22) prophesy the Messiah's death as crucial to achieving Israel's restoration, but these texts are the minority, and they are never directly associated with the repetitions of the Adamic commission. The Adamic expectations and promises of obedience for Israel's patriarchs, the nation, and its king are always stated in positive terms of what they are to do or are promised to do.

The main strands of this biblical story in the OT books are those of Israel (and its king) being commissioned to fulfill the Adamic commission to reign

4. For elaboration of this, see G. K. Beale, *The Temple and the Church's Mission: A Biblical Theology of the Dwelling Place of God*, NSBT 17 (Downers Grove, IL: InterVarsity, 2004).

over a renewed earth but repeatedly failing to do so (e.g., 1 Kings 4:30, 34; 8:1–6; 1 Chron. 29:10–12).[5] As a result of this failure, Israel suffers judgment and exile, and these patterns of renewal and failure become typological patterns of the true, final end-time rule in a new creation that will inevitably come (e.g., Isa. 51:1–3; 54:2–3; Jer. 3:16; Ezek. 36:10–12). Promises of future restoration in a new creation continue to be reiterated in the OT narratives.

One significant aspect of the biblical narrative beginning also in Genesis 1–3 is God's glorious tabernacling presence with his priestly people in a sanctuary as the goal of God's redemptive work. Adam was not only a king but also a priest in Eden, a primordial sanctuary of sorts (Gen. 2:15). Functioning as a priest in the Eden temple was essential to carrying out the commission of Genesis 1:26–28. The Adamic commission often is combined with the notion of priestly service in a temple when it is repeated to Noah, the patriarchs, Israel, and in the promises to end-time Israel.[6]

The major episodes of OT history were seen to be reiterations, to varying significant degrees, of the pattern of beginning kingship in a beginning new creation. These subsequent episodes in the OT appear to commence an end-time process that is never completed. In the postfall sinful cosmos, in contrast to prefall Eden, it seems more understandable that the beginning process of restoration from sin would be charged with notions of a commencement toward an end-time consummation. This is the case with Isaiah's prophecy of new creation, which is portrayed as a part of Israel's return from exile (though Isaiah portrays it as an apparently single event and not an extended new-creational process).[7] The prophecies of Israel's restoration from exile are said explicitly to take place "in the latter days" (Deut. 4:30; 31:29; Hosea 3:5; and possibly Jer. 23:20; 30:24, the latter especially in light of 31:1–40).

The "Latter Days" in the Old Testament

Now that we have outlined the basic story line of the OT, we will focus our attention on the final phase of that story line and sketch the OT conception of the "latter days." The phrase "latter days" occurs at points throughout the OT to refer to the culmination of history from the various writers' perspectives (e.g., Gen. 49:1; Num. 24:14; Deut. 4:30; 31:29; Hosea 3:5; Isa. 2:2; Jer. 23:20;

---

5. For a broad thumbnail sketch of this theme but from somewhat different angles than traced in this chapter, see T. Desmond Alexander, *From Eden to the New Jerusalem: An Introduction to Biblical Theology* (Grand Rapids: Kregel, 2008), 74–89.

6. On which see Beale, *Temple and the Church's Mission*, 93–121.

7. On which see Beale, *New Testament Biblical Theology*, 527–55.

Dan. 2:28–29, 45).[8] In other words, the "latter days" (and other synonymous expressions) are "eschatological" in that they represent a specific period of time that occurs at the very end of history. All the events that take place within this period, whether acts of judgment or restoration, are eschatological. Although earlier OT authors have more vague or "thicker" prophetic portraits of the latter days, all authors include reference to a future period that represents an irreversible radical break with a former period. I define these uses of "latter days" to be overtly eschatological because *all refer to a permanent and radical break with the preceding historical epoch.* A filling out of "the latter days" occurs as the OT writings develop and revelation progresses, like a seed germinating, sprouting, growing into a small plant, and then developing into a full plant.

The following conditions represent the conceptual thrust of the eschatological discontinuity between the two epochs.

1. After a final, unsurpassed, and incomparable period of tribulation for God's people instigated by an end-time opponent who deceives and persecutes, in the face of which they will need wisdom not to compromise, they are
2. delivered and
3. resurrected, and their kingdom is reestablished.
4. At this future time, God will rule on earth
5. through a coming Davidic king, who will defeat all opposition and reign in peace in a new creation over both
6. the nations and
7. restored Israel,
8. with whom God will make a new covenant, and
9. upon whom God will bestow the Spirit, and
10. among whom the temple will be rebuilt.

In various OT contexts these ten ideas compose the essential content of the expression "the latter days" (and its near equivalents in Daniel [10:14; 11:27; 12:1, 10, 13]). The notions of kingdom, king, and rule over nations are sometimes developed in connection with the fulfillment of the Adamic-patriarchal promises of blessing.

---

8. See John T. Willis, "The Expression *be'acharith hayyamim* in the Old Testament," *ResQ* 22 (1979): 54–71. Willis argues, unpersuasively in my view, that every use of "latter days" in the OT, Dead Sea Scrolls, and NT refers to mere indefinite future. This position is held by no one else whose work I have surveyed.

In this connection, Genesis 1–3 reveals the expectation that Adam should have reigned as a consummate eschatological priest-king in God's perfect image.[9] His failure to accomplish this end-time reign left open the necessity for another Adam figure to accomplish the first Adam's commission. Subsequent chapters of Genesis, and indeed of the OT, show repeated allusion to Genesis 1:28 and hope for such an eschatological figure. No significant fulfillment occurs, though. It had to await another who would come after the formal close of the OT period of expectation.[10]

The Basic Story Line of the Old Testament in Relation to the New Testament

With the basic story line of the OT in view, and particularly the time period known as the "latter days," we now turn to the NT's continuation of that same story. *All that the OT foresaw would occur in the end times has begun already in the first century and continues on until the final coming of Christ.*[11] This means that the OT end-time expectations of such things as the great tribulation, God's subjugation of the gentiles, deliverance of Israel from oppressors, Israel's restoration, Israel's resurrection, the new covenant, the promised Spirit, the new creation, the new temple, a messianic king, and the establishment of God's kingdom have been set in motion irreversibly by Christ's death and resurrection and the formation of the Christian church. Of course, other eschatological themes are present, but they tend to be subsets of the preceding ones listed.

This already–not yet eschatological concept may be pictured in the following manner:[12]

9. For the eschatological sense of Gen. 1–3, see Beale, *New Testament Biblical Theology*, 29–46.

10. Some scholars view the expression "in the latter days" as referring to the indefinite future. Others acknowledge this meaning in some cases, but also see, at times, an overt eschatological nuance to the phrase (e.g., BDB 31; H. Seebass, "אַחֲרִית *'achᵃrîth*," *TDOT* 1:207–12; Jack R. Lundbom, *Jeremiah 21–36*, AB 21B [New York: Doubleday, 2004], 197. Lundbom understands this to be the consensus among commentators). The focus of the expression "in the latter days" refers to a period at the end of history, but it also includes secondarily what we may call "protoeschatological" or apparent "semieschatological" events (e.g., tribulation, return from exile) that occur at points in the OT epoch before the climactic world-ending happenings and are inextricably linked to and lead up to such final happenings.

11. Earlier I have qualified this exclusively futuristic assessment of the OT by contending that some of the expressions there later find apparent inaugurated fulfillment still within the OT period itself (e.g., Israel's end-time restoration begins at the time of the return of the remnant from Babylon: see Deut. 4:30; 31:29), yet these were not "true" inaugurated eschatological fulfillments, since these apparent fulfillments did not involve irreversible conditions.

12. Illustration adapted from Anthony A. Hoekema, *The Bible and the Future* (Grand Rapids: Eerdmans, 1979), 20.

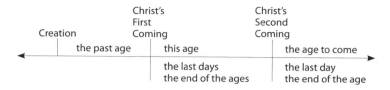

The expression "already–not yet" refers to two stages of the fulfillment of the latter days. It is "already" because the latter days have dawned in Christ, but it is "not yet" since the latter days have not consummately arrived. Scholars often use the phrase "inaugurated eschatology" to describe the beginning stage of the latter days.

Christians live between D-day and V-day. D-day was the first coming of Christ, when the opponent was defeated decisively; V-day is the final coming of Christ, when the adversary will finally and completely surrender.[13] "The hope of the final victory is so much the more vivid because of the unshakably firm conviction that the battle that decides the victory has already taken place."[14] Anthony Hoekema concludes:

> The nature of New Testament eschatology may be summed up under three observations: (1) the great eschatological event predicted in the Old Testament has happened; (2) what the Old Testament writers seemed to depict as one movement is now seen to involve two stages: the present age and the age of the future; and (3) the relation between these two eschatological stages is that the blessings of the present [eschatological] age are the pledge and guarantee of greater blessings to come.[15]

How should the NT story line be stated in light of its relation to the OT's? I propose the following: *Jesus's life of covenantal obedience, trials, death for sinners, and resurrection by the Spirit has launched the fulfillment of the eschatological already–not yet new-creation reign, bestowed by grace through faith and resulting in worldwide commission to the faithful to advance this kingdom and judgment for the unfaithful, unto God's glory.* This statement of the NT's narrative line is to be understood from two angles. First, it is the central concept from which the rest of the other major notions in the NT are derived;[16] therefore, second, this idea is the overarching concept or organizing structure of thought within which the other NT concepts are best understood.

---

13. Ibid., 21.
14. O. Cullmann, *Christ and Time* (Philadelphia: Westminster, 1950), 87.
15. Hoekema, *Bible and Future*, 21–22.
16. Frank Thielman, *Theology of the New Testament: A Canonical and Synthetic Approach* (Grand Rapids: Zondervan, 2005), 231–32, sees this as one way to understand a "center."

We should think of Christ's life, trials, and especially his death and resurrection as the central events that launched the latter days. These pivotal events are eschatological in particular because they launched the beginning of the new creation and kingdom. This already–not yet, end-time, new-creational kingdom has not been recognized sufficiently heretofore as of vital importance to understanding the essence of NT theology and especially its application to pastoral ministry.

The OT prophesied that the destruction of the first creation and the re-creation of a new heavens and earth were to happen at the very end of time. Christ's work reveals that the end of the world and the coming new creation have begun in his death and resurrection: 2 Corinthians 5:15 and 17 says Christ "died and rose again . . . so that if any are in Christ, they are a new creation, the old things have passed away; behold, new things have come." Revelation 1:5 refers to Christ as "the firstborn from the dead," and then Revelation 3:14 defines "firstborn" as "the beginning of the [new] creation of God."[17] Likewise, Colossians 1:18 says that Christ is "the firstborn from the dead" and "the beginning," so that "he himself might come to have first place in everything." In Galatians 6:14–15 Paul says that his identification with Christ's death means that he is a "new creation."

Indeed, the resurrection was predicted by the OT to occur at the end of the world as part of the new creation. God would make redeemed humanity a part of the new creation by re-creating their bodies through resurrection (cf. Dan. 12:1–2). Of course, we still look forward to the time when our bodies will be raised at Christ's final parousia, and we will become part of the consummated new creation. Christ's resurrection, however, placed him into the beginning of the new creation. The resurrected Christ is not merely spiritually the inauguration of the new cosmos, but he is literally its beginning, since he was resurrected with a physical, newly created body. Recall that when Matthew 27:50 narrates Jesus's death, Matthew immediately adds in verses 51–53, "the earth shook; and the rocks split, and the tombs were opened; and many bodies of the saints who had fallen asleep were raised; and coming out of the tombs after his resurrection they entered the holy city and appeared to many." These strange phenomena are recorded by Matthew to signal to his readers that Christ's death was the beginning of the end of the old creation and the inauguration of a new creation. Likewise, 1 John 2:17–18 can say "the world is passing away; . . . it is the last hour." Hence, Christ's death is not

---

17. For the notion of new creation in the 2 Cor. 5 and Rev. 3 texts, see G. K. Beale, "The Old Testament Background of Reconciliation in 2 Corinthians 5–7 and Its Bearing on the Literary Problem of 2 Corinthians 6.14–7.1," *NTS* 35 (1989): 550–81; and G. K. Beale, "The Old Testament Background of Rev. 3.14," *NTS* 42 (1996): 133–52.

just any death but rather the beginning of the destruction of the entire world, which will not be consummated until the very end. Likewise, 1 Corinthians 15:22–24 says the resurrection launched in Christ will be consummated when he returns, when resurrected saints will become a part of the final form of the eternal new creation.

The Use of the Phrase "Latter Days" (and Synonyms) in the New Testament

In order for us to grasp more firmly the story line of the NT, we will now consider its conception of "latter days." The NT repeatedly uses precisely the same phrase "latter days" as is found in the OT prophecies, though other, synonymous expressions are also employed ("last days," "last time," "last hour," etc.). Many of these uses may be echoes of the OT expression, and some uses appear to be specific allusions to some of the "latter day" OT texts. The eschatological nuance of the phrases is generally identical to that of the OT expression, except for one difference: in the NT the end days predicted by the OT are seen as beginning fulfillment with Christ's first coming and culminating in a final consummated fulfillment at the very end of history.

All that the OT foresaw would occur in the end times has begun already in the first century and continues on into our present day. This means that the OT prophecies of the great tribulation, God's deliverance of Israel from oppressors, God's rule over the gentiles, and the establishment of his kingdom have been set in motion by Christ's life, death, and resurrection and the formation of the Christian church. The resurrection marked the beginning of Jesus's messianic reign, and the Spirit at Pentecost signaled the inauguration of his rule through the church (see Acts 1:6–8; 2:1–43). On the other hand, persecution of Jesus and the church indicated the beginning of the final tribulation. What the OT did not foresee so clearly was the ironic reality that the kingdom and the tribulation could coexist, to this extent, at the same time. For example, John says in Revelation 1:9 (NASB), "I, John, your brother and fellow partaker in the tribulation and kingdom and perseverance which are in Jesus. . . ." Therefore, the latter days do not take place only at some point in the future but occur throughout the whole church age, which means that we in the twenty-first century are still experiencing the latter days.

The first time the wording "last days" appears in the NT is Acts 2:17. Here Peter understands that tongues at Pentecost are a beginning fulfillment of Joel's end-time prophecy that a day would come when God's Spirit would gift not merely prophets, priests, and kings but also all of God's people. Peter says, "For these men are not drunk as you suppose, for it is only the third hour of the day; but this is what was spoken of through the prophet Joel: 'And it shall be in the last days, God says, that I will pour forth of my Spirit upon all mankind'"(Acts 2:15–17a; cf. Joel 2:28).

In 1 Corinthians 10:11 Paul says that the OT was written to instruct the Corinthian Christians about how to live in the end times, since upon them "the ends of the ages have come." And in Galatians 4:4 (NASB) he refers to Jesus's birth as occurring "when the fullness of the time came," in fulfillment of the messianic prophecies. Likewise, in Ephesians 1:7–10 (NASB) (esp. in view of 1:20–23) "the fullness of the times" alludes to when believers were redeemed and Christ began to rule over the earth as a result of his resurrection. The expressions "the last times" and "end days" in 1 Timothy 4:1–3 and 2 Timothy 3:1–5 refer to the presence of tribulation in the form of false, deceptive teaching. That the "latter days" in 1 and 2 Timothy is not a reference only to a distant, future time is evident from recognizing that the Ephesian church is already experiencing this latter-day tribulation of deceptive teaching and apostasy (see 1 Tim. 1:3–4, 6, 7, 19–20; 4:7; 5:13–15; 6:20–21; 2 Tim. 1:15; 2:16–19, 25–26; 3:2–9).

In his opening two verses, the author of Hebrews proclaims that in his own day, "in these last days," Jesus had begun to fulfill the Psalm 2 prophecy that God's Son would judge the evil kingdoms and receive the earth as an inheritance from his Father (cf. Ps. 2:1–12 with Heb. 1:2–5). In like manner, in Hebrews 9:26 (NASB) he says, "At the consummation of the ages He [Christ] has been manifested to put away sin by the sacrifice of Himself." And James 5:1–9 warns readers not to trust in riches because the "last days" have already come. James attempts to motivate his audience to trust in Christ and not worldly possessions by imparting to them a comprehension of what God has accomplished through Christ in these "last days."

In identical fashion 1 Peter 1:19–21 (NASB) says that Christ has died as a sacrificial lamb and been resurrected "in these last times." Second Peter 3:3 (NASB) also pronounces that "in the last days mockers will come with their mocking" (see 1 Tim. 4:1; 2 Tim. 3:1). That this is not mere prophecy of the future in 2 Peter 3 but description of the present is clear from noticing that Peter recognizes that the mockers are presently spreading false teaching in the church that he is addressing (2 Pet. 3:16–17; note the imminent threat of false teachers in 2:1–22). Jude 18 has exactly the same idea (cf. Jude 4, 8, 10–13). In a similar context of false teaching, 1 John 2:18 says, "Children, it is the last hour; and just as you heard that antichrist is coming, even now many antichrists have arisen; from this we know that it is the last hour." These "antichrists" were manifesting themselves by attempting to deceive others through erroneous teaching (see 1 John 2:21–23, 26; 4:1–5). Indeed, one of the indications that the latter-day tribulation is continuing during the present interadvent period is the pervasive presence of false teaching within the purported covenant community.

The last days predicted by the OT began with Christ's first coming, although there is other terminology besides "latter days" in many other passages that could also be adduced as further evidence (e.g., see Paul's use of "now" in 2 Cor. 6:2; Eph. 3:5, 10). Also, many passages convey end-time concepts but do not use technical eschatological expressions.

Christ's life, death, resurrection, and establishment of the church community have ushered in the fulfillment of the OT prophecies of the tribulation, the Messiah's conquering of gentile enemies, Israel's deliverance, and the long-expected kingdom. In this initial phase of the end times, Christ and the church begin to fulfill the prophecies concerning Israel's tribulation and end-time kingdom, because Christ and the church are seen by the NT as *the true Israel* (see Rom. 2:25–29; 9:6, 24–26; Gal. 3:29; 6:15–16; Eph. 2:16–18; 3:6; 1 Pet. 2:9; Rev. 1:6; 3:9; 5:9–10).[18] This notion of inaugurated fulfillment is best expressed by 2 Cor. 1:20: "For as many as may be the promises of God [in the OT], in him [Christ] they are yes."

Of course, there are passages in the NT that speak of the future consummation of the present latter-day period. That is, there are still aspects of many end-time prophecies that have not yet been fulfilled but will be when Christ returns a second time, such as the bodily resurrection of all people, the destruction of the present cosmos, the creation of a completely new heavens and earth, the final judgment, the eternal Sabbath, and so on.

Therefore, the apostles understood eschatology not merely as futurology but also as a mind-set for understanding the present within the climaxing context of redemptive history. The apostles grasped that they were already living in the end times and that they were to perceive their present salvation in Christ as already an end-time reality. Every major doctrine of the Christian faith is eschatological in nature and must be seen through the lens of the inauguration of the latter days. Pastoral ministry, too, should not relegate eschatology to the fringes but should attempt to integrate it fully into faith and life.

Most pastors rarely connect eschatology to their pastoral ministry. When properly understood, eschatology is central to all facets of church ministry. The gospel itself is saturated with eschatology: Jesus experienced selective end-time tribulation throughout his ministry, climaxing in the absolute tribulation of

---

18. See further H. K. LaRondelle, *The Israel of God in Prophecy* (Berrien Springs, MI: Andrews University Press, 1983); and esp. Beale, *New Testament Biblical Theology*, 649–749.

death on the cross; by the power of the Spirit, Jesus's resurrection from the dead initially launched the latter-day kingdom and the new creation. At the heart of the Christian message lies an event that is eschatological at its core. If the gospel is eschatological, then, by extension, so is pastoral ministry.

That is why I am excited about the present book. In the pages that follow, Benjamin Gladd and Matthew Harmon explore how inaugurated eschatology should shape pastoral ministry and the life of the church. As former students of mine, they understand and have embraced my approach to biblical theology. In many respects this book is a natural extension of my own work *A New Testament Biblical Theology*, so I am very happy to have a small part in this book. I pray that God will use this book to help pastors lead the eschatological people of God to live out his mission in this world in the power of the Spirit so that God's glorious presence may extend to the ends of the earth.

2

The Nature of the End-Time Church

Pastoral ministry is fraught with challenges. As those called to "shepherd the flock of God that is among you" (1 Pet. 5:2), pastors, like the apostle Paul, experience "the daily pressure on me of my anxiety for all the churches" (2 Cor. 11:28). They serve with the knowledge that "we who teach will be judged with greater strictness" (James 3:1). Because they live in a fallen world, they experience "the desires of the flesh and the desires of the eyes and pride in possessions" (1 John 2:16), as well as an adversary that "prowls around like a roaring lion, seeking someone to devour" (1 Pet. 5:8). On top of all that, pastors serve in "the last days," when the Spirit specifically warns that false teachers will seek to lead people astray to demonic and self-indulgent beliefs and practices that lead to eternal destruction (1 Tim. 4:1–3; 2 Tim. 3:1–9).

Given these sobering realities, we believe that pastors need to understand how the life and ministry of the church should be shaped by the already–not yet. But in order for this to happen, we need to have a good grasp of the nature of the church itself. What is the nature of the church that pastors are called to lead, feed, and serve? For many people, the first thing that comes to mind when they hear the word "church" is a building. Others think of an organization or perhaps a religious service. While the word "church" can be used in a variety of ways (the website dictionary.com lists fourteen different uses of the noun!), in the NT the word consistently refers to the assembly of people identified as followers of Jesus Christ. Thus the church is first and foremost a people before it is anything else, such as a building, organization, or a religious service.[1]

But what kind of people is the church? How is it defined, and how is it distinct from other groups of people? The NT speaks about the church in many different ways, using a variety of images and metaphors. Each of them enhances our understanding of the church, bringing out different aspects of its nature. But when one looks at the earliest preaching of the apostles in both Acts and the Epistles, one consistent emphasis that emerges is that God has at last fulfilled his promises through the life, death, and resurrection of Jesus and the pouring out of the Holy Spirit. The time of eschatological fulfillment has been inaugurated in anticipation of its future, final consummation. The church, as the eschatological people of God, experiences the blessings promised to a renewed and restored people of God.[2] When pastors fully grasp this reality, they will be able to lead God's people to live in a way that embodies God's purpose for us. So let's examine how the Bible presents the church as the eschatological people of God.

The Church as the Eschatological People of God

In order to see how the NT presents the church experiencing the fulfillment of God's promises of a restored and renewed people, we need to begin by tracing the consistent failure of God's people under the old covenant. In the midst of that failure, God promised a day when a renewed and restored people of God would be marked by Spirit-empowered obedience. To accomplish this, God would raise up a Son who would obey where God's people had failed and would take upon himself the punishment for their failure. All those identified with this obedient Son would become part of the end-time people of God who receive the promised inheritance.

The People of God Repeatedly Fail

One of the most consistent themes of the OT is God's people failing to keep his covenant with them. Genesis 3 gives the impression that Adam and Eve had not lived in Eden very long before they disobeyed God's command

---

1. For an overview of how the Greek word *ekklēsia* ("church") is used in the NT, as well as in the LXX and the broader Greek world, see K. L. Schmidt, "ἐκκλησία," *TDNT* 3:501–36. The LXX regularly uses *ekklēsia* to refer to the people of Israel gathered for worship.

2. By "eschatological people of God" we mean the restored, renewed people of God that would come into existence when God inaugurated the time of fulfillment of his promises, often referred to as "the latter days" (see "The 'Latter Days' in the Old Testament" in chap. 1).

not to eat from the tree of the knowledge of good and evil. As a result sin and death spread throughout creation to the point where God brought judgment through the flood. Noah, however, "found favor in the eyes of the LORD" and "was a righteous man, blameless in his generation" (Gen. 6:8–9). But not long after the flood subsided, Noah ends up drunk, passed out, and lying naked in his tent (Gen. 9:21)!

This pattern of failure continues with Noah's descendants. Despite God's command to "be fruitful and multiply and fill the earth" (Gen. 9:1), they joined together to make a name for themselves lest they "be dispersed over the face of the whole earth" (Gen. 11:4). Shortly after God promised to multiply Abram into a great nation and give him the promised land (Gen. 12:1–3), Abram instructed his wife, Sarai, to deceive Pharaoh into thinking she was Abram's sister (Gen. 12:10–20). Rather than trust God to provide a promised descendant, Abram had a son with Sarai's servant Hagar (Gen. 16:1–15). Abraham's grandson Jacob even deceived his father, Isaac, into blessing him instead of his brother Esau (Gen. 27:1–46).

The nation of Israel did not fare any better. Not long after Moses ascended Mount Sinai to receive the rest of the law, the people broke the covenant by convincing Aaron to make a golden calf for them to worship (Exod. 32:1–34:35). Standing on the edge of the promised land, the people refused to trust the Lord and enter because they feared its inhabitants (Num. 14:9). As a result, God condemned that generation to forty years of wandering in the wilderness (Num. 14:20–38). During those forty years Israel frequently grumbled against the Lord, provoking his judgment (see, e.g., Num. 16:1–50; 20:2–13; 21:4–9; 25:1–18). Yet even when they finally entered the promised land under Joshua's leadership and defeated Jericho, the Israelites "broke faith in regard to the devoted things" when Achan kept some of them for himself (Josh. 7:1). And the entire book of Judges repeats a depressing cycle: (1) Israel turns away from the Lord; (2) The Lord hands Israel over to its enemies; (3) Israel cries out for deliverance; (4) The Lord has mercy and raises up a judge to deliver the people; (5) Israel has rest as long as the judge lives but then returns to idolatry.

When Israel finally demands a king so they can be like the other nations around them, God gives them a king (Saul) who is just like the kings of the surrounding nations (1 Sam. 8:1–10:27). Because of Saul's disobedience (1 Sam. 13:1–15:34), God anoints a man after his own heart as king—David (1 Sam. 16:1–13). Despite God promising to establish the kingdom of his descendant(s) forever (2 Sam. 7:1–29), even David breaks faith by committing adultery and murder (2 Sam. 11:1–12:25). His son Solomon, despite being the wisest man alive (1 Kings 3:1–15), turns away from the Lord by marrying foreign wives and going after their gods (1 Kings 11:1–8). When the nation splits into northern

(Israel) and southern (Judah) kingdoms, both spiral further downward into apostasy. As a result, God sends both Israel (722 BC) and Judah (586 BC) into exile for their idolatry (2 Kings 17:1–23; 2 Chron. 36:11–21). The nation that had been called to be "a kingdom of priests and a holy nation" (Exod. 19:6) eventually did "more evil than the nations whom the LORD destroyed before the people of Israel" (2 Chron. 33:9).

The Prophets Promise an Obedient People of God

Yet amid Israel's repeated failure and downward spiral into further rebellion against the Lord, God promised a day when his people would obey him. Standing on the plains of Moab and preparing the people to enter the promised land, Moses foresaw a day when God would send his people into exile for their rebellion (Deut. 30:1–4). But just as God promised restoration to Adam and Eve in the aftermath of their sin (Gen. 3:15), so too the Lord promises to eventually restore his people. Central to that restoration was God circumcising their hearts: "And the LORD your God will circumcise your heart and the heart of your offspring, so that you will love the LORD your God with all your heart and with all your soul, that you may live" (Deut. 30:6).

Israel's rebellion was rooted in their failure to "love the LORD your God with all your heart and with all your soul and with all your might" (Deut. 6:5). But God promised a day when he would circumcise the hearts of his people to enable wholehearted devotion to him so that they would "obey the voice of the LORD your God, to keep his commandments and his statutes that are written in this Book of the Law" (Deut. 30:10). When that day came, God would dwell with his people, and they would reflect his glorious presence.

As the kingdoms of Israel and Judah deteriorated into further idolatry, God raised up prophets to announce not only impending judgment but also the hope of restoration. When Amos prophesied during the first half of the eighth century BC, both Israel and Judah were experiencing a period of prosperity. But this prosperity simply masked Israel and Judah's turning away from their covenant with the Lord (Amos 2:4–6:14). Therefore Amos delivers a series of oracles announcing the coming judgment (7:1–9:15). In the final oracle (9:1–15), this judgment is portrayed as sweeping and decisive (9:1–11). There will be no place to hide because the Lord is sovereign over all creation (9:1–6). While Israel will be destroyed, Judah will not face total annihilation (9:7–10).

Yet not all hope is lost! Amos continues:

"In that day I will raise up the booth of David that is fallen and repair its breaches, and raise up its ruins and rebuild it as in the days of old, that they may possess the remnant of Edom and all the nations who are called by my name," declares the LORD who does this. "Behold, the days are coming," declares the LORD, "when the plowman shall overtake the reaper and the treader of grapes him who sows the seed; the mountains shall drip sweet wine, and all the hills shall flow with it. I will restore the fortunes of my people Israel, and they shall rebuild the ruined cities and inhabit them; they shall plant vineyards and drink their wine, and they shall make gardens and eat their fruit. I will plant them on their land, and they shall never again be uprooted out of the land that I have given them," says the LORD your God. (Amos 9:11–15)

Amos foresees a day when a new people of God, consisting not merely of Jews but of gentiles as well, will live under the rule of a Davidic king. God will transform not only his people but also creation itself, so that he may dwell with them forever.

Not long after the ministry of Amos, Hosea prophesied to both the northern kingdom of Israel in its final years and the southern kingdom of Judah in the years afterward. To vividly portray the idolatry of God's people, the Lord commands Hosea to "take to yourself a wife of whoredom and have children of whoredom, for the land commits great whoredom by forsaking the LORD" (Hosea 1:2). Their first child is named Jezreel ("God will sow") because "in just a little while I will punish the house of Jehu for the blood of Jezreel, and I will put an end to the kingdom of the house of Israel" (Hosea 1:4). The second child is named No Mercy because "I will no more have mercy on the house of Israel, to forgive them at all" (Hosea 1:6). The third child is named Not My People because "you are not my people, and I am not your God" (Hosea 1:9). Yet judgment will not have the final word; hope still remains:

> Yet the number of the children of Israel shall be like the sand of the sea, which cannot be measured or numbered. And in the place where it was said to them, "You are not my people," it shall be said to them, "Children of the living God." And the children of Judah and the children of Israel shall be gathered together, and they shall appoint for themselves one head. And they shall go up from the land, for great shall be the day of Jezreel. (Hosea 1:10–11)

Although Israel and Judah broke God's covenant with them at Mount Sinai, the Lord remains committed to fulfilling his promise to Abraham of innumerable descendants who are faithful to him (Gen. 13:16). God will sow a remnant from both Israel and Judah to live in the land under one Davidic king.

Hosea further describes this restoration in 2:14–23. God will betroth his redeemed people to himself, put an end to their idolatry, and make a new covenant with them that will transform creation itself (Hosea 2:14–20). When that day comes,

> I will answer, declares the LORD, I will answer the heavens, and they shall answer the earth, and the earth shall answer the grain, the wine, and the oil, and they shall answer Jezreel, and I will sow her for myself in the land. And I will have mercy on No Mercy, and I will say to Not My People, "You are my people"; and he shall say, "You are my God." (Hosea 2:21–23)

Like Amos, Hosea also foresees a day when God will act to create a faithful people dwelling with him in a renewed creation.

The prophet Jeremiah builds on the prophecies of Amos and Hosea when he announces God's promise of a new covenant. In the final days before the Babylonians destroyed Jerusalem and its temple (586 BC), God promised a day when he would restore his people (Jer. 30:1–33:26). At the heart of this Book of Consolation is an oracle (31:31–34) that not only announces a new covenant but also compares and contrasts it with the Mosaic covenant. While the heart of this new covenant will still be expressed by the familiar covenant formula "I will be their God, and they shall be my people" (31:33; cf. Lev. 26:12), the Lord stresses that this new covenant will not be like the Mosaic covenant that Israel broke. The first difference is that God will write his law directly onto the hearts of his people (31:33). Second, whereas under the Mosaic covenant some people who were part of the community did not truly know the Lord, in the new covenant "they shall all know me, from the least of them to the greatest" (31:34). Third, and perhaps most important, the new covenant will provide complete and final forgiveness of sins (31:34). The future establishment of this new covenant is so certain that God connects it to the order of creation itself (31:35–37). As Peter Gentry helpfully summarizes, "The new covenant looks beyond judgment to a future in which God will provide a solution to the stubbornness of his partner in the old covenant. The direction and instruction of God for righteous relationships will be internalised and written upon the heart. Since the heart of the people will be transformed, they will be a faithful covenant partner."[3] Thus when this new covenant is established in the days that are coming (31:31, 33), there will be a people of God marked by a personal knowledge of the Lord based on final forgiveness of sins and expressed in greater heart-level obedience.

Although not using the specific expression "new covenant," the prophet Ezekiel describes the same reality. At the heart of a section announcing the

---

3. Peter J. Gentry and Stephen J. Wellum, *Kingdom through Covenant: A Biblical-Theological Understanding of the Covenants* (Wheaton: Crossway, 2012), 503.

future salvation of God's people (34:1–39:29) stands an oracle in which God promises to restore the honor of his name (36:22–38).[4] Because Israel has profaned his name among the nations, he will act to vindicate his holiness so that the nations will know that he is the Lord (36:22–23). He will do this by gathering them from among the nations (36:24) and transforming them into a new people (36:25–28). That transformation consists of at least four components.

First, God will cleanse his people from their impurity and idolatry (36:25). To reflect the holiness of the Lord, his people must have their sins taken away. Second, God will change his people from the inside (36:26). This change is so sweeping that it is described in terms of a new heart and a new spirit; the old heart of stone will be exchanged for a heart of flesh that will respond to God. Third, the Lord will put his Spirit within his people (36:27). The same Spirit who came upon key figures in God's redemptive plan would take up permanent residence in all of God's new-covenant people. This would lead to the fourth aspect of transformation: God causing his people to obey him (36:27). Unlike the persistent rebellion that characterized Israel, this new-covenant people will be empowered by God's Spirit to obey. In that day, they will be God's people, he will be their God (36:28), and they will dwell together in a renewed creation (36:35–36).

Other passages could be discussed, but these are more than sufficient to establish our point. The OT looks forward to a day when there will be a new people of God that is not characterized by their repeated failure to remain faithful to the Lord. This eschatological people of God will be brought into existence by God through the work of a descendant of David who will establish a new covenant and rule over Jews and gentiles united together in this new people of God. Their sins will be completely forgiven, they will have new, circumcised hearts, and they will be empowered to obey by the Spirit of God dwelling within them. It is this OT background that forms the sure foundation of the gospel that pastors are called to faithfully proclaim.

Others, however, see the extent of continuity and discontinuity between the people of God under the old covenant and the people of God under the new covenant differently, with a much greater emphasis on points of continuity between the covenants.[5]

---

4. Here we are loosely following the structure of Daniel I. Block, *The Book of Ezekiel*, 2 vols., NICOT (Grand Rapids: Eerdmans, 1997), 2:349–59.

5. Most who subscribe to "covenant theology" (including Ben Gladd) tend to argue for more continuity between the old and new covenants (e.g., one covenant community). This brief discussion is dependent on G. K. Beale, *A New Testament Biblical Theology: The Unfolding of the Old Testament in the New* (Grand Rapids: Baker Academic, 2011), 730–49. For further

For example, let us return to the key text of Jeremiah 31. Jeremiah predicts that a remnant of Israelites (31:7) will benefit from two end-time blessings:

> This is the covenant that I will make with the house of Israel. . . . *I will put my law within them, and I will write it on their hearts.* And I will be their God, and they shall be my people. And *no longer shall each one teach his neighbor and each his brother, saying, "Know the* LORD," *for they shall all know me, from the least of them to the greatest,* declares the LORD. (Jer. 31:33–34, italics added)

The prophet states that all end-time Israelites will have access to God's revelation and will be in a position to "teach" one another. Within the Mosaic administration, only prophets and priests were in a position to teach the Israelites. Certainly the OT mentions parents instructing their children about God's law (e.g., Deut. 4:10; 6:7), but teaching outside of the family was restricted to prophets and priests. Teaching God's law also presupposes a deep knowledge of it. Notice how Jeremiah claims that the Israelites under the new covenant will "all know me." In other words, the remnant will possess a more robust understanding of God's law and therefore be in a position to "teach his neighbor." The NT writers explicitly claim that with the arrival of the already–not yet, all NT saints function as "priests" before God (e.g., 1 Pet. 2:9; Rev. 1:6; 5:10; 20:6).

Understood this way, Jeremiah 31 is thus not so much about the qualitative difference in the internalization of God's law (though certainly the law will be more deeply emblazoned on the human heart) as it is about a democratization of the priestly and prophetic roles within the end-time community of faith. Recall, for example, the psalmist's obedience in Psalm 119 that springs from the heart, demonstrating the internalization of God's law. This understanding of the new covenant in Jeremiah 31 falls in line with Joel's prophecy about the Spirit coming "on all flesh," enabling "sons" and "daughters" to "prophesy" (2:28). The Spirit will also be poured out on "male and female servants" (2:29). There is also qualitative similarity between new-covenant believers and those faithful Israelites under the Mosaic administration who were redeemed by their faith in God's promises and declared righteous. Though only a remnant, old-covenant saints possessed a saving knowledge of God.

From this perspective, one central area of discontinuity between the two covenants is the temporal nature of the Mosaic covenant. The first covenant was intrinsically temporal and designed for the Israelite nation. The sacrificial

---

elaboration of the relationship between the Mosaic covenant and the new covenant, see Beale's discussion there.

and civil laws were installed for a specific time and for a specific people group, and they anticipate Christ's work.[6] This covenant was able to be "broken" (Jer. 31:32). The new covenant, however, is "eternal" and unable to be broken (Heb. 13:20). "The fulfillment of the new covenant will never be abrogated, so that what begins to be fulfilled in it will come to final, consummate completion for eternity."[7]

Jesus Obeys Where God's People Have Failed

The NT opens by explicitly linking Jesus to the OT hope. He is "the son of David, the son of Abraham" (Matt. 1:1). But the question remains: will he manage to obey where God's people had consistently failed?

The answer that emerges is a resounding yes! Matthew in particular makes this clear at several points in his opening chapters. In a variety of ways, Matthew portrays Jesus as "recapitulating" Israel's history.[8] In other words, Jesus "relives" Israel's experiences so that he can obey where Israel had failed and fulfill the mission that Israel had failed to complete. Although there are strong hints of this throughout Matthew 1:1–2:12, the account of Jesus's journey to and eventual departure from Egypt makes this clear:

> Now when they had departed, behold, an angel of the Lord appeared to Joseph in a dream and said, "Rise, take the child and his mother, and flee to Egypt, and remain there until I tell you, for Herod is about to search for the child, to destroy him." And he rose and took the child and his mother by night and departed to Egypt and remained there until the death of Herod. This was to fulfill what the Lord had spoken by the prophet, "Out of Egypt I called my son." (Matt. 2:13–15)

Matthew claims that these events happened to fulfill what God had spoken in Hosea 11:1.[9] Rather than being a direct promise of a future event, Hosea 11:1 refers to the historical event of God bringing his son Israel out of Egypt. Despite Israel's repeated failure, God promises to restore the nation in a new exodus (11:2–11). Hosea sees in Israel's first exodus a historical pattern that will culminate in a final exodus. Matthew observes that same pattern and asserts that it finds its fulfillment in Jesus's exodus from Egypt. Beale helpfully summarizes what Matthew is doing:

---

6. See Vern Poythress, *The Shadow of Christ in the Law of Moses* (Brentwood, TN: Wolgemuth & Hyatt, 1991).

7. Beale, *New Testament Biblical Theology*, 731.

8. See further ibid., 406–22.

9. See further G. K. Beale, "The Use of Hosea 11:1 in Matthew 2:15: One More Time," *JETS* 55 (2012): 697–715. The discussion here attempts to summarize his argument.

Matthew contrasts Jesus as the "son" (2:15) with Hosea's "son" (11:1). The latter who came out of Egypt was not obedient, and was judged but would be restored (11:2–11), while the former did what Israel should have done: Jesus came out of Egypt, was perfectly obedient, did not deserve judgment but suffered it anyway for guilty Israel and the world in order to restore them to God. Matthew portrays Jesus to be recapitulating the history of Israel because he sums up Israel in himself. Since Israel disobeyed, Jesus has come to do what they should have, so he must retrace Israel's steps up to the point they failed, and then continue to obey and succeed in the mission Israel should have carried out.[10]

The portrait of Jesus as the one who obeys where Israel failed continues with his baptism (Matt. 3:13–17).[11] John the Baptist is the messenger sent in advance of the new exodus (Matt. 3:1–12; note the quote from Isa. 40:3). Just as Israel had passed through the waters of the Red Sea on their way out of Egypt (Exod. 14:1–31) and the second generation passed through the Jordan River on their way into the promised land (Josh. 3:1–17), God promised to restore his people in a new exodus through water (Isa. 11:15; 42:15; 43:2, 16–17; 44:27–28; 50:2; 51:9–11). Thus in his baptism Jesus passes through the waters of the Jordan, the heavens open, and the Spirit descends on him. This description echoes the language of Isaiah 63:11–15 and 64:1, where the prophet looks back to the first exodus in anticipation of an even greater future exodus.[12] The declaration of the heavenly voice, "This is my beloved Son, with whom I am well pleased" (Matt. 3:17), harks back to 2:15, where Jesus was identified as God's Son who came out of Egypt.[13]

Just as the Spirit of God led God's Son Israel into the wilderness after they passed through the Red Sea, so now the Spirit leads Jesus into the wilderness (Matt. 4:1–11).[14] In contrast to Adam, whose temptation took place in the lush

10. Ibid., 710.

11. This section is indebted to Beale, *New Testament Biblical Theology*, 412–17.

12. The mention of waters separating, the Spirit of God, and placing people in a new land may further suggest echoes of Gen. 1. If so, the new exodus would be connected with a new creation, which is evident in several Isaianic texts (e.g., Isa. 43:14–21). See further ibid., 412–14.

13. The expression "This is my beloved Son" is an echo of Ps. 2:7, where Yahweh says to his anointed king, "You are my Son." An echo of the Isaianic Servant is also present in the expression "in whom I am well pleased" (cf. Isa. 42:1). These allusions, along with several others, reinforce that Matthew is presenting Jesus as recapitulating Israel's experiences; see further ibid., 412–17.

14. Luke puts his genealogy of Jesus (3:23–38) between the baptism (3:21–22) and the wilderness temptation (4:1–13). Unlike Matthew, Luke traces the descent of Jesus beyond Abraham all the way back to Adam. In the final lines Luke writes that Jesus was "the son of Seth, the son of Adam, the son of God" (3:38). Although Genesis never explicitly refers to Adam as the son of God, it is clearly implied. Adam was made in the likeness and image of God just as Seth was in the likeness and image of Adam his father (Gen. 5:1–3). Later, in Exod. 4:22–23, God refers to

confines of Eden, Jesus is attacked by Satan in the barren wilderness. Jesus's forty days of temptation echo Israel's forty years of wilderness wandering as well. Satan begins by challenging Jesus's identity as "the Son of God" (4:3). In response to the first temptation to turn stones into bread, Jesus responds by quoting Deuteronomy 8:3, "Man shall not live by bread alone, but by every word that comes from the mouth of God" (Matt. 4:4). When Satan challenges Jesus to throw himself down from the pinnacle of the temple, Jesus quotes Deuteronomy 6:16, "You shall not put the Lord your God to the test" (Matt. 4:7). To the third temptation of receiving all the world's kingdoms in exchange for worshiping Satan, Jesus dismisses the devil with a quote from Deuteronomy 6:13, "You shall worship the Lord your God and him only shall you serve" (Matt. 4:10).[15]

Jesus's choice of these texts is not haphazard. By quoting three different verses from Deuteronomy 6–8, Jesus is intentionally identifying himself with Israel. In these chapters Moses is recounting Israel's wilderness wanderings to a new generation that has not experienced the exodus from Egypt firsthand. But whereas Israel repeatedly failed in the wilderness when tempted by Satan, Jesus obeys! Unlike Adam, who rebelled against God in Eden at the prompting of the serpent, Jesus defeats the devil in the wilderness.

Having successfully passed his wilderness testing as the one who obeys where Israel failed, Jesus then enters the promised land to establish his rightful rule over it (Matt. 4:12–17; cf. Luke 4:14–30). He begins to gather the tribes of Israel around himself by calling the twelve disciples (Matt. 4:18–22). Through his ministry of preaching, teaching, healing, and casting out demons, Jesus is crushing the serpent's head and gathering the eschatological people of God (Matt. 4:23–25). The promised restoration of God's people has begun through the one who obeys where Adam, Israel, and all of God's people failed. That is the heart of the good news that the church is called to preach.

The Church Is the Eschatological People of God

Because we are identified with Jesus Christ, we as the church, consisting of Jew and gentile together, are the eschatological people of God.[16] The restoration

---

Israel as his firstborn son as well. Thus by using sonship language in his genealogy, Luke prepares the reader to see Jesus obey where both Adam and Israel failed. For a much fuller treatment of the OT allusions and echoes in the wilderness temptation accounts, see ibid., 417–22.

15. For a helpful and practical exposition of Jesus's wilderness temptation, see Russell Moore, *Tempted and Tried: Temptation and the Triumph of Christ* (Wheaton: Crossway, 2011).

16. For texts in the Gospels that indicate this reality, some more directly than others, see, e.g., Matt. 3:9; 5:44–48; 10:34–39; 12:46–50; 19:29; Luke 11:27–28. For further discussion of these texts, see Beale, *New Testament Biblical Theology*, 423–27.

of God's people that began with Jesus calling the twelve disciples accelerates dramatically with the outpouring of the Spirit at Pentecost.[17]

In the forty days between Jesus's resurrection and his ascension, he spends significant time "speaking about the kingdom of God" to his disciples (Acts 1:3). They are instructed to remain in Jerusalem until they receive the promised Holy Spirit (1:4–5). Given that Jesus is teaching them about the kingdom, we should not be surprised that the disciples ask, "Lord, will you at this time restore the kingdom to Israel?" (1:6). Jesus's response combines the already and the not yet. The specific times or seasons of God's plan to consummate his promises are not theirs to know (1:7), but they will receive power to be witnesses of the kingdom to the ends of the earth when the Spirit comes upon them (1:8). Thus the Spirit is directly tied to the restoration of the kingdom to Israel. With those words Jesus ascends into heaven to sit at the right hand of the Father until his return in glory (1:9–11).

When the day of Pentecost arrives, the Spirit is finally poured out on Jesus's followers (Acts 2:1–4). Just as God's descent on Mount Sinai was accompanied by fire, so too the descent of the Spirit here is signified by tongues of fire and a rushing wind. God's presence has broken forth from his heavenly sanctuary and filled his new-covenant people. Moses's dream of a day when the Lord would put his Spirit on all his people (Num. 11:29) has now become a reality. Because they are filled with the Spirit, the apostles begin proclaiming "the mighty works of God" to Jews from every nation under heaven (Acts 2:5–12). The judgment rendered at the tower of Babel (Gen. 11:1–9) is now being reversed through the outpouring of the Spirit and the proclamation of the gospel, even if some miss it through their mockery (Acts 2:12).

In response to those who suggest that the apostles are drunk, Peter steps forward to explain what is happening (Acts 2:14–41). God is fulfilling his promise in Joel 2:28–32 to restore his people (Acts 2:16–21).[18] That restoration includes God pouring out the Spirit on all his people in advance of the day of the Lord, and all who call on the name of the Lord will be saved. In other words, they will be included within the end-time people of God, the faithful remnant who are saved through judgment (Joel 2:32).

---

17. For a detailed treatment of Acts 2, see esp. G. K. Beale, "The Descent of the Eschatological Temple in the Form of the Spirit at Pentecost, Part 1: The Clearest Evidence," *TynBul* 56.1 (2005): 73–102; and G. K. Beale, "The Descent of the Eschatological Temple in the Form of the Spirit at Pentecost, Part 2: Corroborating Evidence," *TynBul* 56.2 (2005): 63–90. The discussion that follows is indebted to these articles at several points.

18. Not to be overlooked is that the phrase "in the last days" (Acts 2:17) echoes Isa. 2:2, a passage that envisions an eschatological temple to which all the nations come to worship. See further David W. Pao, *Acts and the Isaianic New Exodus* (Grand Rapids: Baker Academic, 2002), 156–59.

This restoration has been accomplished through Jesus Christ (Acts 2:22–36). God identified him as the Christ through his miraculous signs, his death, and his resurrection from the dead (Acts 2:22–24). These events are confirmed by David's words in Psalm 16:8–11 and the promise made to him in 2 Samuel 7:12–16, as well as the eyewitness testimony of the apostles themselves (Acts 2:25–32). As the one exalted to the right hand of the Father (promised in Ps. 110:1), Jesus has poured out the Spirit on his people, proving that Jesus is both Lord and Christ (Acts 2:33–36).

Luke's description of the results of Peter's sermon further demonstrates that he is describing the formation of the eschatological people of God (Acts 2:37–41). In response to the crowd's question of what they should do (Acts 2:37), Peter's answer is full of OT allusions from passages that refer to the end-time people of God (Acts 2:38–41). Baptism in the name of Jesus for the forgiveness of sins echoes the promise of God to sprinkle clean water on his people to forgive their sins and put his Spirit within a renewed people (Ezek. 36:25–27; Jer. 31:31–34). The promise of the Spirit is for those who are near and far off, language borrowed from a text (Isa. 57:19) that envisions a renewed people of God who bear fruit. The reference to "everyone whom the Lord our God calls to himself" (Acts 2:39) returns to the language of Joel 2 as a means of inviting the crowd to respond in the way that God has mandated in order to be part of the remnant. And the call to be saved from "this crooked generation" takes up language describing rebellious Israel (Deut. 32:5, 20) in a passage that promises their eventual restoration (Deut. 32:36–43). These allusions make it clear that we are witnessing the formation of the eschatological people of God.

Numerous other NT passages present the church as the end-time people of God. One of the clearest is Galatians 3:1–5:1.[19] Sometime after Paul planted the churches in Galatia, troublemakers who distorted the gospel began leading them astray (Gal. 1:6–10). They were teaching that in order for one to be a full member of the people of God, it was necessary to keep the Mosaic law (or at least be circumcised; see 2:3–5, 11–21; 3:2, 5; 4:8–11, 21; 5:2–12). Paul responds by arguing in no uncertain terms that all who are united to Christ by faith are the promised eschatological people of God, regardless of whether they are Jew or gentile (2:15–5:1). Paul begins by stressing that a person is justified—that is, declared not guilty before God—on the basis of faith in the person and work of Jesus Christ, not by works of the law

---

19. For a fuller treatment of this passage, see Matthew S. Harmon, *She Must and Shall Go Free: Paul's Isaianic Gospel in Galatians*, BZNW 168 (Berlin: de Gruyter, 2010), 123–203. The brief discussion here is an attempt to summarize what is argued at much greater length there.

(2:15–16).[20] Believers have died to the law and been made alive to God by being crucified with Christ, who now lives in us (2:17–21).

Paul sets up the heart of his argument by asking the Galatians whether they received the Spirit on the basis of works of the law or hearing with faith (3:1–5). From that starting point he introduces the central issue that drives the rest of the argument: Who are the true children of Abraham (3:6–9)? Paul starts with Abraham's faith in God (Gen. 15:6) and his promises (Gen. 12:3; 18:18) as the basis for being declared righteous. Taking his cues from Isaiah 51–54, he contends that the salvation of the gentiles through the proclamation of the gospel fulfills both the promise to Abraham and the restoration of Israel. Therefore all who have faith in Christ, regardless of whether they are Jew or gentile, inherit the blessing promised to Abraham and his descendants.

But those who attempt to rely on the works of the law to receive this blessing receive a curse instead (Gal. 3:10–14). Echoing the language of the Suffering Servant of Isaiah 53, Paul asserts that Christ redeemed his people from this curse by becoming a curse for us (3:13). As a result, believers—including gentiles—receive the blessing of Abraham and the promised Spirit (3:14). The restoration of God's people marked by possession of the Spirit foretold in Isaiah 44:1–5 has now taken place.

The blessing of Abraham comes to Jew and gentile alike through their identification with Jesus Christ by faith, the promised singular offspring of Abraham (Gal. 3:15–29). The giving of the law did not change God's covenant with Abraham that his offspring would inherit the blessing through the promise (3:15–20). The law was never intended to bring life but rather acted as a guardian over God's people until the promised seed of Abraham came (3:21–24). But now that Christ has come, all who are united to Christ by faith—regardless of whether they are Jew or gentile, slave or free, male or female—are children of God and Abraham's offspring, heirs according to the promise (3:25–29).

Before Christ came, we all were children enslaved to the elementals (4:1–3),[21] but in the fullness of time God sent his Son to lead us in the new exodus promised in Isaiah (4:4–7).[22] As the Suffering Servant, Jesus Christ redeemed

---

20. The precise meaning of "works of the law" has been hotly debated over the past twenty-five years; for a helpful yet concise discussion, see Douglas J. Moo, *Galatians*, BECNT (Grand Rapids: Baker Academic, 2013), 157–61. We understand the phrase to refer to keeping the requirements of the Mosaic law.

21. Scholars continue to debate the meaning of the Greek expression *ta stoicheia tou kosmou*, woodenly translated "the elements of the world"; for a helpful summary of the various views, see ibid., 260–63.

22. Although the new exodus is a repeated theme in many of the prophetic books, the way Paul speaks of it here is indebted to Isaiah's particular presentation of it; see Harmon, *She Must and Shall Go Free*, 161–67.

those under the law and made them adopted children who have the Spirit. Now that we have been set free from the elementals, why would we ever want to go back to them by trying to keep the law (4:8–20)?

The climax of Paul's argument comes in 4:21–5:1.[23] He revisits Genesis 16–21 to draw a contrast between Sarah/Isaac and Hagar/Ishmael. All who are identified with Christ by faith, regardless of their ethnicity, are Spirit-born children of the promise made to Abraham, while all who define themselves by the law are children of the flesh. Again taking his cues from Isaiah, Paul argues that the Abrahamic covenant and the promised restoration of Israel have now been fulfilled in and through the promised offspring of Abraham, Jesus Christ.[24] Through his death and resurrection, Jesus is the firstborn of the eschatological people of God, and all who are identified with him by faith experience freedom from the dominion of this present evil age and all its powers—including the law, sin, death, and the devil himself.[25]

Paul also identifies the church as the eschatological people of God in 1 Corinthians 10:1–13. To steer the Corinthians away from immorality and idolatry, Paul reminds them of Israel's failures in the wilderness (1 Cor. 10:1–10). He says that "these things happened to them as an example, but they were written down for our instruction, on whom the end of the ages has come" (10:11). Because of our union with Christ, believers (regardless of whether they are Jew or gentile) experience the inaugurated blessings that God promised would come in the messianic age.

But perhaps the most common way the NT authors identify the church as the end-time people of God is to apply to the church the OT passages promising a renewed people. We will focus our discussion on the NT passages that either quote or allude to the OT texts mentioned in our discussion of the OT hope of a renewed people.

We begin with Acts 15. As gentiles began responding to the gospel, some Jewish believers "were teaching the brothers, 'Unless you are circumcised

---

23. For further discussion of this passage, see ibid., 173–201; and Matthew S. Harmon, "Allegory, Typology, or Something Else? Revisiting Galatians 4:21–5:1," in *Studies in the Pauline Epistles: Essays in Honor of Douglas J. Moo*, ed. Matthew S. Harmon and Jay E. Smith (Grand Rapids: Zondervan, 2014), 144–58. Several key themes in Galatians converge in this paragraph: being "under the law," Abraham and his descendants, the contrast between slave and free, the contrast between flesh and promise, and the contrast between flesh and Spirit.

24. See esp. Isa. 51–54, where the Abrahamic covenant, the restoration of Israel, and a new creation are accomplished through the sacrificial death and resurrection of the Servant.

25. When Gal. 3:1–5:1 is understood this way, it seems likely that when Paul refers to the "Israel of God" in 6:16, he has in view the church consisting of Jew and gentile together; see further G. K. Beale, "Peace and Mercy upon the Israel of God," *Bib* 80 (1999): 204–23; and Harmon, *She Must and Shall Go Free*, 236–38.

according to the custom of Moses, you cannot be saved'" (Acts 15:1). The controversy was so great that Paul and Barnabas make their way to Jerusalem to settle the issue with the apostles and elders in Jerusalem (15:2–6). After they deliberate for some time (15:7–12), James steps forward to weigh in (15:13–21). His starting point is the outpouring of the Spirit on the gentiles through Peter's preaching, which James describes as God visiting the gentiles "to take from them a people for his name" (15:14).[26] James finds confirmation of this conclusion in Amos 9:11–12, which he then quotes (Acts 15:16–17). Thus James sees the repentance and faith of the gentiles as the fulfillment of God's promise to rebuild the tent of David and bring into existence the eschatological people of God.[27] Through the resurrection of Jesus, David's fallen tent has been rebuilt, and as a result Jews and gentiles together form the new tabernacle where God's presence dwells. Therefore it is unnecessary to require the gentiles to be circumcised or keep the Mosaic law, since God has accepted them into the end-time people of God on the same basis as the Jews: faith in Jesus, the son of David.

The promise of restoration in Hosea 1–2 is developed in two places. In 1 Peter 2:4–6, believers are identified as living stones being built into a spiritual house because they are united to Christ, the living stone who is precious in God's sight. In contrast to those who stumble over Christ through their unbelief (2:7–8), believers are described with language used in the OT to describe Israel (2:9–10). They are "a chosen race, a royal priesthood, a holy nation, a people for his own possession," language applied to Israel at Mount Sinai (Exod. 19:5–6). But the remainder of the description in 1 Peter 2:9–10 comes from texts that describe what restored Israel will be like. God intends the church to "proclaim the excellencies of him who called you out of darkness into his marvelous light," which in Isaiah 43:21 refers to a restored Israel experiencing a new exodus and a new creation. The description continues in 2:10 with "Once you were not a people, but now you are God's people; once you had not received mercy, but now you have received mercy." As we saw above, these words are taken from Hosea 1–2, where they unambiguously refer to rebellious Israel being restored to God's favor in a new exodus. Yet Peter applies them to the church, composed of Jew and gentile together.[28]

26. In both the OT and NT, God "visiting" his people regularly refers to him acting to bring redemption (e.g., Exod. 3:16; Zeph. 2:7; Luke 1:68, 78). The Greek verb is *episkeptomai*, which regularly renders the Hebrew verb *pāqad*.

27. Of course, simply because this text is fulfilled in the formation of the church does not automatically mean that it has no remaining future fulfillment. Many of God's promises have multiple fulfillments, often with both initial and final fulfillments.

28. After the language quoted here (Hosea 1:6, 9), there is a reference to God's commitment to fulfill the Abrahamic covenant in Hosea 1:10–11. Might the promise of all the families being

Paul is even more explicit in applying the promise of Hosea 1–2 to the church in Romans 9. In an effort to explain how the widespread Jewish rejection of the Messiah fits within God's redemptive plan, Paul begins by explaining that the word of God has not failed because inheriting the promise of Abraham was never solely linked to ethnicity (9:6–13). Just as in the exodus, God is free to show mercy to whomever he wills, and to harden whomever he wills (9:14–18). As the potter, God has the sovereign right to display his glory in both vessels of wrath and vessels of mercy (9:19–23). By "vessels of mercy" Paul means those whom God has called from the Jews and the gentiles—in other words, the church (9:24). As the eschatological people of God, the church is the fulfillment of the promise that those who were once not a people are "my people, . . . beloved . . . sons of the living God" (Rom. 9:25–26, citing Hosea 1:23 and 2:1).

The promise that the end-time people of God would have circumcised hearts (Deut. 30:6) also finds its fulfillment in the church. Paul contends that when it comes to being right with God, physical circumcision is not what matters (Rom. 2:25–28). Rather, "A Jew is one inwardly, and circumcision is a matter of the heart, by the Spirit, not by the letter. His praise is not from man but from God" (Rom. 2:29). Believers experience the heart circumcision that God promised would characterize God's restored people. This is true not just of Jewish believers but of gentiles as well. In response to Judaizers who insist on circumcising the flesh, Paul says that as believers "we are the circumcision, who worship by the Spirit of God and glory in Christ Jesus and put no confidence in the flesh" (Phil. 3:3; cf. Col. 2:11).

In a number of places the NT authors explicitly identify the church as receiving the blessings of the new covenant promised to Israel. In 2 Corinthians 3:1–18, Paul explicitly contrasts the glory of the Mosaic covenant experienced by Moses and Israel with the new-covenant glories experienced by believers. He describes the Corinthians as "a letter from Christ delivered by us, written not with ink but with the Spirit of the living God, not on tablets of stone but on tablets of human hearts" (2 Cor. 3:3). The expression "tablets of human hearts" comes from Ezekiel 36:26–27, where God promises to remove the heart of stone, replace it with a heart of flesh, and put his Spirit in his people to cause them to obey him. There is also an echo of the promise in Jeremiah 31:33 to write God's law on the hearts of his people. Believers experience these blessings of the new covenant through believing in the gospel of Jesus Christ (2 Cor. 3:4–6). Explaining and reminding believers of these realities is central to the calling of the pastor.

---

blessed through the offspring of Abraham have led the NT authors to see the inclusion of the gentiles within the promise of Israel's restoration?

Conclusion

Although more texts could be mentioned, the ones we have discussed are more than sufficient to establish that the church is the eschatological people of God. Through our identification with Jesus Christ by faith, we have begun to experience the promised blessings of the new covenant. Foremost among these blessings is the gift of the Holy Spirit dwelling in us to empower us to obey God. He is the "guarantee of our inheritance until we acquire possession of it, to the praise of his glory" (Eph. 1:14). As those who have this inheritance that is "imperishable, undefiled, and unfading, kept in heaven" for us, we "by God's power are being guarded through faith for a salvation ready to be revealed in the last time" (1 Pet. 1:4–5). Because we have been rescued from the powers of this present evil age yet still live within it (Gal. 1:4), we experience trials and persecution that test the genuineness of our faith until the day when God consummates all his promises (1 Pet. 1:6–9).

Implications

Now that we have seen that the NT presents the church as the eschatological people of God, we need to draw out several implications.

The Church Is Not a Parenthesis

In some theological circles the church is described as a parenthesis in God's larger plan. Not only is such language unhelpful; it is ultimately unbiblical. Nowhere does Scripture portray the church as an interruption in God's plan for the world, occasioned only by the Jewish people's rejection of Jesus as the Messiah. Biblically speaking, if anything can be described as a parenthesis in God's plan, it is the Mosaic law. In Galatians 3:15–29, Paul explains that the giving of the Mosaic law 430 years after God's covenant with Abraham in no way nullified that covenant. Instead, it was a temporary provision of God until Jesus Christ, the promised seed of Abraham, came. Because Christ has come, the law has played its role in God's plan and has exited the stage.

From before the foundation of the world, God intended to create a people consisting of Jew and gentile together in one body known as the church. Because of our union with Christ, we are the eschatological people upon whom the end of the ages has come.

The Church Does Not "Replace" Israel

Other theological traditions argue that the church "replaces" Israel. There are at least two problems with this statement. First, as our discussion above showed, Jesus relives Israel's experiences and obeys where they (as well as Adam) had failed. Jesus is the embodiment of everything that Israel was supposed to be but never was because of their rebellion and idolatry. Therefore Jesus is the "true Israel," the faithful seed of Abraham who inherits the promises. It is by our faith in Christ, then, that the church, composed of believing Jews and gentiles, can be identified as the restored and renewed people of God promised in the OT. To argue that the church "replaces" Israel misses the central place of Christ in understanding the identity of God's people.

Second, the notion of "replacement" misses the repeated NT emphasis that the church experiences the (partial) fulfillment of what God promised in the OT. The way in which these promises have been fulfilled is at one level surprising and unexpected, yet at the same time it stands in continuity with the OT when understood in light of Christ.[29] There is an organic relationship between the faithful remnant of God's people under the old covenant and the church under the new covenant (Rom. 11:13–24).

God Is Not Done with the Jewish People

The emphasis on the church experiencing the initial fulfillment of the new-covenant promises does not mean that God is done with the Jewish people. Paul addresses this most clearly in Romans 11:1–32. Despite the widespread rejection of Jesus as the Messiah by the Jewish people, there is a remnant "chosen by grace" that has believed in Christ (11:1–10). The Jewish rejection of the Messiah has opened the door for the gentiles to experience salvation while at the same time provoking jealousy among the Jews (11:11–16). Because gentiles are "wild olive shoots" grafted into the holy root of the olive tree of God's people that runs from Genesis to Revelation, they must not become arrogant toward the Jews ("natural branches") who have been broken off because of their unbelief (11:17–22). God is more than capable of grafting back into the olive tree Jews who come to faith in Jesus as the Messiah (11:23–24). This partial hardening of Israel until the full number of gentiles has come into the people of God is a mystery that will result in all Israel being saved (11:25–27). Although many Jews oppose the gospel, God is not yet finished with them (11:28–29). Just as gentile believers were once disobedient to God but now have received mercy, so too there will come a

---

29. The NT frequently uses the word "mystery" (*mystērion*) to capture this reality; see further G. K. Beale and Benjamin L. Gladd, *Hidden but Now Revealed: A Biblical Theology of Mystery* (Downers Grove, IL: InterVarsity, 2014).

day when the Jewish people will turn from their disobedience to the gospel and receive mercy (11:30–32).[30]

While there are many different ways of working out the specifics, the larger point stands clear. God has not once and for all rejected the Jewish people, and there remains hope for all—Jew and gentile alike—who turn from their sins and trust in Jesus the Messiah.

Practical Suggestions

In the chapters that follow, we will attempt to spell out in practical terms how the church's identity as the eschatological people of God should shape different aspects of ministry. Because we have already experienced the blessings of the messianic age, our lives as individuals and as a body of believers should reflect this reality. However, we have not yet experienced the final consummation of all that God has promised! So as God's end-time people, our lives are also shaped by the hope that we have of the day when we will see the face of our Lord and Savior Jesus Christ, and his name will be written on our foreheads (Rev. 22:4). In the meantime, we experience the tension that comes from living between the cross and consummation. As those who have experienced the firstfruits of the Spirit, we "groan inwardly as we wait eagerly for adoption as sons, the redemption of our bodies" (Rom. 8:23).

In the rest of this book we will seek to explain how this already–not yet dynamic works itself out in the life and the ministry of the church. Because pastors are called to shepherd the flock, we will focus special attention on their role in equipping the eschatological people of God to live, love, and serve in the power of the Spirit.

Suggested Reading

While the various titles suggested below differ in how they understand the relationship between Israel and the church, they are all sensitive to the already–not yet aspect of the church's identity.

Beale, G. K. *A New Testament Biblical Theology: The Unfolding of the Old Testament in the New*, 651–749. Grand Rapids: Baker Academic, 2011.

---

30. There may be an already–not yet dynamic to this as well. The conversion of Jews in the present day anticipates a larger scale conversion in the future. Some, however (including Ben Gladd), believe not in a wide-scale future conversion of Jews but that ethnic Jews are currently being provoked to "jealousy" through gentiles being saved.

Clowney, Edmund P. *The Church*. Contours of Christian Theology. Downers Grove, IL: InterVarsity, 1995.

Dever, Mark. *The Church: The Gospel Made Visible*. Nashville: B&H, 2012.

Ladd, George E. *A Theology of the New Testament*, 576–94. Rev. ed. Grand Rapids: Eerdmans, 1993.

Ware, Bruce A. "The New Covenant and the People(s) of God." In *Dispensationalism, Israel and the Church: The Search for Definition*, edited by Craig A. Blaising and Darrell L. Bock, 68–97. Grand Rapids: Zondervan, 1992.

3

Life in the Overlap of the Ages

Several years ago, I was sitting in a pew and listening to a pastor wax eloquent about living in light of eternity. He then made a statement that has never left me: "Christians, live as though you are on the other side of heaven. Live like you are in the future." The point was forcefully made, and a number of the congregants readily nodded in agreement. The pastor had asked the audience to imagine that they were already living in eternity, dwelling in the new heavens and earth. After I gave this sermon some thought, it dawned on me that many pastors share a similar conviction. This popular teaching is not heresy, but it is unbiblical and can lead to a grave misunderstanding of the Christian life. Christians need not merely imagine that they live "on the other side," because in reality they are *already* there.

The present chapter, like the previous one, is foundational to our book. Our main purpose here is to sketch how believers live in accordance with the "latter days," particularly, how they are to behave as kingdom citizens, spiritually resurrected beings, and Spirit-led believers. Pastors and church leaders need a firm grasp of these realities if they are to minister in keeping with the "overlap of the ages."

We will look at some often-discussed topics and some that are less often treated. What we hope to discover is a more robust, more biblical way of viewing the Christian life. As end-time kingdom citizens, Christians are responsible to maintain certain ethics, and as resurrected and Spirit-filled saints, believers have the power to overcome sin and persevere in the midst of difficult circumstances.

Living in Light of the Kingdom

At the time of Jesus's arrival onto the scene in the early part of the first century, the Jews in Jesus's day, for the most part, were yearning for the arrival of the long-awaited messiah.[1] They expected that the messiah, or the "anointed one," would usher in the long-awaited kingdom of God in a period known as the "latter days." The "latter days" (and other synonymous expressions) are eschatological in that they represent a specific period of time that occurs at the very end of history. All the events that take place within this period, whether acts of judgment or restoration, are eschatological. The OT describes in some detail how God would intervene in history, restore Israel to its promised land, remove pagan oppression, and install his messiah to rule over Israel (e.g., Gen. 49:8–10; Num. 24:5–8; Dan. 2:44–45; 7:11–12). These end-time events were to occur at the very end of an epoch, the culmination of Israel's history.

When we turn to the Gospels, we soon realize that God's long-awaited kingdom has indeed broken into history through the person and work of Jesus. Jesus's defeat of the devil during his wilderness temptation (Matt. 4:1–11 and par.) is nothing short of the fulfillment of OT promises that portray God annihilating Israel's enemy through the messiah. But the true enemy of Israel is not ultimately Rome—but Satan.[2] Jesus, as the "stone" that had been "cut out without hands," has "crushed" the devil and his demonic forces (Dan. 2:34 NASB; cf. Luke 20:18). Moreover, Jesus's exorcism of demons is a result of his victory over the devil and further advancement of the kingdom. Matthew 12:28 says, for example, "But if it is by the Spirit of God that I cast out demons, then the kingdom of God has come upon you." At the very end of the age, the physical enemies of God (behind whom stand Satan and the forces of evil) will be completely and finally defeated. We thus have an already–not yet defeat of evil: first the unseen powers of evil in the first century and then the physical opponents of God and his people at the very end of history.[3]

1. For a brief overview of messianic expectations in the first century, see N. T. Wright, *Jesus and the Victory of God* (Philadelphia: Fortress, 1996), 481–86.

2. Ibid., 451–61.

3. For further discussion of the already–not yet state of the end-time kingdom in the Gospels, see George Eldon Ladd, *The Presence of the Future: The Eschatology of Biblical Realism* (Grand Rapids: Eerdmans, 1974); and G. R. Beasley-Murray, *Jesus and the Kingdom of God* (Grand Rapids: Eerdmans, 1986).

In his work on the notion of heaven and earth in the book of Matthew, Jonathan T. Pennington cogently argues that Matthew's preference for "heavenly" language[4] stems not from a desire to avoid the title "God" but to draw a distinction between heaven and earth.[5] In addition, Matthew's "heaven" terminology refers to the arrival of the heavenly kingdom on earth. The heavenly dimension of God's kingdom irrupts into the earthly ministry of Jesus. This end-time kingdom "of heaven" has begun its descent and has initially broken into the earthly sphere.

With the arrival of God's long-awaited kingdom comes what we will label "kingdom ethics." In other words, when God installs his eschatological kingdom, he establishes ethics that are in keeping with arrival of the kingdom. The OT, on occasion, anticipates these ethics. Isaiah 11:1–5, for example, states that the coming messiah will rule with perfect justice and righteousness ("righteousness shall be the belt of his [the messiah's] waist, and faithfulness the belt of his loins" [v. 5]). Not only will equity and justice characterize his rule, but the inhabitants of the kingdom will also enjoy great peace (v. 8; cf. vv. 6–9). Another passage from Isaiah 32:16–20 describes several similar characteristics of living in the "new age":

> Then *justice* will dwell in the wilderness, and *righteousness* abide in the fruitful field. And the effect of *righteousness* will be *peace*, and the result of *righteousness*, *quietness and trust* forever. My people will abide in a *peaceful habitation*, in secure dwellings, and in *quiet resting places*. And it will hail when the forest falls down, and the city will be utterly laid low. Happy are you who sow beside all waters, who let the feet of the ox and the donkey range free. (italics added)

These brief examples from Isaiah 11 and 32 illustrate the importance of God's end-time work among his people. To repeat, the advent of the long-awaited kingdom of God ushers in particular ethics, ethics that are in line with the eschatological kingdom. Therefore, Jesus's emphasis on the arrival of the kingdom and its accompanying ethics signals the fulfillment of OT prophetic passages (e.g., Isa. 9:6–7; 11:1–16). Though largely invisible, God's kingdom and its ethics have broken into the world. Once this concept is grasped, Jesus's teaching on the "kingdom" becomes much more biblically sensible and rooted in the story line of the Bible.

4. Matthew generally has "kingdom of heaven" (e.g., Matt. 3:2; 4:17; 5:3, 10), whereas Mark and Luke prefer the phrase "kingdom of God" (e.g., Mark 1:15; 4:11; Luke 4:43; 6:20; 7:28).
5. Jonathan T. Pennington, *Heaven and Earth in the Gospel of Matthew*, NovTSup 126 (Leiden: Brill, 2007; repr. Grand Rapids: Baker Academic, 2009).

The "Love Command"

Now that we have begun to grasp this idea, let us probe Jesus's teaching a bit more deeply and tease out some implications. We will first look at his teaching on love and then turn to his emphasis on ministering to the poor. Love, according to Jesus, is a prime expression of kingdom citizenship. We will first turn to Matthew 22:36–37: "'Teacher, which is the great commandment in the Law?' And he [Jesus] said to him, 'You shall love the Lord your God with all your heart and with all your soul and with all your mind.'" Jesus's response is directed toward one of the Pharisees, an expert in the law. Jesus here quotes Deuteronomy 6:5 and claims that the weightiest or "greatest" commandment of the Torah is to love God above all else. In the next verse, Jesus states the second greatest commandment: "You shall love your neighbor as yourself" (Matt. 22:39; cf. Lev. 19:18). What needs to be kept in mind is that loving one another is rooted in loving God. Believers cannot love one another without first loving God (see Exod. 20 and Deut. 5).

We can now proceed to Matthew 5:43–44: "You have heard that it was said, 'You shall love your neighbor and hate your enemy.' But I say to you, Love your enemies and pray for those who persecute you." Jesus's teaching on love here in verses 43–44 is an integral part of the Sermon on the Mount (Matt. 5–7), but what is often overlooked is Jesus's relationship to the law in the immediate context (vv. 17–20). Before we can grasp Jesus's message on love, we must first understand his relationship to the Mosaic covenant, a topic that continues to be heavily debated.[6] Verses 17 and 19 state, "Do not think that I have come to abolish the Law or the Prophets; I have not come to abolish them *but to fulfill them*. . . . Therefore whoever relaxes one of the least of these commandments and teaches others to do the same will be called least in the kingdom of heaven, but whoever does them and teaches them will be called great in the kingdom of heaven" (italics added). Jesus is essentially claiming that he and his teaching, particularly the Sermon on the Mount, are a "fulfillment" of OT patterns and expectations (cf. Matt. 2:15).[7] The OT, especially the Mosaic covenant, anticipated Jesus's person, his acts, and his teaching on kingdom ethics.[8] The OT expected that the coming messiah

6. For a general introduction to the debate, see Stanley N. Gundry, ed., *Five Views on Law and Gospel* (Grand Rapids: Zondervan, 1996).

7. Cf. Robert Banks, "Matthew's Understanding of the Law: Authenticity and Interpretation in Matthew 5:17–20," *JBL* 93 (1974): 226–42; D. A. Carson, "Matthew," in *The Expositor's Bible Commentary*, ed. F. E. Gaebelein (Grand Rapids: Zondervan, 1984), 8:143–46; Douglas J. Moo, "Jesus and the Authority of the Mosaic Law," *JSNT* 20 (1984): 3–49; Vern Poythress, *The Shadow of Christ in the Law of Moses* (Brentwood, TN: Wolgemuth & Hyatt, 1991), 263–69.

8. In his concluding paragraph, Robert Banks helpfully explains Matthew's view of the law: "It is not so much Jesus' stance towards the Law that he is concerned to depict; it is how the Law stands with regard to him, as the one who brings it to fulfillment and to whom all attention must

would establish ethics or norms that are in keeping with the future kingdom. This explains Jesus's statement "Do not think that I have come to abolish the Law or the Prophets; I have not come to abolish them but to fulfill them" (v. 17; Luke 16:16–17).

With Jesus's establishment of the new age, his people are called and empowered to live as citizens of his kingdom. In commenting on the Sermon on the Mount in Matthew 5–7, R. T. France claims, "Far from being a philosophical discourse on ethics, this is a messianic manifesto, setting out the unique demands and revolutionary insights of one who claims an absolute authority over other people and whose word, like the word of God, will determine their destiny."[9] These ethics are not antithetical to those in the old covenant or Mosaic administration (see Deut. 6:5!), but they are internalized, reaching their intended state of fulfillment (Jer. 31:31–34; Ezek. 36:25–27). This is not to say that the Mosaic covenant lacked an internal dimension (Exod. 20:17), but it was largely external in nature.

These end-time kingdom ethics are not deeply intertwined with Israel's status as a theocratic nation living in the "old age." Instead, they are intended for a community of saints that has been reconstituted around King Jesus in the "new age."[10]

For example, one function of the Torah in the OT was to separate Israel from the surrounding pagan neighbors, but this function of the law has ceased to be the case. In the new age, God's people are marked not by external trappings (dietary regulations, festivals, clothing, etc.) but by their allegiance to Jesus, the Messiah, through faith. This is particularly true of gentile believers (Eph. 3:1–13). The same could be said of the ceremonial regulations. Since Jesus ultimately fulfills the requirements of the temple and its cult, there is no longer any need to keep them in the "new age" (Heb. 9:11–10:18). G. K. Beale summarizes this well:

> The external rites (dietary laws, special cultic feast days, Sabbaths, circumcision, etc.) of the law are no longer necessary in that their redemptive-historical

---

now be directed. For Matthew, then, it is not the question of Jesus' relation to the Law that is in doubt but rather its relation to him!" ("Matthew's Understanding," 242).

9. R. T. France, *The Gospel of Matthew*, NICNT (Grand Rapids: Eerdmans, 2007), 156.

10. Richard Hays argues within this vein, "The community of Jesus' followers lives now in anticipation of ultimate restoration by God. They do not seek to enforce God's way through violence; rather, they await God's act of putting things right. . . . The teachings of the rest of the Sermon [on the Mount], then, specify the character of a community that seeks to embody this eschatological vision of God's righteousness" (*The Moral Vision of the New Testament: Community, Cross, New Creation; A Contemporary Introduction to New Testament Ethics* [San Francisco: HarperSanFrancisco, 1996], 98).

purpose was to function as a "shadow of things about to come . . ." (Col. 2:17).
. . . The various external expressions of the OT law pointed to the coming
Messiah, who has now arrived. Therefore, the law's preparatory adumbrating
function has come to an end because the messianic "substance" to which it
pointed has arrived.[11]

Since all believers equally participate in the kingdom, we are now bound
to a set of "latter-day kingdom ethics." The phrase "latter-day kingdom ethics" is appropriate, as it pertains to living in a particular stage of redemptive
history. All Christians belong to the new age and are required to live accordingly. We have seen how love plays a pronounced role in the Gospels, and as
kingdom citizens, we ought to pursue an ethic of love. First John 4:7–8 states
the matter succinctly: "Beloved, let us love one another, for love is from God,
and whoever loves has been born of God and knows God. Anyone who does
not love does not know God, because God is love." Above all, Christians' love
of God and others must shine brightly in the new age.

Kingdom and Service to the Poor

One of the most remarkable features of Jesus's kingdom message is its
counterintuitiveness—a teaching that flies in the face of culture and worldly
expectations. The Greco-Roman and Jewish cultures of the first century certainly differ from our Western culture. Dress, language, and family and social
structures looked quite different two thousand years ago. Yet certain social
principles and expectations transcend time and culture. The poor, for example,
have always been relegated to society's fringes, whereas wealth commands
authority, respect, and the ear of the populace. One need only observe the
checkout counters of grocery stores. Magazines covering the rich and famous,
movie stars, and society's elite litter the aisles. Culture idolizes the wealthy
and talented but marginalizes the weak, even the ordinary.

Jesus's kingdom message, however, flips society's expectations and values
on their heads. The kingdom is characterized not by wealth and talent but
by humility and service to those caught in the fringes of society. Jesus often
spoke on this topic, and we have scores of texts from which to choose.[12] Two
poignant examples are the parable of the wedding and the parable of the
banquet (Luke 14:7–24; Matt. 22:1–14).

11. G. K. Beale, *A New Testament Biblical Theology: The Unfolding of the Old Testament
in the New* (Grand Rapids: Baker Academic, 2011), 805.
12. For a good, biblical-theological study of poverty and wealth, see Craig L. Blomberg,
Neither Poverty nor Riches: A Biblical Theology of Possessions, NSBT (Downers Grove, IL:
InterVarsity, 1999).

At the beginning of Luke 14, Jesus shares a meal with a "ruler of the Pharisees" on the Sabbath (v. 1). Chapter 14 begins with what appears to be a discourse on healing a diseased individual on the Sabbath (cf. Mark 3:1–6), and Jesus's words affirm this observation: "Is it lawful to heal on the Sabbath, or not?" (v. 3). The Jewish leaders are unable to give a response, so they keep their mouths shut (v. 6). Then in verse 7 Jesus transitions into a parable about a wedding celebration. What ties the parable (vv. 7–11) and the healing episode (vv. 1–6) together is not Sabbath or the like, but an individual with dropsy (v. 2). As such, this particular individual would, to a certain degree, be socially marginalized. In the following two parables, Jesus tugs on this thread and relates it to the nature of the kingdom. What we have then is a discussion on how the kingdom relates to the pariahs of society.

Verse 7 further reveals why Jesus delivered this parable: "He [Jesus] told a parable to those who were invited, when he noticed how they chose the places of honor." In both Greco-Roman and Jewish society, the more prestigious individuals sat in certain seats of honor. For example, the Qumran community, a Jewish sect living in the desert at the time of Jesus, proves our point. In the *Community Rule* (1QS), the community sat its council according to rank: "Each one [council member] by his rank: the priests will sit down first, the elders next and the remainder of all the people will sit down in order of rank" (VI, 8–9; cf. II, 1–8).[13]

This sect's council not only sat according to rank but also scrupulously screened its members, refusing to grant membership to individuals with any sort of malady or deformity. Qumran's outlook is akin to the Jewish leaders' treatment of the man with dropsy (v. 2) and their insistence that they assume the "places of honor" (v. 7).

Jesus's kingdom message inverts this worldview: "When you [Jewish leaders] are invited, go and sit in the lowest place. . . . For everyone who exalts himself will be humbled, and he who humbles himself will be exalted" (vv. 10–11). Jesus is essentially claiming that even though the Jewish leaders deserve (at least according to the cultural norms of the day) to sit in seats of honor, they are to choose willingly the "lowest place" (v. 10). The paradoxical nature of the kingdom (Matt. 13:11–14 and par.) corresponds to the paradoxical nature of Jesus's kingdom ethics: "Everyone who exalts himself will be humbled, and he who humbles himself will be exalted" (v. 11).

We see this in greater detail in the following section, the parable of the banquet (vv. 15–24). Jesus's second parable concerns a prominent individual

---

13. I became aware of this Jewish text in J. D. G. Dunn, *The Christ and the Spirit: Christology*, 2 vols. (Grand Rapids: Eerdmans, 1998), 1:106–9. Unless otherwise noted, all quotations of the Dead Sea Scrolls are from *The Dead Sea Scrolls Study Edition*, ed. F. García Martínez and Eibert J. C. Tigchelaar, 2 vols. (Leiden: Brill, 2000).

who decided to host a great feast. The host invited not a few guests, and many of them appear to be wealthy individuals (vv. 18–19). Instead of making it a priority to come to the feast, the guests were ensnared with their business and personal affairs. In reaction, the host of the party became enraged and commanded his servant to seek out the culturally unsophisticated and those on the fringes of society. The servant was to bring back "the poor and crippled and blind and lame" (v. 21). Once all these folks arrived at the banquet, room still remained for more (v. 22). The host then ordered that the servant should "go out to the highways and hedges and compel people to come in" (v. 23). The banquet thus looked remarkably different from expectations. The host and his servants anticipated that the culturally elite and the rich would attend, but lo and behold, they were too consumed with their own affairs. In the end, the banquet was filled with outsiders, probably gentiles, and the poor. The upshot of this parable is Jesus's insistence that the kingdom is counterintuitive on a variety of levels, and one of those levels pertains to those who gain admittance. From a worldly perspective, the kingdom belongs to the sophisticated, the culturally significant. But Jesus reverses these values and claims the exact opposite—only the weak and the lowly are admitted.

This teaching strikes at the heart of the gospel and Christian living. This is not to say that money is wrong or being culturally sophisticated is to be shunned. The gospel is, though, for the *spiritually* bankrupt, the "poor in spirit" (Matt. 5:3). When we arrive at the cross, we must not do so with our talents or money in hand. All that is required of us is faith in God's promises, faith that lays hold of Christ and all that he offers. Jesus's teaching on the kingdom reminds us of this truth.

Now that the kingdom has arrived, our lives are to be in accordance with its principles. Kingdom living demands that we recognize the world's values and, once we have done so, overturn them. This means that we treat people differently. We view them from God's perspective and not ours. We embrace those who are spiritually poor and weak.[14] Whatever the case may be, we are compelled to demonstrate our kingdom citizenship by reflecting its values in our daily lives.

What makes living out these kingdom ethics particularly challenging is what scholars call the "overlap of the ages." Generally, the OT did not envision that the eschatological kingdom would arrive, for the most part, invisibly (Matt. 13:1–52). With a few exceptions, the OT largely anticipated its arrival to happen physically and all at once. To rehearse what G. K. Beale argued in chapter 1, above, Christians are caught living, on the one hand, in the new creation

---

14. Note that sometimes the spiritually poor are indeed physically poor.

and all that accompanies it (the kingdom, the pouring out of the Spirit, the forgiveness of sins, etc.). On the other, believers still wage war against sin, the devil, and the world around them. Restoration has arrived and the new creation has dawned in Christ, but it has not done so in its fullness. Strangely, kingdom saints live in the midst of an unbelieving world.[15] Living out end-time kingdom ethics is difficult, since we await the full restoration of all things. Until then, we can anticipate great hostility, both internally and externally, in conducting ourselves in light of the overlap of the ages.

Living in Light of Our Spiritual Resurrection

The doctrine of the resurrection, though central to the NT, is often one of the least understood teachings of the Bible.[16] Many Christians view resurrection as a future event and generally unrelated to the believer's daily walk with God. In one sense, this position is partially justified, since the OT expected that the resurrection would occur at the very end of Israel's history, when the righteous saints would rise and gain eternal life, and the unrighteous would rise and receive eternal punishment (e.g., Dan. 12:1–3). From the OT perspective, the resurrection was indeed a future doctrine. But when we take into account the NT's teaching on the resurrection, we soon realize that the end-time resurrection, an event that was to take place at the very end of the "latter days," has been pushed up into the present. Though the resurrection has not come in its fullness, a spiritual resurrection[17] of the saints has begun through the person of Christ. The implications of this already–not yet conception of the resurrection are staggering.

We will first listen to Jesus's teaching on this issue in John 5, and then we will move into Paul and discover what he has to say on the topic. John 5 opens

15. For further discussion of this theme, see G. K. Beale and Benjamin L. Gladd, *Hidden but Now Revealed: A Biblical Theology of Mystery* (Downers Grove, IL: InterVarsity, 2014).

16. This portion of the chapter is conceptually dependent on Beale, *New Testament Biblical Theology*, 131–36, 234–38.

17. We do not use the term "spiritual" in the hermeneutical sense of a deeper meaning of Scripture or the like but by way of contrasting the physical mode of existence. This does not mean that a great divide exists between the spiritual and physical within the totality of a person in a Platonic sense (see Anthony A. Hoekema, *Created in God's Image* [Grand Rapids: Eerdmans, 1986]). Saints now enjoy a partially resurrected status, which entails the resurrection of their souls. Though believers are spiritually resurrected, they still possess indwelling sin and, until their bodily resurrection, will continue to sin. We must also note that the OT, particularly Dan. 12:1–3, predicted the resurrection not only of the saints' bodies but also of their souls. The saints will enjoy the complete restoration of soul and body. In this way, the NT authors are right to claim that Daniel's prophecy has indeed been fulfilled, at least initially.

with Jesus healing a disabled man (vv. 1–15). This particular healing episode, however, was not primarily about the disabled person but about Jesus's actions on a certain day of the week. Verses 9–17 are the heart of the discourse, and verse 9b introduces the problem: "Now that day was the Sabbath." Evidently the newly healed man had violated Sabbath regulations because he did "work" by taking up his bed and walking. For our purposes, we need only note that according to the Jews, this man had broken the Sabbath, an action that incurred the gravest of penalties.

We now arrive at the heart of the problem in verses 16–17: The Jews were "persecuting Jesus, because he was doing these things on the Sabbath." Throughout Jesus's ministry, the Sabbath is one of the most important issues that Jesus confronts. Jesus is the Lord of the Sabbath; therefore, he has authority over it (Mark 2:23–28). Furthermore, in verse 17, Jesus makes one of the most tantalizing statements in all of John: "My Father is working until now, and I am working." Jesus claims that God is "working." Jesus then goes on to say that just as God is working, he too is "working." Jesus is placing his activity on par with God's. As God is sovereign over the affairs of the cosmos, so is Jesus.

Verse 18 summarizes verses 19–47 and is the main point of verses 1–18: "This was why the Jews were seeking all the more to kill him, because not only was he breaking the Sabbath [vv. 6–16], but he was even calling God his own Father, making himself equal with God." In other words, Jesus is explicitly identifying himself with Israel's God. We now enter into an arena that both the Father and the Son share, namely, raising the dead (v. 21). Since the theme of "raising the dead," or resurrection, permeates this section, we will briefly sketch this theme.

Though the OT writers did not develop fully the concept of the resurrected state, they do mention it in a few passages (see Job 19:26–27; Isa. 26:19; Hosea 6:2; Dan. 12:1–2).[18] By the time of the NT, the issue of resurrection had undergone considerable development in Judaism. Various sects of Judaism held to different views of the resurrection. The Sadducees did not believe in the resurrection, whereas the Pharisees did (Acts 4:1–2; 23:8; 26:6–8). Yet the NT is very clear: there will be a bodily resurrection (1 Cor. 15:35–53), which is

18. In the ancient Near East, particularly in Egypt, a good amount of discussion exists concerning the afterlife. Death is the greatest enemy of all, and the grave is a place of shadows, confinement, darkness, etc. Evidence points to some sort of afterlife, but only in the sense of a spirit—not *a renewed existence*. The ancient Near Eastern and Greco-Roman views of resurrection stand in stark contrast to the OT and Jewish conception of the resurrection (see Philip S. Johnson, *Shades of Sheol: Death and Afterlife in the Old Testament* [Downers Grove, IL: InterVarsity, 2002]; N. T. Wright, *The Resurrection of the Son of God* [Minneapolis: Fortress, 2003], 32–84).

tied to God's promise of creating a new heavens and a new earth (Rev. 21–22). God is committed to his creation and to his people. Believers will conform to the body of the second, resurrected and glorious Adam (while at the same time enjoying some continuity with their old body), according to 1 Corinthians 15:35–53. The church will participate in this great act of the creation of a new heavens and earth. We will not be garbed in our old mortal bodies but will be fashioned in a new, resurrected physical body, just like the body of Christ (1 John 3:2).

Coming back to John 5:21, we can now understand in more detail what this text is communicating. The "Father raises the dead" means that God is committed to the great act of redeeming the cosmos and humanity. Verse 21 ends with the Son also "giving life" and implicitly "raising the dead." Just as the Father raises the dead, so does Jesus, because he too is divine.

The beginning of verse 24 highlights the need for faith in Christ in order to obtain "eternal life." But how is "eternal life" defined here in John 5? Verse 24b says the one who believes "does not come into judgment, but has passed from death into life." According to this verse, eternal life is *the transfer from death to life*. Notice how this is past tense: the believer has crossed the line, as it were, from death to life. We see no hint of Platonic immortality or anything of the sort. Instead, we see a more glorious doctrine—the resurrection of the soul.[19]

The phrase "passing from death to life" sets the tone for the next several verses. In fact, verses 25–29 further explicate the meaning of eternal life. Verse 25 begins with a very strange yet salient description: "An hour is coming and is now here." Most pass over this statement, but doing so defangs the point of the verse, for the clause tells us "*when* the dead shall hear the voice of the Son of God" (italics added). The term "hour" (*hōra*) plays a prominent role in John (4:21, 23; 12:23; 16:25, 32; 17:1) and originates from the book of Daniel (8:17, 19; 11:6, 35, 40).[20] Of special interest to us is Daniel 12:1–2:

> At that time [lit., "hour"; Gk. *hōra*] shall arise Michael, the great prince who has charge of your people. And there shall be a time of trouble, such as never has been since there was a nation till that time. But at that time your people shall be delivered, everyone whose name shall be found written in the book. And many of those who sleep in the dust of the earth shall awake, some to everlasting life, and some to shame and everlasting contempt.

19. D. A. Carson deems v. 24 as "perhaps the strongest affirmation of inaugurated eschatology in the Fourth Gospel" (*The Gospel according to John*, PNTC [Grand Rapids: Eerdmans, 1991], 256); cf. William J. Dumbrell, *The Search for Order: Biblical Eschatology in Focus* (Grand Rapids: Baker, 1994), 247.

20. See Beale, *New Testament Biblical Theology*, 131–36; and Stefanos Mihalios, *The Danielic Eschatological Hour in the Johannine Literature*, LNTS (New York: T&T Clark, 2011).

The Greek translation of Daniel 12:1–2 uses the same word found here in John 5:25.[21] What confirms the allusion to Daniel 12:1–2 is the following verses. In verses 28–29, John continues to allude to Daniel 12:1–2 when he states, "An hour [hōra] is coming when all who are in the tombs will hear his voice and come out, those who have done good to the resurrection of life, and those who have done evil to the resurrection of judgment."

So when we read Jesus's statement that "an hour is coming, and is now here," we can now fully appreciate his saying. The "hour" or timing of the resurrection has *now begun in the ministry of Christ, especially his resurrection*. Jesus's teaching on the already–not yet aspect of resurrection entails a radical new way of viewing the Christian life. For example, here in John 5 Jesus gives "life" to those who have faith or "believe" in him (vv. 24, 40). But obtaining "life" or "eternal life" does not primarily mean living forever (though, obviously, that is secondarily in view) but being joined, here and now, to God's future redemption in the new heavens and earth. The future (Isa. 65:17; 66:22) has broken into the present. In commenting on John 5, Mathison rightly adds, "The resurrection life of the future age reaches back into the present and is available now to the spiritually dead. Believers now receive a foretaste of the resurrection life that they will experience in fullness on the last day."[22]

Christ transforms and renews (regenerates) the dead soul of the individual unto resurrection life. Carson aptly comments on John 5:25, "The resurrection life for the physically dead in the end time is already being manifest as life for the spiritually dead."[23] Recall the famous miracle involving Lazarus in John 11. Jesus reassures Martha, "Your brother will rise again" (v. 23). But Martha affirms this truth in the following verse: "Martha said to him, 'I know that he will rise again in the resurrection on the last day.'" Jesus responds to her in verses 25–26: "Jesus said to her, 'I am the resurrection and the life. Whoever believes in me, though he die, yet shall he live, and everyone who lives and believes in me shall never die. Do you believe this?'" Remarkably, Jesus claims that he himself is the locus of resurrection life (John 6:39–40, 44, 54; 11:24; 12:48) and proceeds to demonstrate that resurrection power by raising Lazarus from the grave (vv. 43–44).

That explains the "now" part, but there is still a side of the resurrection that has yet to arrive. Notice the phrase "is coming" in 5:25a. Though the

---

21. The Old Greek version of the Septuagint reads *hōra* ("hour"), whereas the Theodotion version has *kairos* ("time").

22. Keith A. Mathison, *From Age to Age: The Unfolding of Biblical Eschatology* (Phillipsburg, NJ: P&R, 2009), 437.

23. Carson, *Gospel according to John*, 256.

resurrection and new creation have broken in through the ministry of Christ, the bodily resurrection has yet to occur. A few verses later, we see this line of thinking: "Do not marvel at this, for an hour *is coming* when all who are in the tombs will hear his voice and come out, those who have done good to the resurrection of life, and those who have done evil to the resurrection of judgment" (vv. 28–29, italics added). John 5, therefore, teaches a two-stage resurrection. On the one hand, all those who have faith or "believe" in Jesus have been spiritually raised in fulfillment of Daniel 12:1–2. On the other, believers do not yet have their resurrected bodies (1 Cor. 15:12–54) and still must battle against indwelling sin.

That believers would enjoy a two-stage resurrection (spiritual then physical) is largely foreign to the OT. But what must be kept in mind is that both fulfillments remain literal. The "spiritual" resurrection is just as literal as the physical, since Daniel's prophecy certainly included the resurrection of bodies together with resurrected spirits (Dan. 12:1–3)! The prophecy is not fulfilled all at once, since the spiritual resurrection occurs first, followed later by the physical. Therefore, it is not the nature of fulfillment that has changed, but its timing. That is, the fulfillments of the spiritual and physical resurrections are not spiritualized nor allegorized but merely staggered. This two-stage temporal fulfillment is the revelation conceptually of an OT "mystery," since it was not clear in Daniel that there would be such a staggered fulfillment.[24]

We have attempted to show that Jesus's teaching in John 5 pertains to the already–not yet aspect of resurrection. But this theme is not restricted to John 5; several passages in the Pauline corpus reinforce this belief. Here are two of the more prominent ones:

> But God, being rich in mercy, because of the great love with which he loved us, even when we were dead in our trespasses, made us alive together with Christ—by grace you have been saved—and *raised us up with him and seated us with him* in the heavenly places in Christ Jesus. (Eph. 2:4–6, italics added)

> If then *you have been raised with Christ*, seek the things that are above, where Christ is, seated at the right hand of God. (Col. 3:1, italics added)

Ephesians 2:4–6 is perhaps the most explicit reference to the already–not yet aspect of resurrection. Taken together, the phrases "made us alive" and being "raised up" certainly refer to a present resurrected state of believers. Some prefer to read this passage metaphorically or as a figure of speech, but

---

24. For further discussion of the notion of a two-stage resurrection in the NT, see Beale and Gladd, *Hidden but Now Revealed*, 289–91, 300–304.

the same wording is used elsewhere in Paul as a reference to Christ's physical resurrection (Rom. 8:9–11). Peter O'Brien comments on Ephesians 2:5, "Paul's readers have come to life with Christ, who was dead and rose again; their new life, then, is a sharing in the new life which he received when he rose from the dead."[25] At present, Christians are enjoying their resurrected state, albeit spiritually. Certainly we anticipate the day when our body will "catch up" to our spirit.

We have devoted some energy to this topic because many Christians today have not fully grasped this doctrine, if at all. Those who have put their faith and trust in the gospel are spiritually resurrected beings.[26] Their existence has been radically and incontrovertibly altered; Christians have been joined to God's future redemption in the new heavens and earth.

This doctrine is not esoteric, with little or no application to our daily lives. Indeed, this NT teaching on the resurrection has manifold and concrete applications. This principle resembles a wheel: at the center of the wheel is our resurrected state, and the protruding spokes are the various ways in which the resurrection affects our walk with God.

Though believers are spiritually resurrected (the "already"), they still await a future time when God will redeem them fully (the "not yet"). At Christ's second coming, God will eradicate indwelling sin and transform believers' sin-wrecked bodies into the body of Christ (1 Cor. 15:51–53). We will be transformed into a perfect body that is fit for the new heavens and earth. Presently believers are caught between these two events. Inaugurated eschatology reminds Christians that sin still remains, and believers will struggle continuously with the effects of the fall. Recall Paul's words in Romans 8 where he reminds believers that they are counted righteous in God's sight and no longer under "condemnation" (8:1). They are joined to the risen Christ by God's life-giving Spirit but still battle the effects of the fall (8:11). Christians "suffer" and, like creation itself, await the final restoration of all things (8:18–21). While caught between the overlap of the ages, all believers are called to eradicate sin and put down the "deeds of the body" (i.e., the works of the old age; 8:13).

This understanding of the already–not yet of our resurrection dramatically affects our assurance of salvation. Confidence in our salvation resembles a triangle.[27] At one point lies faith in God's promises, at another is good works that spring forth from our initial, spiritual resurrection, and at the third point is the Spirit's work in our lives.

25. Peter T. O'Brien, *The Letter to the Ephesians*, PNTC (Grand Rapids: Eerdmans, 1999), 167.
26. Though believers have been spiritually resurrected and participate in the new creation (2 Cor. 5:17), indwelling sin remains until the final resurrection (cf. Gal. 5:13–26).
27. This illustration is taken from Beale, *New Testament Biblical Theology*, 867.

Each of these three points reinforces the others, assuring believers that they can be confident that God will "bring it [salvation] to completion at the day of Jesus Christ" (Phil. 1:6).

Living in Light of the Spirit

Old Testament Expectations of the Spirit

One of the hallmarks of the new age is the arrival of the Spirit. According to the OT, God's promise to establish an end-time people of God that enjoys his presence in a new creation (the original intention of Gen. 1–2) is actualized through the coming of the Spirit in the "latter days." The Holy Spirit, therefore, plays a central role in achieving God's purpose of redemption, climaxing in the restoration of all things in a new heavens and earth. The Spirit's role is far reaching, encompassing a variety of themes throughout the OT, so we will only focus our attention on the Spirit's work in the "latter days" and how he relates to creation, temple, God's law, and kingdom. All four of these categories have considerable overlap, and each informs the others.

CREATION

From the very beginning, we discern that the Spirit participates in God's work of creation: "The Spirit of God was hovering over the face of the waters" (Gen. 1:2). Throughout the OT, especially in the Prophets, the Spirit is the agent of God's creative power. Isaiah prophesies that in the "latter days" the Spirit will remove God's curse upon the land and bring about the new creation: "For the palace is forsaken, the populous city deserted . . . until the Spirit is poured upon us from on high, and the wilderness becomes a fruitful field, and the fruitful field is deemed a forest. Then justice will dwell in the wilderness, and righteousness abide in the fruitful field" (Isa. 32:14–16; see also 44:3). The prophet Ezekiel portrays the restoration of Israel through the use of resurrection language; it is striking that his description most likely alludes to Genesis 2 and the creation of Adam and Eve (Gen. 2:7): "Thus says the Lord GOD: Behold, I will open your graves and raise you from your graves. ... And you shall know that I am the LORD, when I open your graves, and raise you from your graves, O my people. And I will put my Spirit within you, and you shall live, and I will place you in your own land" (Ezek. 37:12–14; see 37:3–11). These texts and others like them (e.g., Ps. 104:30) associate the Spirit with God's great act of creating. Just as the Spirit played a vital role in the original creation, so too will he play a role in the end-time new creation.

TEMPLE

Throughout the OT, the Spirit occasionally dwells with certain individuals (prophets, kings, etc.) for specific tasks, but the prophets predict that God will one day dwell with all believers in a special way.[28] Not only will his Spirit dwell more fully with humanity on a qualitative level in the new creation, but his Spirit will also dwell with all of the redeemed in a special manner. Take, for example, Joel's famous prophecy: "And it shall come to pass afterward, that I will pour out my Spirit on all flesh; your sons and your daughters shall prophesy, your old men shall dream dreams, and your young men shall see visions. Even on the male and female servants in those days I will pour out my Spirit" (2:28–29; cf. Num. 11:29).

GOD'S LAW

The Spirit's coming signals a more intense stage, whereby God's law is more deeply emblazoned on the heart. One of the most explicit texts in this regard is Ezekiel 36:26–27: "And I will give you a new heart, and a new spirit I will put within you. And I will remove the heart of stone from your flesh and give you a heart of flesh. And I will put my Spirit within you, and cause you to walk in my statutes and be careful to obey my rules" (cf. Ezek. 11:19–20; Jer. 31:31–33). In light of humanity's plight, we are not able to obey God's law perfectly. God must therefore send his Spirit to create the heart anew, enabling it to internalize his laws more deeply in the new creation.

KINGDOM

Lastly, the Spirit empowers believers to fight sin and gain victory over evil. We mentioned above that God's Spirit filled certain individuals for specific tasks in the OT (prophets, temple artisans, kings, etc.). In this vein, the OT predicts that the Spirit will fill God's messiah in a unique way, equipping him

---

28. This Spirit most likely, at some level, dwelled with all OT saints (Gal. 4:29). Since the process of salvation is the same in both Testaments (the Spirit "regenerates" individuals' hearts), the Spirit must have dwelled, to some degree, in all OT saints. But the indwelling of the Spirit in NT saints appears to be in an escalated manner.

to judge wisely and rule over Israel and the nations. In Isaiah 11:1–4, the Spirit plays a role in the messiah's victory over the rebellious nations: "And the *Spirit of the* LORD *shall rest upon him*, the Spirit of wisdom and understanding, the Spirit of counsel and might, the Spirit of knowledge and the fear of the LORD. . . . *He shall strike the earth with the rod of his mouth*, and with the breath of his lips *he shall kill the wicked*" (italics added; cf. Isa. 42:1–3; 61:1–3). The Spirit will thus enable the messiah to defeat Israel's enemies and install God's eschatological kingdom.

New Testament Fulfillment of the Spirit's Arrival

The above OT prophecies associated with the Spirit's coming within the period of the "latter days" were "in the air" in the first century AD. The Jewish people longed for the day when God would pour out his Spirit and anoint them and his messiah.

CREATION

The NT closely associates the role of the Spirit with the doctrine of the resurrection, both the resurrection of Christ and of the saints. Romans 8:11 is explicit in this regard: "If the Spirit of him who raised Jesus from the dead dwells in you, he who raised Christ Jesus from the dead will also give life to your mortal bodies through his Spirit who dwells in you" (cf. Rom. 1:4). Elsewhere in Paul, the Spirit is called a "life-giving Spirit" (1 Cor. 15:45; cf. 2 Cor. 3:6; 1 Pet. 3:18), a title that recalls the creation account in Genesis and Adam passing his image along to his son, Seth.[29] God's promise to create a new heavens and earth at the very end of time has initially been fulfilled through God's creative Spirit.

TEMPLE

The NT writers connect the coming of the Spirit with the arrival of God's end-time temple. One of the central themes running through the book of Acts, particularly in the account of Pentecost, is the inauguration of the church as God's latter-day temple through the Spirit's descent upon the covenant community (Acts 2:1–41).[30] Peter even claims that the prophecy of Joel 2 has indeed been fulfilled at Pentecost (Acts 2:16). On several occasions, the apostle Paul explicitly identifies the church as God's temple: "Or

---

29. See Benjamin L. Gladd, "The Last Adam as the 'Life-Giving Spirit' Revisited: A Possible Old Testament Background of One of Paul's Most Perplexing Phrases," *WTJ* 71 (2009): 297–309.

30. G. K. Beale, *The Temple and the Church's Mission* (Downers Grove, IL: InterVarsity, 2004), 201–44.

do you not know that your body is a temple of the Holy Spirit within you, whom you have from God?" (1 Cor. 6:19; cf. 2 Cor. 6:16; Eph. 2:20–22). God's heavenly presence, which was partially present in the Most Holy Place in the tabernacle/temple, now dwells more fully in believers. God's original intention was never to dwell permanently in a building, but in people and creation (see Rev. 21–22!).

GOD'S LAW

The Spirit internalizes God's law within believers. God's law, according to the Mosaic covenant, was largely external, making it incredibly difficult to obey. But the Spirit's coming in the new age signals a new stage whereby God's law is more deeply emblazoned upon the human heart (2 Cor. 3). Believers have fulfilled all the requirements of the law since they are joined to Jesus (Rom. 8:3–4), the one who perfectly obeyed God's law (Rom. 10:4), and continue to fulfill the law's demands through God's Spirit.

KINGDOM

The Spirit assisted Jesus in his victory over Satan and establishment of God's end-time kingdom. Mark 1:12–13 makes this connection explicit: "The Spirit immediately drove him out into the wilderness. And he was in the wilderness forty days, being tempted by Satan." During Christ's forty-day temptation, he wages a cosmic war against Satan. With the Spirit's help, Jesus dislodges Satan's rule over the world (e.g., Luke 10:18; Rev. 12:7–9). Indeed, one of the markers of the establishment of God's eschatological kingdom and the overthrow of Satan's rule is Jesus's ability to cast out demons by the power of the Spirit: "But if I cast out demons by the Spirit of God, then the kingdom of God has come upon you" (Matt. 12:28 NASB). The upshot is that the Spirit plays a critical role in the establishment of God's kingdom and the believers' victory over sin.

Implications

Assurance of Our Future Resurrection and Salvation

Since God has already "regenerated" or, perhaps better, spiritually resurrected us, we are assured that our future, bodily resurrection will come to pass. The process has already begun, and at some point in the future, it will be completed. The OT viewed the saints' resurrection as one event (Dan. 12:1–3), whereas the NT further develops this deeply eschatological doctrine and splits the resurrection into two stages (initial and final fulfillment). This observation is remarkably encouraging because believers, who have been initially resurrected in Christ, can hold fast to God's promise of their final resurrection. The Spirit's new-creational work in the hearts of believers cannot be undone. This view of the resurrection gives us courage and hope in the midst of trials and tribulations. The world and the devil are powerless against it, and they can do nothing to prevent it. We are already victorious and participants in God's end-time program of restoration, and we will one day be granted final victory.

Victory over Sin

As resurrected beings, we now have power to gain victory over sin, though we still possess indwelling sin. Sin is no longer our master (Rom. 6:1–23); instead, the Spirit who pours forth righteousness now rules over us. As resurrected saints, we now have the power to obey God's law. The God-given ability to obey through the Spirit's work increases our desire to follow Scripture's commands. For example, I (Ben) enjoy woodworking as a hobby, and one of my least favorite parts of the process was sanding the finished pieces. Wood dust settles all over my garage, and my arms become quickly fatigued. But when I acquired a nice sander with accompanying vacuum, my attitude soon changed; I finally had the *power* and *ability* to sand effectively without layers of dust. I noticed that my motivation to finish projects radically changed. Likewise with our resurrected status: now that we have the power to obey, we ought to have a change of motivation. Obeying God's laws is no longer burdensome but flows freely from a heart that has been created anew by the Spirit.

Church members often visit pastors and share with them their shortcomings and addictions. Pastors should help them see that the gospel brings resurrection life to believers and offers freedom from sin and addictions. We need to recognize that the Spirit's new-creational work in our lives enables us to obey God's commands and gives us the motivation to do so (Gal. 5:22–26).

Participating in God's Story Line

We also should remind ourselves that God has truly begun a good work in us (Phil. 1:6), and we are part of God's larger story line. Once we have grasped our place in the history of redemption, particularly how our resurrection fits into the overall landscape of the Bible, we realize that we are part of something grand, something remarkable. A proper view of the resurrection prevents us from becoming too isolated and individualistic. We are part of God's magnificent plan to redeem creation! Richard Hays punctuates this theme when he comments on the apostle Paul's ethics: "Paul sees the community of faith being caught up into the story of God's remaking of the world through Jesus Christ. Thus, to make ethical discernments is, for Paul, simply to recognize our place within the epic story of redemption."[31] The apostles often reminded their congregations that they were living in the period known as the "latter days," and they expected their audiences to act accordingly.

Practical Suggestions

1. *Study the topic of "kingdom" in Matthew 13.* Matthew 13:24–52 is one of the longest explanations of the kingdom in all of the NT. In the form of parables, Jesus explains how the kingdom stands in both continuity and discontinuity with the OT. Jesus calls this the "mysteries of the kingdom" (13:11 NASB). In other words, the kingdom contains both "new" and "old" elements. Spend some time studying each of the parables and take note of the nature of the kingdom, particularly how we participate in the unusual fulfillment of the long-awaited kingdom. For example, in Matthew 13:44–46 the kingdom is compared to two individuals who sell all of their possessions to procure "treasure" and "pearls." The point of the parables is to demonstrate the immense worth of the kingdom and to underscore the genuine fulfillment of the end-time kingdom. Jesus expects his audience to respond in belief that God's eternal kingdom, which the OT spoke about so often (e.g., Dan. 2:24–45), has commenced and that God has begun to vanquish the pagan empires and their leader, the devil.

2. *Teach the counterintuitiveness of Jesus's kingdom message.* Much of the NT teaches counterintuitiveness, and we mentioned a few examples above. The general OT pattern of eschatology is that suffering and persecution of the saints precede their restoration (Dan. 7, 11–12). But the NT contends that the saints' suffering and restoration have now been fused together. Believers can be confident that they now participate in the end-time kingdom, even *while* they presently endure the great tribulation. This central NT principle is also reflected in the nature of the kingdom and those gaining admittance to it. For example, the prophet Isaiah predicts that in the latter days, God's "servants" will "eat," "drink," and "rejoice" in the new creation, and those unfaithful to God's commands will be "hungry," "thirsty," and "put to shame" (Isa.

31. Hays, *Moral Vision of the New Testament*, 46.

65:12–14). Though Jesus ushers in this end-time kingdom that the prophet Isaiah longed for, NT saints are often physically "hungry" and "thirsty" (but spiritually well fed!). The OT prophets anticipated the spiritual and physical dimensions of the kingdom as occurring simultaneously, whereas the NT tends to divide these two. The kingdom welcomes the physically poor and outcast, so that they may gain spiritual wealth within the end-time kingdom, whereas society inverts this principle. It is not until Christ's second coming when the saints will fully enjoy the physical and spiritual benefits of the latter-day kingdom. Until then, we Christians must expect dissonance with our surrounding culture. Compile a list of examples in which our culture promotes pride and self-adulation, and then determine how much the culture has influenced you in those areas. Perhaps even reflect on how this principle affects your local church. This is a great way to become aware of integrating end-time kingdom principles into the culturally engrained areas of life.

3. *Perform a word study of "Spirit."* If you do not own a good Bible concordance, sell all your possessions and buy one. A concordance is a valuable resource for every Christian, and is absolutely essential for the pastor. Online resources are readily available (http://www.esvbible.org/search) as well as desktop software (Logos, Accordance, Bible Works, etc.). Look up the word "Spirit" in the Letters of Paul and take note of how the Spirit relates to creation, law, temple, and kingdom. In doing so, write down how the Spirit relates to the believer in each of the aforementioned categories. One good example of this type of study is found in Galatians 5:22–26, where the Spirit is linked to several prominent characteristics of the end-time new creation.[32] Paul says that the "fruit" of the Spirit's work is "love, joy, peace, patience, kindness, goodness, faithfulness," and so on (Gal. 5:22–23). Not coincidentally, these characteristics are found in Isaiah 32:14–17 and 57:15–19, two prominent passages that feature the work of the Spirit in the new creation. Paul, therefore, weaves these prophecies from Isaiah into Galatians 5 to reaffirm the identity of Galatian gentiles as true, end-time Israel, who are participating in Isaiah's promises of the new creation.

---

32. See further Matthew S. Harmon, *She Must and Shall Go Free: Paul's Isaianic Gospel in Galatians*, BZNW 168 (Berlin: de Gruyter, 2010), 214–21.

Suggested Reading

Beale, G. K. *A New Testament Biblical Theology: The Unfolding of the Old Testament in the New*. Grand Rapids: Baker Academic, 2011.

Carson, D. A. "Partakers of the Age to Come." In *These Last Days: A Christian View of History*, edited by Richard D. Phillips and Gabriel N. E. Fluhrer, 89–106. Phillipsburg, NJ: P&R, 2011.

Ladd, George Eldon. *The Presence of the Future*. Rev. ed. Grand Rapids: Eerdmans, 2000.

Pate, C. Marvin. *The End of the Age Has Come*. Grand Rapids: Zondervan, 1995.

Part 2

Pastoral Leadership

Leading God's End-Time Flock in the Already—Not Yet

Now that we have described how the already–not yet shapes our understanding of the nature of the church and the Christian life (chaps. 2–3), we will apply this eschatological framework to three key areas of pastoral leadership. Pastors play a unique role in shaping the church, and their leadership naturally flows from a robust understanding and application of inaugurated eschatology.

The Bible presents pastors as shepherds of the flock of God (1 Pet. 5:2), and we capitalize on this metaphor in framing each of these chapters. A good shepherd must nourish the flock, so chapter 4 explores how the pastor feeds the end-time people of God through preaching that is shaped by the already–not yet. Faithful shepherds must also guard the flock from dangerous predators, so chapter 5 focuses on the role of the pastor in protecting the church from the false teaching of the antichrist(s) and in equipping God's people to endure the great tribulation. Chapter 6 unpacks how the already–not yet shapes the way the pastor leads by example, disciples others, and casts vision, since he is called to guide the flock.

4

Feeding the Flock

Instead of spring cleaning, my (Matt's) family has the summer purge. During a recent purge we discovered several boxes of letters and cards that my wife and I had written to each other through the years. Some were as early as our freshman year in college, three years before we began dating. Many of these letters and cards were from our five-month engagement, when we were living 1,200 miles apart. In those days, things like email, cell phones, and texting either did not exist or were in their early stages of development. Long-distance calls were expensive. So we depended on letters to maintain and deepen our relationship as we anticipated our wedding day.

As I read back through these, I noticed a consistent trend: we constantly reminded each other of what God had already done to bring us together. These milestones in our relationship provided a foundation for us to deal with new challenges that arose and to pursue needed growth in certain areas. They also stirred even greater anticipation of our wedding day.

Biblical preaching functions in a similar way. It is grounded in what God has already done for us in Christ and calls us to grow into greater Christlikeness. Furthermore, it stirs within us a longing for the day when Christ returns to consummate his kingdom in a new heavens and new earth. To help us see this, we will first explore examples of the apostolic preaching in Acts. How did the apostles' conviction that the latter days had dawned in and through Jesus Christ shape the way they preached the gospel? Second, we will look at Paul's approach to preaching. Is there any indication that the already–not yet determined the content, manner, and goal of his preaching? Third, we will discuss the relationship between the indicative and the imperative. How should the inauguration of the messianic age inform the way we preach what God has already done for us as well as what he commands us to do? We will then conclude by applying what we learn to the task of preaching.

The Apostolic Preaching in Acts

From the moment the Spirit is poured out on the apostles at Pentecost, we see the already–not yet dynamic embedded within their preaching. A brief look at two key examples will demonstrate this.

Acts 2:14–41

In response to the charge that the apostles are drunk (Acts 2:13, 15), Peter begins his sermon by claiming that these events fulfill what God promised through the prophet Joel regarding the outpouring of the Spirit (Joel 2:28–32; Acts 2:17–21). The Spirit has now been poured out on God's new-covenant people, regardless of their gender, age, or social status (Acts 2:17–18). The rushing wind and tongues of fire (Acts 2:2–3) demonstrate that the great and magnificent day of the Lord has come (Acts 2:19–20). As a result, everyone who calls on the name of the Lord will be saved (Acts 2:21).

Peter introduces his quote from Joel 2:28–32 with a subtle but important expression: "in the last days" (Acts 2:17). This phrase is taken not from Joel but from Isaiah 2:2.[1] By borrowing this phrase from Isaiah 2:2, Peter intensifies the end-time emphasis of Joel 2:28–32 and signals that the last days have truly begun in the life, death, and resurrection of Jesus.[2] The rest of Peter's sermon demonstrates this claim by summarizing the basic facts about Jesus (Acts 2:22–24), proving that Jesus is David's promised heir based on his resurrection (2:25–32), and arguing that the exalted Lord Jesus has poured out the Holy Spirit (2:33–36).[3]

---

1. See David W. Pao, *Acts and the Isaianic New Exodus* (Grand Rapids: Baker Academic, 2002), 156–59; and G. K. Beale, *The Temple and the Church's Mission: A Biblical Theology of the Dwelling Place of God*, NSBT 17 (Downers Grove, IL: InterVarsity, 2004), 209.

2. Additionally, by linking these two texts Peter interprets "the Spirit's coming in fulfillment of Joel to be also the beginning fulfillment of Isaiah's prophecy of the end-time temple, under the influence of which the nations would come" (Beale, *Temple and the Church's Mission*, 209).

3. This outline is adapted from Eckhard J. Schnabel, *Acts*, ZECNT (Grand Rapids: Zondervan, 2012), 133–34.

To prove that the last days began with the life, death, and resurrection of Christ (2:22–24), Peter states that Jesus was "attested to you by God with mighty works and wonders and signs that God did through him in your midst" (2:22). Rather than being a tragic accident, Jesus's crucifixion at the hands of the Jews and gentiles was central to God's eternal plan (2:23). God raised Jesus from the dead because death had no rightful claim on him (2:24).[4] By virtue of his resurrection, Jesus is shown to be David's rightful heir (2:25–32). After quoting Psalm 16:8–11 (Acts 2:25–28), Peter asserts that, because God promised him an heir to sit on his throne (2 Sam. 7:12–16), David spoke as a prophet, foretelling the resurrection of Christ (Acts 2:29–31). Indeed, Peter and the rest of those speaking "the mighty works of God" (2:11) are witnesses of God raising Jesus from the dead (2:32).

The final stage of Peter's message connects the risen Lord Jesus to the outpouring of the Spirit that has just taken place (2:33–36). As the resurrected and exalted Lord, Jesus has received the promised Holy Spirit from the Father and has poured out that Spirit on God's people (2:33). Once again David is brought forth to testify, this time from Psalm 110:1. Jesus is the Lord to whom the Lord said, "Sit at my right hand, until I make your enemies your footstool" (Acts 2:34–35). Peter's punch line is direct: "Let all the house of Israel therefore know for certain that God has made him both Lord and Christ, this Jesus whom you crucified" (2:36).

When the crowds ask how they should respond (2:37), Peter gives two commands: "Repent and be baptized . . . in the name of Jesus." All who do so will receive forgiveness of sins and the gift of the Spirit (2:38). This "promise is for you and for your children and for all who are far off, everyone whom the Lord our God calls to himself" (2:39).[5] These final words pick up the language of Joel 2:32, where it refers to those who are saved from God's wrath and receive the Spirit. Peter applies that promise to his audience to drive home his point: the proper response to the last days arriving in Jesus is to repent and be baptized to receive forgiveness and the gift of the Spirit.

The central thrust of Peter's message is that Jesus's life, death, and resurrection have triggered the last days. Now that he has ascended to the right hand of God, the Lord Jesus Christ has poured out the Holy Spirit on his new-covenant

---

4. The connection between resurrection and the last days is rooted in the OT; see esp. Dan. 12:1–4. For further discussion of the links between the last days, resurrection, and the Spirit, see G. K. Beale, *A New Testament Biblical Theology: The Unfolding of the Old Testament in the New* (Grand Rapids: Baker Academic, 2011), 136–38.

5. When Peter refers to "all who are far off," he echoes the language of Isa. 57:19, a passage also connected with the outpouring of the Spirit; see Matthew S. Harmon, *She Must and Shall Go Free: Paul's Isaianic Gospel in Galatians*, BZNW 168 (Berlin: de Gruyter, 2010), 214–21; and Beale, *New Testament Biblical Theology*, 585–88.

people. But the final and climactic day of the Lord has not yet come, so there is still time to call on the name of the Lord by repenting and being baptized in the name of Jesus. All who do so will receive forgiveness of sins and the gift of the Spirit, and thus they will be saved from God's eschatological judgment.

Acts 3:1–26

This same already–not yet dynamic appears again in Peter's next sermon, recorded in Acts 3:12–26. As he and John were heading to the temple one afternoon, they encountered a man lame from birth (3:1–3). Instead of giving him money, Peter healed the man in the name of Jesus (3:4–7). Leaping with joy, the man followed Peter and John into the temple courts, attracting a crowd that praised God for this remarkable miracle (3:8–11). In response, Peter addressed the crowds (3:12–26). His sermon falls into two main sections: the identity of the Jesus in whose name the lame man was healed (3:12–16) and the response called for in light of who Jesus is (3:17–26).[6]

Peter begins by identifying Jesus as the Servant of the Lord who through his death and resurrection fulfills God's promise to the patriarchs (3:13).[7] But instead of recognizing him as such, the people rejected "the Holy and Righteous One" and killed the "Author of life, whom God raised from the dead" (3:14–15). It is faith in the name of Jesus that has restored the lame man's health (3:16). Because the exalted Jesus has poured out the Spirit on his people (Acts 2:33), Peter and John were able to heal this man as evidence that the new creation has truly broken into this world (cf. Isa. 35:1–10 and Matt. 11:1–6).

While acknowledging their ignorance (3:17), Peter reiterates that Christ's suffering fulfilled what God promised through all the prophets (3:18). Therefore the proper response is repentance and turning back from their rejection of Jesus (3:19a). Three purpose/result clauses unpack what happens when a person repents. First, "your sins may be blotted out" (3:19b). The picture is of God completely erasing any record of a person's sins; it is as if they never existed. While this imagery occurs in a number of places in the OT, Isaiah 43:25 seems particularly pertinent. As part of his promise to make all things new through a new exodus (43:18–21), the Lord asserts: "I, I am he who blots out your transgressions for my own sake, and I will not remember your sins."

---

6. Here again we are following Schnabel, *Acts*, 202–6.

7. The expression "the God of Abraham, the God of Isaac, and the God of Jacob, the God of our fathers" is likely drawn from Exod. 3:15–16, while the phrase "glorified his servant Jesus" is adapted from Isa. 52:13; see further G. K. Beale, "Colossians," in *Commentary on the New Testament Use of the Old Testament*, ed. G. K. Beale and D. A. Carson (Grand Rapids: Baker Academic, 2007), 544–45. Combining these two passages identifies Jesus as the servant who has fulfilled the promised new exodus (cf. Luke 9:30–31).

What God promised in connection with the new creation can be experienced now through repentance and faith.

Second, "times of refreshing may come from the presence of the Lord" (3:20a).[8] Although there is no exact OT parallel to this expression, Peter may have Isaiah 32:15 in mind.[9] There the definitive sign of the new creation is the outpouring of the Spirit on the eschatological people of God. Since the gift of the Spirit is connected to repentance and the forgiveness of sins in Acts 2:38, it makes sense that a similar connection is present in 3:20, albeit with different vocabulary. Thus the times of refreshing are best understood as the present experience of God's Spirit.

Third, God will "send the Christ appointed for you, Jesus" (3:20b). The apostles had been assured that Jesus would return in the same manner in which he ascended (Acts 1:11). Currently he is in heaven "until the time for restoring all the things about which God spoke by the mouth of his holy prophets long ago" (3:21). After the transfiguration, Jesus himself told Peter, James, and John that "Elijah does come, and he will restore all things" (Matt. 17:11).[10] Thus the restoration of all things is another way of describing what elsewhere is called new creation. This restoration was promised by Moses and all the prophets (Acts 3:22–24). By raising Jesus the Servant from the dead, God has fulfilled his promise to Abraham and now commands all to turn away from their wickedness (Acts 3:25–26).

Like his message in Acts 2, Peter's sermon in Acts 3 emphasizes what God has already done in and through Jesus Christ. He is the promised Servant of the Lord, the Holy and Righteous One, the Author of Life, the Prophet like Moses, and the promised descendant of Abraham. Through his death and resurrection, the "last days" have begun. Forgiveness of sins, times of refreshing by the Holy Spirit, and the restoration of all things can be experienced in the present by those who repent and believe in Christ. But the full realization of these blessings awaits the day when Jesus returns from heaven.

These two sermons from Acts illustrate something that in varying degrees is true of all the messages in Acts: the already–not yet is embedded within the

---

8. The expressions "sins may be blotted out" and "times of refreshing from the presence [lit., face] of the Lord" (3:19–20) may have their origins in Ps. 51:9–11—"Hide your *face* from my *sins*, and *blot out* all my iniquities. Create in me a clean heart, O God, and renew a right spirit within me. Cast me not away from your *presence* [lit., face], and take not your Holy Spirit from me" (italics added).

9. See Pao, *Acts and the Isaianic New Exodus*, 132–35.

10. Although the noun translated "restoration" (*apokatastasis*) occurs nowhere else in the NT or LXX, the cognate verb *apokathistēmi* occurs in both the NT (Matt. 17:11; Mark 9:12) and the LXX (Jer. 16:15; 23:8; 24:6; Ezek. 16:55; Hosea 11:11) in connection with God restoring his people.

structure and content of the apostles' preaching. They emphasize what God has already done in and through Christ to launch the "last days" (characterized especially by the gift of the Holy Spirit), while at the same time pointing forward to the consummation of all God's promises, when he restores all things. The new heavens and earth have broken into this fallen world!

Paul's Approach to Preaching

Although in his letters Paul never includes a transcript of one of his sermons, he does at various points explain the theological convictions that shaped the content, manner, and goal of his preaching. We will focus on two such passages: 1 Corinthians 1:18–2:16 and Colossians 1:24–2:5.

First Corinthians 1:18–2:16

When writing to the church at Corinth, Paul faced a congregation with a number of problems. Many of these problems were connected to the culture of the city itself. One area of difficulty was the prominence of rhetoric and oratory in Corinth. Professional orators who made their living through their performances and competed for a following among the population were a staple of the city. Such competition for followers rivaled the intensity of modern-day sports: "Orators would ridicule one another and compete for prestige before the crowds, who cheered their favorites like modern Americans cheer their favorite ball teams."[11]

Apparently this attitude had infiltrated the church at Corinth. Different factions were forming around different Christian leaders, such as Paul, Cephas (Peter), Apollos, and even Christ himself (1 Cor. 1:11–17). Paul responds to this problem by exposing the true nature of what the world considers wisdom (1:18–31), recalling his own example (2:1–5) and describing God's wisdom (2:6–3:4). Along the way, Paul provides a window into his approach to preaching and the already–not yet dynamic that shapes it.

He begins with the paradox of the "word of the cross" (1:18–25).[12] This unique expression is synonymous with "preach the gospel" and in contrast to the "words of eloquent wisdom" from 1:17. The message of a crucified Messiah seems foolish to those who are perishing in their sin, but in fact it is the power of God that leads to salvation for those who believe (1:18). In

11. David A. deSilva, *An Introduction to the New Testament: Contexts, Methods & Ministry Formation* (Downers Grove, IL: InterVarsity, 2004), 557.

12. When Paul refers to the "cross of Christ," he is not focusing exclusively on the crucifixion of Jesus but rather uses the expression to refer to the totality of Christ's saving work.

1:19, Paul grounds this claim with a citation of Isaiah 29:14, which announces God's judgment on those who think they are wise but in fact only pay lip service to God. By building his argument on Isaiah 29:14, "Paul is trying to teach the Corinthians to perceive reality within the framework of a dialectical 'already–not yet' eschatology."[13] God has done "wonder upon wonder" in the crucifixion and resurrection of Jesus, and in doing so has rendered the wisdom and powers of this age powerless. As a result,

> Paul is calling on the Corinthians to reevaluate their prizing of rhetoric. . . . The argument takes its particular force from Paul's conviction that the transforming action of God prophesied by Isaiah *has now taken place* in the crucifixion of Jesus. Consequently, Paul and his readers now stand in the new eschatological situation where Isaiah's words must be read not merely as a judgment on ancient Judean leaders but also as an indictment of the rhetorical affectations of the Corinthians—and simultaneously as a warning of the destruction that is coming on "the day of our Lord Jesus Christ" (1 Cor. 1:8) for those who do not live according to the word of the cross.[14]

Thus the word of the cross appears as folly to those still under the powers of this age (both Jew and gentile alike), but it is in fact the wisdom of God (1 Cor. 1:20–25). In light of the eschatological manifestation of God's wisdom in Christ, the Corinthians need to reflect on their own conversion so that they boast only in the Lord (1:26–31).[15]

Having laid this groundwork, Paul now reminds the Corinthians of his own preaching ministry in Corinth (2:1–5). In contrast to the professional orators, Paul did not preach with "lofty speech or wisdom" (2:1; cf. "words of eloquent wisdom" in 1:17). The content of Paul's preaching is "the mystery of God" (2:1 marg.).[16] Biblically speaking, "mystery" refers to something that was hidden but has now been revealed. The mystery that Paul proclaims is a crucified Messiah as the wisdom of God (2:2; cf. 1:18–25). In preaching this

13. Richard B. Hays, *The Conversion of the Imagination: Paul as Interpreter of Israel's Scripture* (Grand Rapids: Eerdmans, 2005), 14.

14. Ibid., 15, italics original.

15. Space prohibits discussing Paul's quotation of Jer. 9:23 (or possibly 1 Sam. 2:10 LXX) in 1 Cor. 1:31; for a helpful summary, see Roy E. Ciampa and Brian S. Rosner, "1 Corinthians," in *Commentary on the New Testament Use of the Old Testament*, ed. G. K. Beale and D. A. Carson (Grand Rapids: Baker Academic, 2007), 699–700.

16. While most English translations have "testimony" (*martyrion*) rather than "mystery" (*mystērion*), the earliest manuscripts and internal evidence favor "mystery" (*mystērion*) as the original reading; see further Benjamin L. Gladd, *Revealing the Mysterion: The Use of Mystery in Daniel and Second Temple Judaism with Its Bearing on First Corinthians*, BZNW 160 (Berlin: de Gruyter, 2009), 123–26.

apocalyptic message, Paul was with the Corinthians "in weakness and in fear and much trembling" (2:3). As the recipient and messenger of this mystery, Paul experiences fear and trembling because he performs his preaching ministry in the presence of God himself.[17] As a messenger of this mystery, Paul did not use "plausible words of wisdom" but rather preached "in demonstration of the Spirit and of power" (2:4). His reason for taking this approach is to ensure that their "faith might not rest in the wisdom of men but in the power of God" (2:5). Thus Paul's preaching centers on communicating the unveiled mystery of what God has already done in Christ. By means of Paul's preaching, God manifests his power through the work of the Spirit, who was given to God's people to signal that the age to come had dawned in and through the work of Jesus Christ.

The contrast between the "wisdom of men" and "the power of God" in 2:5 leads Paul to return to the difference between the wisdom of God and human wisdom (2:6–16). Verses 6–8 highlight the stark differences between this age and the age to come:

> Yet we do speak wisdom among those who are mature; a wisdom, however, not of *this age* nor of the rulers of *this age*, who are passing away; but we speak God's wisdom in a mystery, the hidden wisdom which God predestined *before the ages* to our glory; the wisdom which none of the rulers of *this age* has understood; for if they had understood it they would not have crucified the Lord of glory. (NASB, italics added)

The wisdom of this age consists of manipulative rhetoric designed to entertain and gain power over the hearer (see 1:18–25). Although the rulers of this age use this method to maintain their status and influence, they nonetheless "are doomed to pass away" (2:6).[18] Paul uses the present tense to stress that the demise of these rulers is already happening. How? Through the proclamation of the gospel, which is described as "God's wisdom, a mystery that has been hidden and that God destined for our glory before time began" (2:7 NIV). The wisdom of God proclaimed in the gospel of a crucified and risen Messiah is already bringing the wisdom of this age to nothing. Destroying the wisdom and rulers of this age through a crucified Messiah was God's plan "before the ages" (cf. Acts 2:23). Because the rulers of this age were blind to

17. The terms "fear" and "trembling" often occur in contexts where God manifests his presence (e.g., Exod. 15:16; Deut. 2:25; 11:25; Ps. 2:11; Isa. 19:16); see further, ibid., 120–23.

18. Determining whether the "rulers of this age" are spiritual forces, earthly political leaders, or some combination of the two does not ultimately affect our larger point here; for a helpful discussion of the issues, see Anthony C. Thiselton, *The First Epistle to the Corinthians: A Commentary on the Greek Text*, NIGTC (Grand Rapids: Eerdmans, 2000), 233–39.

God's wisdom in the gospel, they unwittingly played their role by crucifying the Lord's Messiah (1 Cor. 2:8). What God promised in Isaiah 64:4 has now come to pass in the crucifixion and resurrection of Jesus (2:9).[19]

These incomprehensible wonders that God has done for his people are revealed by the Spirit, who "searches everything, even the depths of God" (2:10–11). As the eschatological people of God, we have received the Spirit of God to enable us to understand God's wisdom in the cross (2:12). God imparts this wisdom through the proclamation of the gospel empowered by the Spirit (2:13). Those without the Spirit of God are unable to accept what he teaches (2:14), but believers have the mind of Christ to enable them to receive and apply the wisdom of God taught by the Spirit (2:15–16).

This rich passage shows us at least four ways that the already–not yet shaped Paul's approach to preaching. First, preaching centers on what God has already done through the crucifixion and resurrection of Jesus (1:17–25; 2:2). For Paul, preaching the gospel was speaking the message about the cross of Christ. As the proclamation of the word of the cross, preaching announces that God has now revealed the hidden mystery of God's wisdom in Christ (2:1, 6–10). What was present but largely hidden within the OT comes into plain view as God's servants preach the cross of Christ to those who possess God's Spirit.

Second, preaching relies on the power of God's Spirit. As we have already noted, the gift of the Holy Spirit is the defining indicator that the messianic age has begun (Acts 2:1–41) and the guarantee of our full inheritance to come (Eph. 1:14). Just as the Spirit empowered the apostles on the day of Pentecost, so now the Spirit uses the preaching of the cross to make those dead in their sins spiritually alive. As God's messengers proclaim God's wisdom displayed in the cross, the Spirit manifests himself powerfully so that faith is placed in God rather than in people (1 Cor. 2:1–5).

Third, preaching destroys the wisdom and rulers of this age. At the cross God "disarmed the rulers and authorities and put them to open shame, by triumphing over them in him" (Col. 2:15). Despite this decisive defeat, these spiritual forces of evil actively wage war against believers (Eph. 6:11–20) and seek to keep unbelievers blinded by their sin (2 Cor. 4:3–4). But through the Spirit-empowered preaching of the cross, God exposes these spiritual forces for what they are and opens blind eyes to see "the light of the knowledge of the glory of God in the face of Jesus Christ" (2 Cor. 4:6).

---

19. For more on the use of Isa. 64:4 in 1 Cor. 2:9, see Ciampa and Rosner, *First Letter to the Corinthians*, 701. There are also several allusions to Daniel in 1 Cor. 2:1–16; see Gladd, *Revealing the* Mysterion, 129–32. These allusions supply the reason "why the cross, so grand and pivotal in the process of redemptive history, remains an utter mystery to the foolish but wisdom to the wise" (ibid., 132).

Finally, preaching communicates spiritual truth to those with the Spirit. The Spirit dwelling in believers applies the Spirit-empowered preaching of the cross to enable greater understanding and application of what God has done for us in Christ (1 Cor. 2:12–16). As those who have the firstfruits of the Spirit hear the word of the cross preached, their longing for the consummation of God's promises intensifies (Rom. 8:18–25). And this hope compels us to pursue purity because Christ is pure (1 John 3:3).

Colossians 1:24–2:5

Although Paul did not personally plant the church in Colossae, he felt a particular burden for them as a church established through the ministry of his coworker Epaphras. As part of his effort to combat false teaching, Paul gives us a window into how he understands his ministry and the role that preaching/teaching plays in it (Col. 1:24–2:5). He does so by situating his ministry within redemptive history (1:24–29) and within the context of the local church (2:1–5).

Paul begins by situating his ministry within redemptive history (1:24–29). Instead of grumbling about his suffering for the sake of the churches, Paul rejoices (1:24). Such joy is rooted in knowing that he is "filling up what is lacking in Christ's afflictions for the sake of his body, that is, the church" (1:24). Paul is not suggesting that Christ's death is insufficient to save his people. Instead, he is drawing on the Jewish expectation that the last days would be accompanied by a predetermined amount of tribulation and suffering sometimes referred to as the "messianic woes" (Dan. 7:21–27; 12:1).[20] We see this most clearly in Revelation 6:9–11. In response to the souls of the martyrs asking how long before God judges their enemies, John writes, "Then they were each given a white robe and told to rest a little longer, until the number of their fellow servants and their brothers should be complete, who were to be killed as they themselves had been" (6:11). Thus Paul sees his own ministry as helping to fill up the amount of divinely ordained affliction for the eschatological people of God during the last days.[21]

---

20. For a helpful summary of this view, see David W. Pao, *Colossians & Philemon*, ZECNT 12 (Grand Rapids: Zondervan, 2012), 125–26. For further explanation, see Richard F. Bauckham, "Colossians 1:24 Again: The Apocalyptic Motif," *EvQ* 47 (1975): 168–70; and Brant Pitre, *Jesus, the Tribulation, and the End of the Exile: Restoration Eschatology and the Origin of the Atonement*, WUNT 204 (Tübingen: Mohr Siebeck, 2005), 41–130.

21. Although Paul understood himself to have a special role within redemptive history as the lead apostle to the gentiles, experiencing the "messianic woes" is not limited to Paul and his ministry; see, e.g., Acts 14:22; 1 Thess. 3:3, 7. On the possibility that Paul draws on language from the Servant Songs in Isaiah here in Col. 1:24–29, see Harmon, *She Must and Shall Go Free*, 120–21.

As a "minister according to the stewardship from God," Paul sought "to make the word of God fully known" (Col. 1:25). He further explains the content of the word of God: "the mystery hidden for ages and generations but now revealed to his saints" (1:26). Again we see that Paul's preaching centers on the redemptive plan of God in Christ, previously hidden but now revealed to the church. God's purpose is to reveal "the riches of the glory of this mystery" among the gentiles (1:27). This mystery is further explained as "Christ in you, the hope of glory" (1:27). The mystery of God's eschatological kingdom spoken of in Daniel 2 has been inaugurated through the person and work of Christ.[22] That is why Paul proclaims Christ by warning and teaching to "present everyone mature in Christ" on the last day (Col. 1:28). For that goal Paul labors with all the power that God supplies (1:29).

In 2:1–5 Paul situates his ministry within the context of the local church. Even though he has not met the Colossians or the Laodiceans, Paul labors on their behalf (2:1). The goal of his labor is "that their hearts may be encouraged" (2:2). Paul's language here picks up the OT promise of eschatological "comfort" that God would bring to his people in the last days (Isa. 40:1–2, 11; 51:3).[23] Although the next clause is usually rendered along the lines of "being knit together in love" (Col. 2:2), a strong case can be made for translating it "being instructed in love."[24] Thus the preaching and teaching of the gospel in love is the means by which God's eschatological comfort is experienced. The purpose of such instruction is for believers "to reach all the riches of full assurance of understanding and the knowledge of God's mystery, which is Christ" (2:2). Through the proclamation of the gospel, believers grow in their understanding and application of God's mystery in Christ, "in whom are hidden all the treasures of wisdom and knowledge" (2:3). By staying rooted in this gospel, believers are immunized from false teaching that diminishes the sufficiency and supremacy of Christ (2:4–5).

From this rich passage we learn at least four ways the already–not yet shapes preaching. First, the *content* of preaching is the mystery of God revealed in Christ. As those who live in the last days, we are called to "make the word of God fully known" (Col. 1:25) in all its vibrant colors. We do so by preaching in a way that connects a particular passage to its place within the larger story

---

22. See the discussion in Beale, "Colossians," 857–59.

23. Helpfully noted by Pao, *Colossians & Philemon*, 136. Paul uses the same verb here (*parakaleō*) as the LXX does in Isa. 40:1–2; 51:3.

24. See Matthew S. Harmon, "Letter Carriers and Paul's Use of Scripture," *JSPL* 4 (2014): 32–34; and Peter T. O'Brien, *Colossians, Philemon*, WBC 44 (Waco: Word, 1982), 93. Perhaps the strongest argument is that all ten occurrences of this verb (*symbibazō*) in the LXX have the sense of "instruct, make known, teach."

of redemption that runs from Genesis to Revelation. In doing so, we focus on Christ as the fulfillment of God's purposes, which were hidden in ages past but are now revealed in these last days. As the embodiment of God's wisdom and knowledge, Christ has brought the eschatological comfort promised by God long ago.

Second, the *components* of preaching the mystery include explanation, application, and warning. The repeated references to revelation and knowledge make it clear that the mystery of God requires explanation to understand it. But head knowledge is not enough. Preaching must apply those truths to the specifics of our lives. Since Christ, the fullest expression of God's wisdom, dwells in us, we should increasingly come to reflect his wisdom in our everyday lives. In those areas where we are not doing so, preaching sounds the warning and calls for repentance.

Third, the *goal* of preaching is to present believers mature in Christ on the last day. Although Paul does not use the phrase "on the last day," the context indicates that this is what he means. The verb "present" (*paristēmi*) occurs in 1:22, where Paul states that the purpose of God reconciling us is "to present you holy and blameless and above reproach before him."[25] On that last day believers will be "mature" (*teleios*). Paul explains what such maturity looks like in Ephesians 4:13, where he asserts that the work of ministry continues "until we all attain to the unity of the faith and of the knowledge of the Son of God, to mature manhood, to the measure of the stature of the fullness of Christ." Preaching thus aims at the ongoing growth of the believer in godliness in the present in anticipation of standing before God on the last day. As believers hear the mystery of God's work in Christ proclaimed, the Spirit produces faith (Rom. 10:17) that displays itself through good works (Eph. 2:8–10; James 2:14–26).

Fourth, the *power* of preaching comes from God through his Spirit. Paul strives toward the goal of presenting everyone mature in Christ by "struggling with all his energy that he powerfully works within me" (Col. 1:29). Although Paul does not explicitly mention the Holy Spirit, he frequently uses the expression found here (lit., "in power" [*en dynamei*] rather than "powerfully") in connection with the Spirit's work through him (Rom. 15:18–19; 1 Cor 2:4–5; 2 Cor 6:7; 1 Thess. 1:5).[26] As Gordon Fee notes, "The Spirit, therefore, must be understood as the presupposition of this language, not as its direct reference point. God is the obvious subject of the empowering; from all kinds of texts in

---

25. Compare the use of this same verb in other eschatological contexts, such as 2 Cor. 4:14; 11:2; Eph. 5:27.

26. Gordon D. Fee, *God's Empowering Presence: The Holy Spirit in the Letters of Paul* (Peabody, MA: Hendrickson, 1994), 645.

Paul we may assume this means 'by the power of God's Holy Spirit.'"[27] Thus it is the Spirit of God working powerfully through proclamation of the word that makes possible the kind of preaching Colossians 1:24–2:5 envisions. As the mystery of God revealed in Christ is preached, the Spirit of God works through the preacher to cause believers to walk in obedience to God in anticipation of being presented before Christ on the last day (Ezek. 36:27; Phil. 1:9–11).

First Corinthians 1:18–2:16 and Colossians 1:24–2:5 make it apparent that the already–not yet shaped the way Paul preached. Because God has revealed the mystery of his redemptive plan in the person and work of Christ, Paul labored to explain and apply that good news by the power of the Spirit working through him. Therefore he called people to pursue Christlikeness in the present as they anticipated appearing before God on the last day fully mature in Christ.

The Indicative and the Imperative

Another way we see the already–not yet shaping preaching is in the "grammar" of how the Bible calls us to live. When we wish to make a statement or an assertion, we use an indicative verb: "Preachers strive to explain the Bible." It is the kind of verb we use when we inform someone. By contrast, when we want to order someone to do something, we use an imperative verb: "Strive to explain the Bible!" Such a sentence is not meant to provide information but rather call someone to action.

Here is the payoff from our brief grammar lesson: from the very beginning of the Bible all the way to the end, God does something for us (indicative), tells us about it (indicative), and then calls us to respond in certain ways (imperative). After creating human beings in his own image (Gen. 1:26–27), God blessed and commanded them to be fruitful and rule over the earth (Gen. 1:28–31). God redeemed Israel from their slavery in Egypt and brought them to Mount Sinai to make a covenant with them as a nation (Exod. 1:1–19:25). The centerpiece of that covenant is the Ten Commandments (Exod. 20:1–17). What is often overlooked is how that passage begins: "And God spoke all these words, saying, 'I am the LORD your God, who brought you out of the land of Egypt, out of the house of slavery'" (20:1–2). God's redemption of Israel from Egypt (indicative) is the foundation of his commands on how to live (imperative).

Entire NT letters are even structured on this relationship between the indicative and the imperative. Perhaps the clearest example is Ephesians. In the first three chapters Paul paints a panorama of God's redemption in Christ,

27. Ibid., 644.

emphasizing what God has already done for his people (indicative). The only command in these three chapters is "Remember" (2:11). By contrast, in chapters 4–6 Paul uses forty commands to call believers to live a certain way in light of what God has done for them (imperative). Romans has a similar structure. In chapters 1–11, Paul sketches out in significant detail what God has done for his people in the gospel (indicative). Notice then how chapter 12 begins: "I appeal to you therefore, brothers, by the mercies of God, to present your bodies as a living sacrifice, holy and acceptable to God, which is your spiritual worship. Do not be conformed to this world, but be transformed by the renewal of your mind, that by testing you may discern what is the will of God, what is good and acceptable and perfect" (Rom. 12:1–2). What follows in chapters 12–16 is the application of that gospel to specific areas of life as a Christian in community with other believers while living in a fallen world (imperative).

When properly understood, the relationship between the indicative and the imperative is another way of expressing the already and the not yet. The indicative states what God has already done for us in Christ, while the imperative calls us to be in our everyday experience what we are not yet fully. Therefore preaching must explain what God has already done for us in Christ (indicative) and call people to grow in areas where they do not yet fully reflect Christ (imperative). Emphasizing one to the neglect of the other is hazardous to our spiritual health. Focusing on the indicative while ignoring the imperative leads to license, while focusing on the imperative to the neglect of the indicative leads to legalism.

Implications

We Must Center Our Preaching on What God Has Already Done for Us in Christ

The primary purpose of preaching is not to provide helpful tips for daily living, nor is it to provide insightful cultural commentary. Instead, it is to proclaim "Jesus Christ and him crucified" (1 Cor. 2:2) in such a way that we can say to those who hear us, "It was before your eyes that Jesus Christ was publicly portrayed as crucified" (Gal. 3:1). Regardless of what text or topic we are preaching, we must explain how it relates to the person and work of Jesus Christ in the gospel.[28] An important element of this kind of preaching is

28. For helpful explanations of the various ways texts can point to the person and work of Christ, see Sidney Greidanus, *Preaching Christ from the Old Testament: A Contemporary Hermeneutical Method* (Grand Rapids: Eerdmans, 1999), 203–25; and Bryan Chapell, *Christ-Centered*

unfolding the mystery of God's redemptive plan from Genesis to Revelation, so that people see how the latter days have already dawned with the first coming of Christ and will one day be consummated when he returns. By listening to our preaching, hearers should learn how to "put their Bible together."

As a corollary to this implication, our preaching should express passion that is appropriate to the magnitude and wonder of what God has done for us in Christ. "All the promises of God find their Yes" in Christ (2 Cor. 1:20). So in light of the age to come dawning through Christ and his work for us, how can we preach with cold detachment and indifference? How that passion is expressed will vary based on how God has wired each of us, but it should come through clearly to all who hear us preach. Our preaching must boldly announce that the last days have come with the death and resurrection of Jesus and that God's people have the promised Holy Spirit dwelling in us.

We Must Call People to Pursue Spiritual Maturity in Areas Where They Do Not Yet Fully Reflect Christ

Preaching that fails to call God's people to spiritual maturity is not biblical preaching. The reality of what God has already done for us in Christ serves as the starting point for calling people to live in a manner consistent with the gospel. As believers we still face "the desires of the flesh and the desires of the eyes and pride of life" (1 John 2:16), not to mention an enemy who "prowls around like a roaring lion, seeking someone to devour" (1 Pet. 5:8). John captures well this dynamic of calling believers to pursue spiritual maturity in light of what God has already done for us in Christ while awaiting our bodily resurrection on the last day and the final consummation of his promises: "Beloved, we are God's children now, and what we will be has not yet appeared; but we know that when he appears we shall be like him, because we shall see him as he is. And everyone who thus hopes in him purifies himself as he is pure" (1 John 3:2–3). In these two verses we see it all: (1) God has already given us new life in fulfillment of the new-covenant promise (Ezek. 36:25–27); (2) we yearn for our bodily resurrection and our final glorification in a new heavens and new earth (Ezek. 37:1–28); (3) we pursue holiness in the meantime as evidence of our status as the eschatological people of God (1 Pet. 1:13–19). As we preach, we must call for the same response that the early apostles did: repentance and faith. Martin Luther was spot on when he wrote as the first of his 95 Theses: "When our Lord and Master, Jesus Christ, said 'Repent,' He called for the entire life of believers to be one of

Preaching: Redeeming the Expository Sermon, 2nd ed. (Grand Rapids: Baker Academic, 2005), 280–88.

repentance." Far from being restricted to our entrance into the Christian life, repentance and faith are the central means by which we experience the grace of God in the gospel in our daily lives.

We Must Stir in People a Longing for the Consummation of God's Promises

While what God has already done for us in Christ in the latter days is truly breathtaking, it is merely the down payment of what is to come (Eph. 1:13–14). All of creation is groaning in anticipation of the day when our redemption is consummated (Rom. 8:18–25). Because we have the Spirit in us, we too "groan inwardly as we wait eagerly for adoption as sons, the redemption of our bodies" (Rom. 8:23). As preachers, we should preach in a manner that intensifies the Spirit-produced longing for God to sum up all things in Christ in a new heavens and new earth. We are artists painting a portrait of the beauty of Christ so that God's people long to see him face to face. We are heralds proclaiming the imminent return of the King to incite joyful anticipation of the day when "he will wipe away every tear from their eyes, and death shall be no more, neither shall there be mourning, nor crying, nor pain anymore, for the former things have passed away" (Rev. 21:4).

Of course, the consummation of God's promises will not be good news to those who persist in their rebellion against him. When the King returns, his offer of amnesty will expire. So our preaching must warn those outside of Christ that they must turn from their rebellion against the King before it is too late. For a day is coming when "at the name of Jesus every knee [shall] bow, in heaven and on earth and under the earth, and every tongue confess that Jesus Christ is Lord, to the glory of God the Father" (Phil. 2:10–11).

We Must Depend on the Power of God's Spirit

The same end-time Holy Spirit that came upon the apostles at Pentecost dwells in us to empower the preaching of his Word. He is the one who raises the spiritually dead and gives them life. He is the one who empowers obedience in the life of the believer in response to the preaching of the Word. So even as we study God's Word and prepare to proclaim it to others, we must do so in dependence on the Spirit to guide our thoughts and words. As we preach, we must rely on the Spirit so that we can say with Paul, "We also thank God constantly for this, that when you received the word of God, which you heard from us, you accepted it not as the word of men but as what it really is, the word of God, which is at work in you believers" (1 Thess. 2:13).

As we preach the Word in the power of the Spirit, we are waging an end-time battle with the rulers of this age who are seeking to blind the minds of unbelievers. The Lord gives us his very own eschatological armor (Isa. 59:17; Eph. 6:12–18) to push back the forces of the evil one through our proclamation of the good news that "the LORD has bared his holy arm before the eyes of all the nations, and all the ends of the earth shall see the salvation of our God" (Isa. 52:10). Paul reminds us that "the weapons of our warfare are not of the flesh but have divine power to destroy strongholds. We destroy arguments and every lofty opinion raised against the knowledge of God, and take every thought captive to obey Christ" (2 Cor. 10:4–5). By preaching the "foolishness" of the cross, we expose the "wisdom" of the world for what it truly is.

Practical Suggestions

1. *Deepen your understanding of God's redemptive plan.* The starting point is immersing yourself in God's Word. There is simply no substitute for consistent, sustained, thoughtful, reflective, and meditative engagement with Scripture. Combining breadth and depth of reading is especially valuable for grasping the overall story line of Scripture. Pay special attention to what Scripture says takes place in the latter days, as well as key themes that repeatedly occur. Consider using a reading plan that takes you through the entire Bible in one year while at the same time picking a particular biblical book or theme to study in depth.[29] Reading good books on biblical theology can also enhance your understanding of the already–not yet. They enable you to see key themes that run throughout the canon, the overall scope of the biblical story line, and even distinctive contributions of various biblical books and authors. An excellent starting point is the series New Studies in Biblical Theology, edited by D. A. Carson.[30] Another helpful resource is the *New Dictionary of Biblical Theology*, edited by T. Desmond Alexander and Brian S. Rosner.[31] As your grasp of the already–not yet deepens, find specific ways to incorporate it into your regular preaching.[32]

29. A number of reading plans can be found at http://www.biblestudytools.com/bible-reading-plan/. Logos Bible Software also allows you to customize your own Bible reading plan.
30. Downers Grove, IL: IVP Academic, 2001–.
31. Downers Grove, IL: IVP Academic, 2000.
32. For helpful examples of preaching that embodies this, see http://resources.thegospelcoalition.org/library?f%5Bresource_category%5D%5B%5D=Sermons. The various messages and workshops from the 2011 Gospel Coalition Conference are also very helpful and available for free: http://thegospelcoalition.org/conferences/2011/#media.

2. *Intentionally connect the indicative and the imperative.* As part of preparing your sermons, create separate lists of the eschatological indicatives and the end-time imperatives in the passage you are preaching. As we have seen in chapter 4, NT imperatives are rooted in the believers' participation in the new creation. For each indicative, identify an imperative that flows from it; for each imperative, specify an indicative that grounds it. Sometimes the connection is clear in the passage itself, while other times the context must supply it. By connecting the indicative with the imperative, you will remind believers of their identity as the eschatological people of God while calling them to live in the power of the Spirit.

3. *Bathe your preaching in prayer.* God promised that in the latter days he would pour out his Spirit on all of his eschatological sons and daughters, causing them to prophesy/teach (Joel 2:28–29). As God's child, you have been given the Holy Spirit to empower your preaching. Perhaps the most tangible way we depend on the work of the Spirit in preaching is in prayer. By praying we admit that apart from the work of the Spirit, preaching is merely human words. So we cry out to God for him to do what only he can do through the power of the Spirit. Pray that God would open your eyes to see the beauty of Christ and empower you to portray that beauty so that dead sinners are brought to life and God's people are empowered to obey.[33]

Suggested Reading

Chapell, Bryan. *Christ-Centered Preaching: Redeeming the Expository Sermon.* 2nd ed. Grand Rapids: Baker Academic, 2005.

Clowney, Edmund. *Preaching Christ in All of Scripture.* Wheaton: Crossway, 2003.

Greidanus, Stanley. *Preaching Christ from the Old Testament: A Contemporary Hermeneutical Method.* Grand Rapids: Baker, 1999.

Johnson, Dennis E. *Him We Proclaim: Preaching Christ from All the Scriptures.* Phillipsburg, NJ: P&R, 2007.

Piper, John. *The Supremacy of God in Preaching.* Rev. and exp. ed. Grand Rapids: Baker Books, 2015.

---

33. For an excellent suggestion on how to prepare to enter the pulpit in the final moments before preaching, see John Piper, *The Supremacy of God in Preaching*, rev. and exp. ed. (Grand Rapids: Baker Books, 2015), 49–51.

5

Guarding the Flock

The word "antichrist" conjures up a variety of connotations. Some immediately think of the devilish figure Nicolae Carpathia in Tim LaHaye's best-selling Left Behind series. In the series, Nicolae appoints himself as the leader of the Global Community and wages war against Christians during the future known as the great tribulation. The NT, however, claims that this antichrist figure not only will appear physically at the very end of history, at Christ's second coming, but is here presently, albeit in a spiritual and corporate manner.

The second part of our discussion of pastoral leadership stresses the importance of protecting God's flock from demonic assaults. We attempt to articulate *why* and *how* pastors and other leaders within the local church are to lead their staff and congregation within the time period known as the "latter days." Our goal here is to show how pastoral ministry can cope with false teaching and persecution within the overlap of the ages. The NT authors draw a direct correlation between the latter days and the onslaught of this two-pronged attack.

Perhaps the best entry point into this discussion is to evaluate Paul's urgent message in 2 Thessalonians 2:1–7, a text that concerns the end-time figure of the antichrist.[1] This passage may seem like an odd choice, but it provides a theological blueprint for the NT writers' conviction that church leaders must

---

1. For greater treatment of this passage, particularly as it concerns the NT's conception of "mystery," see G. K. Beale and Benjamin L. Gladd, *Hidden but Now Revealed: A Biblical Theology of Mystery* (Downers Grove, IL: InterVarsity, 2014).

shepherd their congregations in light of the already–not yet. We will camp at this text, briefly sketching the immediate context of this passage, and then uncover its OT background. We must wade through a few detailed points of exegesis in order to grasp the significance of Paul's staggering claims. Once we have arrived at the general thrust of 2 Thessalonians 2:1–7, we will turn our attention to other corroborating portions of the NT and then apply our conclusions to pastoral ministry.

False Teaching on the Advent

The pastoral relevance of eschatology is most apparent in 2 Thessalonians. Central to Paul's church-planting effort was teaching the Thessalonians about the nature of the antichrist and his influence within the local church. Paul's frustration with the Thessalonian congregation is easily discernible when he writes: "Do you not remember that when I was still with you I told you these things?" (2 Thess. 2:5). When Paul planted the church at Thessalonica, eschatology played a crucial role in his instruction. Unfortunately, in the short time between Paul's teaching in Thessalonica (Acts 17:1–9) and the writing of 2 Thessalonians, the Thessalonians' doctrinal integrity had begun to erode, negatively affecting their conduct (2 Thess. 3:11–13).

In Paul's First Epistle to the Thessalonians, he corrects those who have set up timetables for Christ's return, explaining why the Thessalonians appear lethargic (1 Thess. 5:12–14). In order to curb their idle behavior, Paul warns them that the day of the Lord is imminent (1 Thess. 5:2–4). By the time we reach 2 Thessalonians, such imminence has been overly developed: the Thessalonians think that Christ has already come! The Thessalonian church again struggles with idleness, since they believe that the eternal state has already been consummately established (2 Thess. 3:6–15). Paul must once again correct an aberrant view of eschatology. By identifying two events that will *precede* the Lord's coming, he explains why the day of the Lord has not already occurred. Bad eschatology leads to bad behavior.

Immediate Context of 2 Thessalonians 2:1–7

Second Thessalonians 2:1–7 contains one of the most staggering claims in the entire NT. Foremost in Paul's mind is the Thessalonians' perseverance in the faith and their willingness to maintain sound doctrine:

> Now concerning the coming of our Lord Jesus Christ and our being gathered together to him, we ask you, brothers, not to be quickly shaken in mind or

alarmed, either by a spirit or a spoken word, or a letter seeming to be from us, to the effect that the day of the Lord has come. Let no one deceive you in any way. For that day will not come, unless the rebellion comes first, and the man of lawlessness is revealed, the son of destruction, who opposes and exalts himself against every so-called god or object of worship, so that he takes his seat in the temple of God, proclaiming himself to be God. Do you not remember that when I was still with you I told you these things? And you know what is restraining him now so that he may be revealed in his time. For the mystery of lawlessness is already at work. Only he who now restrains it will do so until he is out of the way. (2:1–7)

Much of the letter turns on the false teaching that the Thessalonians have embraced. But this false teaching that crept into the church at Thessalonica, like other forms of heresy in the early church, is deeply wedded to eschatology. Apparently, the Thessalonians believed that Christ's return had already come in some invisible, spiritual manner. Paul must now correct their aberrant view of eschatology and explain why the day of the Lord has not already occurred.

In 2:1–12, Paul exhorts the Thessalonian community not to be led astray about the timing of the "day of the Lord." False teachers apparently proclaimed that the final coming of Christ and the resurrection had already arrived. In verse 2, Paul says, "[Do not] become easily unsettled or alarmed by the teaching allegedly from us—whether by a prophecy or by word of mouth or by letter—asserting that the day of the Lord has already come. Don't let anyone deceive you in any way" (2:2–3a NIV). These false teachers claimed that the spiritual resurrection had occurred and that therefore Christ had already come to raise his people to glory (cf. 1 Cor. 15:12–24; 2 Tim. 2:16–18; 2 Pet. 3:3–13).

Paul parries this doctrinal attack by claiming that two events must come to fruition before Christ's return: "Let no one deceive you in any way. For that day will not come, unless the *rebellion* comes first, and the *man of lawlessness* is revealed, the son of destruction" (2 Thess. 2:3, italics added). The "rebellion" or "apostasy" (NASB) probably refers to those within the covenant community who fall away from the faith, and the "man of lawlessness" is the latter-day opponent of Israel—the "antichrist."[2] Since neither of these two events has occurred in its fullness, Christ's return remains a future event.

Paul expounds on the "man of lawlessness" in verse 4. He claims in verses 3–4 that the Thessalonians should not be deceived in thinking that Christ's coming has already happened, since the final apostasy in the church and

2. Within the NT, the term "antichrist" (*antichristos*) appears only in the Johannine Epistles (1 John 2:18, 22; 4:3; 2 John 7).

the final appearance of the antichrist have not yet happened. Perhaps to the surprise of the Thessalonians, in verse 7 Paul reveals that the "mystery of lawlessness is already at work." It is not until "he who now restrains" withdraws that the end-time oppressor of Israel will be physically manifested.[3] Verses 8–10 speak of the demise of this end-time figure and his cooperation with Satan: "Then the lawless one will be revealed, whom the Lord Jesus will kill with the breath of his mouth and bring to nothing by the appearance of his coming" (v. 8). The figure will bring about a great deception within the covenant community and among unbelievers (vv. 10–12). Individuals who succumb to the deception and "had pleasure in unrighteousness" will be on the receiving end of God's judgment (v. 12).

But Paul is thankful for God electing the Thessalonian community and maintaining sound doctrine, the latter of which is due to the protection that election affords, so that the elect are not deceived (v. 13). Yet the readers must continue to live holy lives and keep the gospel free from corruption. It is of utmost importance that they not abandon apostolic tradition but seek to preserve it: "Stand firm and hold to the traditions that you were taught by us, either by our spoken word or by our letter" was Paul's encouragement for them to remain faithful to the gospel (v. 15). We will now examine Daniel's view of Israel's end-time foe in some detail, since it has considerable bearing on Paul's (and other NT writers') admonitions to the church.

The Book of Daniel's Conception of Israel's Antagonist

In order for us to grasp Paul's insightful discussion of the antichrist figure, we must pay careful attention to an important OT allusion. The expression "man of lawlessness" in 2 Thessalonians 2:3 recalls Daniel 11:29–36 and 12:10 (as commentators rightly note).[4]

---

3. Commentators are divided as to the precise identity of "the restrainer." Complicating matters is the neuter gender in v. 6 (*to katechon*), whereas the masculine gender is found in v. 7 (*ho katechōn*). In addition, v. 7b is notoriously difficult to translate. The general options for the identity of the restrainer are the following: the Roman Empire, a nonspecific empire, the Jewish nation, Satan or one of his agents, the influence of false teachers within the local church, God or the Spirit, and the gospel as heralded by an angel. The last view appears most likely: an angel represents God's sovereignty in making the heralding of the gospel effective by prevailing over the devil's influence, especially the devil's desire to bring about the appearance of the "man of lawlessness" in history, when that evil figure will be able temporarily to suppress the growth of the gospel through persecution and deception (see Matt. 16:18; Rev. 20:1–9). For a discussion of this problem, see G. K. Beale, *1–2 Thessalonians*, IVPNT (Downers Grove, IL: InterVarsity, 2003), 213–18.

4. E.g., F. F. Bruce, *1 & 2 Thessalonians*, WBC 45 (Dallas: Word, 1982), 168; I. H. Marshall, *1 and 2 Thessalonians*, NCBC (Grand Rapids: Eerdmans, 1983), 190–91.

Daniel 11:31, 36; 12:10	2 Thessalonians 2:3–4
"Forces from him shall appear and profane the temple and fortress, and shall take away the regular burnt offering. And *they shall set up the abomination that makes desolate*." (11:31, italics added)	"and *the man of lawlessness* [*anthrōpos tēs anomias*] is revealed, the son of destruction, who *opposes and exalts himself above every so-called god* or object of worship, so that he *takes his seat in the temple* of God, *proclaiming himself to be God*." (italics added)
"He shall *exalt himself and magnify himself above every* god and shall speak astonishing things against the God of gods." (11:36, italics added)	
"Let many choose and be made white and be refined and the *lawless act lawlessly* [*anomēsōsin anomoi*]. And *the lawless* [*anomoi*] will not understand, and the intelligent will understand." (12:10 LXX [Theodotion]; *NETS*, italics added)	

The immediate OT context of this allusion to Daniel is particularly illuminating to Paul's argument. Chapters 10–12 constitute Daniel's final vision. Those who are "wise" will instruct the "many" and undergo severe affliction (11:33–35). In 12:1 we are told that a great persecution will come, "a time of trouble, such as never has been." But in the midst of this tribulation, a remnant will remain and "be delivered" (12:1). They will eventually be resurrected, and those who have "understanding" will "shine brightly" (12:2–4 AT). The end-time events in chapters 11–12 largely comprise the rise and fall of kings, the antagonism of Antiochus IV (the Seleucid king), and a latter-day opponent of God and his people (11:36–45). It is not entirely clear whether Antiochus IV should be identified with the figure in verses 36–45. At the very least, Antiochus IV certainly functions as a precursor to or type of this antagonist.

In the immediate context of Daniel 11:36–45, a final opponent of God besieges the covenant community. Verse 36, to which Paul directly alludes, characterizes the opponent in stunning terms: "And the king shall do as he wills. He shall exalt himself and magnify himself above every god, and shall speak astonishing things against the God of gods. He shall prosper till the indignation is accomplished; for what is decreed shall be done" (cf. Dan. 2:8, 11, 25; 8:9–12; Isa. 14:12–14). This figure will commit great blasphemy by exalting and magnifying himself "above every god." In other words, he places himself on a pedestal above God. Not only does this opponent promote himself above God, but he also disparages God by "speaking astonishing things against the God of gods."

In addition, the end-time attack on Israel manifests itself in two ways. First, an opponent will persecute righteous Israelites. Verse 31 says, "Forces from him will arise, desecrate the sanctuary fortress, and do away with the regular sacrifice. And they will set up the abomination of desolation" (NASB). Here the enemy will wage war against the temple precinct and defile it by setting up "the abomination of desolation." Verses 33–35 further describe the attack against the "wise" within the covenant community: "Those who have insight among the people . . . will fall by sword and by flame, by captivity and by plunder for many days" (v. 33 NASB). The righteous, nevertheless, will persevere under pressure (v. 32), though they will "stumble" and be "refined" and "purified" (v. 35).

Second, Israel's latter-day enemy will deceive some within the Israelite community through enticing speech. His deception will be accompanied by "smooth words," leading some within the covenant community to "forsake the holy covenant" (v. 30, 32 NASB). His influence also extends to those "who violate the covenant" to become even more godless themselves (v. 32), to compromise, and to foster deception and further compromise among others. Verse 34 claims that "many will join with them [the faithful] in hypocrisy" (NASB), claiming to be faithful but not being so.

Daniel 12:10 describes in general the conduct of two groups in the latter days. The righteous Israelites will enjoy great discernment of God's actions. From the outside, it seems as though the wicked have the upper hand, especially in light of grave persecution, but those who have insight into God's plan (the "wise") will grasp the significance of the end-time turmoil. God has decreed that the wicked become increasingly hostile to those within the covenant community ("many shall purify themselves and make themselves white and be refined"). On the other hand, the "wicked" or lawless ones have been, it seems from 11:29–34, deceived by the end-time opponent. These lawless ones spiral into greater wickedness and deception: "The wicked will act wickedly" (Dan. 12:10 NASB).[5] This lawless behavior is even directly linked to, if not partly explained by, "the time of the removal of the perpetual sacrifice, when the abomination of desolation shall be set up" (AT).

The book of Daniel, as a whole, significantly develops this great oppressor of Israel. Foremost is the end-time context of the antagonist. The key passages are contextualized with phrases like "latter days" (10:14), "days yet to come" (10:14), and "time of the end" (8:17). In other words, this figure will arrive on the scene when the "latter days" dawn in Israel's history. In addition to the end-time component, the opponent will commit grave blasphemy by exalting

5. Daniel 11:32 LXX-Theodotion also includes the theme of "lawlessness"; however, Theodotion's translation differs in that it replaces the end-time opponent with a group of "lawless ones": "And *those who are lawless* will introduce a covenant by means of slipperiness" (*NETS*, italics added).

himself above God (11:36–37). The figure will be characterized primarily by two traits: (1) he will wage war against Israel on a number of fronts (7:25; 8:24; 9:26; 11:31, 33–35); (2) he will deceive many within the covenant community (though not the remnant or the "wise") and will further delude the wicked (8:25; 9:27; 11:30, 32, 34; 12:10).

Daniel's description of a latter-day tyrant and deceiver could be a development of Deuteronomy's earlier prediction. At the end of Deuteronomy, Moses predicts that Israel will turn from the Lord and become wicked in the "latter days": "For I know that after my death you will surely act corruptly and turn aside from the way that I have commanded you. And in the days to come [lit., "in the latter days"] evil will befall you, because you will do what is evil in the sight of the LORD, provoking him to anger through the work of your hands" (31:29; cf. Deut. 4:30). Earlier in Moses's appeal to Israel, he states precisely how Israel will turn away from God: "You [the present generation of Israelites] are about to lie down with your fathers. Then this people will rise and whore after the foreign gods among them in the land that they are entering, and they will forsake me and break my covenant that I have made with them. . . . And many evils and troubles will come upon them" (31:16–17). Within this period known as the "latter days," Israel will succumb to false teaching and commit heinous idolatry. Since Israel breaks the covenant, God promises to pour out his wrath upon them and send them into exile (cf. 30:15–20). Daniel supplements Moses's prophecy by refining the particulars of the false teaching and the extent of the heresy.

Therefore, when Paul alludes to Daniel 11:31, 36 and 12:10 in 2 Thessalonians 2:4, he likely has the full context of Daniel 11:31–12:10 in his mind (and perhaps other texts in Daniel that describe a similar or identical opponent: 7:7–12, 24–25; 8:9–12, 23–25; 9:26–27). He claims that through the individual "man of lawlessness" (2 Thess. 2:3), these things will surely come to pass in the future.

The Mysterious Presence of the Antichrist

In light of our brief analysis of Daniel, we can now understand Paul's admonitions to the Thessalonian community more richly. As mentioned above, Paul corrects the church's confusion over the second coming of Christ. He makes clear that Christ's second coming has not yet occurred, since that day will be preceded by two events—"apostasy" and the unveiling of the "man of lawlessness" (2 Thess. 2:3 NASB).[6]

6. On the "man of lawlessness," see Craig S. Keener, *A Commentary on the Gospel of Matthew: A Socio-Rhetorical Commentary* (Grand Rapids: Eerdmans, 2009), 570–71.

In verse 3 Paul claims that Daniel's "man of lawlessness" has not yet arrived on the scene, but alarmingly, there is a sense in which the end-time oppressor is already on the scene. This suggestion explains the language in verse 7: "The mystery [*mystērion*][7] of lawlessness is already at work." It is important to maintain the continuity of subject matter between verse 3 and verse 7. In verse 3 Paul mentions the future coming of the "man of lawlessness," and in verse 7 he further describes this same figure but in terms of his present existence. Verse 7 refers not to a general form of wickedness and persecution, as some presume, but to a specific end-time deception and persecution that ought to be attributed to Israel's end-time antagonist. The term "mystery," as found in the book of Daniel and the NT, refers to a specific end-time revelation, a particular doctrine or event that was previously hidden but has now been unveiled (e.g., Matt. 13:11; Rom. 11:25; 1 Cor. 2:7). Paul employs this unique term here in 2 Thess. 2:7 to describe a unique situation with startling ramifications: according to Daniel, the end-time persecutor will appear to the covenant community in his full bodily presence in the future; yet Paul argues that the antagonist is already at work in the community (though he is not bodily present at Thessalonica). In other words, the book of Daniel did not predict a two-stage fulfillment of the antagonist's arrival, first spiritual (through corporate false teachers present within the church) and then bodily.

Twice the book of Daniel also mentions how Israel's antagonist will desecrate the sanctuary:

> Forces from him will arise, desecrate the sanctuary fortress, and do away with the regular sacrifice. And they will set up the abomination of desolation. (11:31 NASB)

> From the time that the regular sacrifice is abolished and the abomination of desolation is set up, there will be 1,290 days. (12:11 NASB)

These two texts describe the end-time oppressor as entering Israel's temple precinct and defiling the sanctuary, actions initially fulfilled by Antiochus IV in 167 BC. With this in mind, Paul says in 2:4 that the antichrist will "[take] his seat in the temple of God." Though heavily debated among scholars, "temple" (*naos*) here probably does not refer to a rebuilt, physical temple in Jerusalem sometime in the future. Rather, "temple" (*naos*) refers to the community of believers, the church.[8] In other words, the antichrist will assume a position of

---

7. Some translations incorrectly render *mystērion* as "secret power" (TNIV) or "hidden power" (NET). Instead, the term ought to be translated as "mystery" (NASB; ESV; NRSV; ASV).
8. See 1 Cor. 3:16–17; 2 Cor. 6:16; Eph. 2:19–21; 1 Pet. 2:4–7; Rev. 3:12; 21:22.

authority in the church and thereby promulgate widespread deception. This event is thus a fulfillment of Daniel's tyrant setting up the abomination of desolation in the temple.[9]

The thrust of Paul's argument is that Daniel's prophecy is initially and uniquely fulfilled: although the latter-day foe has not yet come in physical form, the antagonist inspires the false teachers at Thessalonica, who deceive and persecute the church.

The Antichrist's Mysterious Presence in Other New Testament Texts

In addition to Paul's teaching in 2 Thessalonians, the antichrist plays a stark role in the Gospels and early Christianity.[10] In the Olivet Discourse, Jesus discusses an end-time figure who will deceive and bring about the destruction of many:[11]

> For many will come in my name, saying, "I am the Christ," and they will lead many astray. (Matt. 24:5; pars. Mark 13:6; Luke 21:8)

> And many false prophets will arise and lead many astray. And because lawlessness will be increased, the love of many will grow cold. (Matt. 24:11–12)

> Then if anyone says to you, "Look, here is the Christ!" or "There he is!" do not believe it. For false christs and false prophets will arise and perform great signs and wonders, so as to lead astray, if possible, even the elect. See, I have told you beforehand. So, if they say to you, "Look, he is in the wilderness," do not go out. If they say, "Look, he is in the inner rooms," do not believe it. (Matt. 24:23–26; par. Mark 13:21–22)

These passages reinforce our previous conclusions about the nature of the end-time opponent. Jesus envisions an antichrist figure(s) who will deceive Israel during a time preceding the destruction of the temple in AD 70.[12] His influence

---

9. For further discussion, see G. K. Beale, *The Temple and the Church's Mission*, NSBT 17 (Downers Grove, IL: InterVarsity, 2004), 274–92.

10. See also Rev. 13:1–8; 17:7–8; and 19:19–20. For a survey of this theme in the early church, see L. J. Lietaert Peerbolte, *The Antecedents of Antichrist: A Traditio-Historical Study of the Earliest Christian Views on Eschatological Opponents*, JSJSup 49 (Leiden: Brill, 1996), 63–220; P. H. Furfey, "The Mystery of Lawlessness," *CBQ* 8 (1946): 179–91.

11. *Apocalypse of Elijah* (first to fourth century AD), partly under the influence of Matt. 24 and 2 Thess. 2:3, includes both deception (3.1, 5–18; 4.15) and persecution (1.10; 4.2, 7–10; cf. *Apocalypse of Peter* 2; *Didache* 16.3–4).

12. See Anthony A. Hoekema, *The Bible and the Future* (Grand Rapids: Eerdmans, 1979), 148–49, 156.

will be a sign that Israel's destruction is near. In Matthew 24:5, the oppressor will be characterized by deception, claiming to be the Messiah and therefore upsetting the faith of many. Verses 11–12 may even allude to the emissaries of the antichrist, since they, like the end-time antagonist, will "mislead many" (see v. 5).

Jesus thus also refers to the same prophecy from Daniel to which Paul is referring (see Matt. 24:4–5, 10–13, 23–26). Just as the main point in 2 Thessalonians 2:1–7 is "let no one deceive you" in verse 3, the main point of the Matthew 24 passage is that no one mislead Jesus's followers about his second coming (vv. 3–4). Jesus predicts that before he returns, many antichrists will indeed come. He is focusing not on the final coming of one antichrist but on the coming into the church of many antichrists, who are the semifulfillments and forerunners of the final predicted opponent of God (Matt. 24:5, 10–15, 24). These are the same false prophets to whom 2 Thessalonians is referring (and, as we will see, 1 John 2:18 is referring). In Matthew 7:21–23 Jesus says that even some who were regarded as teachers of the church will be judged as false teachers at the final judgment.

In 2 Thessalonians 2:1–7 Paul claims that even now the false teachers that have been prophesied by Daniel and Jesus (cf. Matt. 24:4–5, 23–24, etc.) are operating within the church. Therefore, the end-time "great tribulation" has begun in the first century! The prophecy of the "apostasy" and coming of "the man of lawlessness" has been initially fulfilled.

Perhaps the most detailed discussion of the antichrist appears in 1 John 2:18–23. Whereas Jesus's primary focus in the Olivet Discourse is on the relationship between the antichrist(s) and the coming destruction of the temple, John highlights the inauguration of the latter-day deceiver as it pertains to heresy within the local church:

> Children, it is the last hour; and just as you heard that antichrist is coming, even now many antichrists have appeared; from this we know that it is the last hour. They went out from us, but they were not really of us; for if they had been of us, they would have remained with us; but they went out, so that it would be shown that they all are not of us. But you have an anointing from the Holy One, and you all know. I have not written to you because you do not know the truth, but because you do know it, and because no lie is of the truth. Who is the liar but the one who denies that Jesus is the Christ? This is the antichrist, the one who denies the Father and the Son. Whoever denies the Son does not have the Father; the one who confesses the Son has the Father also. (NASB)

This passage appears to depend on Jesus's prediction of "antichrists" in the Olivet Discourse and the discussion of the "man of lawlessness" in 2 Thessalonians 2. Verse 18 says that the writer's audience "heard" about the antichrist's arrival, suggesting that the audience was familiar with a circulating oral form of the expectations in the Synoptics and 2 Thessalonians 2.

John's words echo much of what we saw in the book of Daniel and in 2 Thessalonians 2:7. First, John claims that the coming of an antichrist(s) signals the inauguration of the "last hour." The phrase "last hour" or equivalent wording, found here and in John's Gospel (4:21, 23; 12:23; 16:25, 32; 17:1), stems from the book of Daniel (8:17, 19; 11:6, 35, 40; 12:1).[13] Now that the church is aware that the "latter days" or the "last hour" has begun, they are to remain sober minded and be on heightened alert for deceivers in the church, as Daniel prophesied long ago.

Second, the church can be confident that the "last hour" has been inaugurated because the end-time oppressor has arrived on the scene corporately through the false teachers: "Even *now* many *antichrists* have appeared" (italics added). John's words in 2:18 are remarkably similar to Paul's in 2 Thessalonians 2:7: "The mystery of lawlessness *is already at work*" (italics added). Like 2 Thessalonians 2, John claims that the end-time opponent of Israel is present in the local congregations, not physically but corporately. John does not label this a "mystery," but perhaps the force of "now" in 2:18 comes close to this idea.

Finally, as we have repeatedly observed in this chapter, the antichrist is marked by two characteristics—persecution and deception. Here John highlights the latter. Verse 22 describes in some detail the falsehood that the antichrists are proclaiming: "Who is the liar but the one who denies that Jesus is the Christ? This is the antichrist, the one who denies the Father and the Son." The majority of commentators are convinced that these "antichrists" or false teachers "denied that Jesus is the Christ" by espousing the view that Christ was not fully human.

How to Deal with False Teaching: Jude

We have spent some time underscoring *why* pastors must lead their congregations in accordance with the latter days, particularly as this relates to false teaching. We will now turn to *how* pastors should do so. Though only spanning twenty-five verses, Jude's letter is highly instructive on how to engage false teachers.

Jude's primary concern is to address the ingress of false teachers into house churches. The majority of the epistle is dedicated to condemning these false

---

13. Cf., e.g., Dan. 11:13, 20, 27, 29, 35. See Stefanos Mihalios, *The Danielic Eschatological Hour in the Johannine Literature*, LNTS 436 (New York: T&T Clark, 2011); and G. K. Beale, "The Eschatological Hour in 1 John 2:18 in the Light of Its Daniel Background," *Bib* 92 (2011): 231–54.

teachers and telling the churches how to respond to them. Evidently, false prophets have furtively crept into the believing community, offering a self-indulgent life-style. It seems as though this group is analogous to those rebuked in 2 Peter 2.

At the heart of this epistle lies Jude's condemnation of the false teachers. The NT reserves its harshest words for false teachers, and Jude proves to be no exception. In a straightforward manner, Jude condemns this pernicious group and outlines their destructive ways. Not only does he resolutely condemn these teachers (vv. 5–10, 14–16), but he also describes their sinful conduct in some detail (vv. 11–13). One of the most unique, even dizzying, aspects of the epistle is Jude's close reading and use of the OT. In a span of just eleven verses, the OT (and two Jewish texts) plays a formative role in his condemnation of the false teachers. Few texts in the NT drip with as many references to the OT as this section in Jude. What makes Jude's reading of the OT instructive is his conviction that several events and large swaths of passages anticipate the condemnation of these false teachers.

After condemning and describing the heretics, Jude tells the churches how they are to respond to these nefarious teachers. First, they should expect the arrival of false teachers: "You must remember, beloved, the predictions of the apostles of our Lord Jesus Christ. They said to you, 'In the last time there will be scoffers, following their own ungodly passions'" (vv. 17–18; cf. 2 Pet. 3:2). As mentioned above, pastors and leaders must expect and anticipate the presence of false teaching and prepare accordingly, since the period of the "last times" dawned in the first century and continues into the present.

Second, the churches must cultivate a robust relationship with God through prayer and meditation on his Word: "By building yourselves up in your most holy faith and praying in the Holy Spirit, keep yourselves in God's love as you wait for the mercy of our Lord Jesus Christ to bring you to eternal life" (vv. 20–21 NIV). Jude does not unpack with great precision what he means by "building yourselves up in your most holy faith," but we can be pretty confident that he has in mind studying Scripture and learning more about the Christian "faith." As the apostles begin to die off, the early church must proactively preserve apostolic teaching. Paul's words to Timothy are relevant here: "Follow the pattern of the sound words that you have heard from me, in the faith and love that are in Christ Jesus. By the Holy Spirit who dwells within us, guard the good deposit entrusted to you" (2 Tim. 1:13–14; cf. Titus 1:9; Rev. 3:3).[14] Accompanying Jude's exhortation to study God's Word is the

14. Like Jude, the apostle Paul commands believers, and especially Christian leaders, to maintain sound doctrine, because the "latter days" have dawned, and with them has come false teaching (1 Tim. 4:1; 2 Tim. 3:1; cf. 2 Pet. 3:3).

admonition to pray in the Holy Spirit. Church leaders must be characterized not only by studying Scripture but also by prayer. The twin habits of studying and prayer are crucial for engaging false teachers.

Third, Jude asks that his church be merciful and attempt to preserve those who struggle with false teaching: "And have mercy on those who doubt; save others by snatching them out of the fire; to others show mercy with fear, hating even the garment stained by the flesh" (vv. 22–23). Though his words are somewhat enigmatic here, Jude exhorts the church to have mercy on and make an attempt to save those who have bought into aberrant teaching. Notice how Jude draws a strong distinction between the false teachers and those who have been deceived by false teaching. Jude reserves his harshest words of judgment for the purveyors of falsehood (vv. 5–10, 14–16) but asks his congregation to extend a merciful hand toward those who have succumbed to it. Jude even exhorts the church to rescue the misled congregants, an act that most likely entails patience and mature faith. This last point is particularly helpful in that it serves as a wonderful model for current methods of combating false teaching. Pastors and church leaders must be mature Christians who handle false teaching with great care, being patient with those who have been deceived but intolerant toward those who are steeled in their resolve to promote their false teaching.

Elders and Eschatological Tribulation

The origin of ecclesiology, particularly with respect to the hierarchical structure of the church, is to be viewed, at least in part, within this context of the latter-day tribulation of false teaching.[15] On the one hand, "elders" or "bishops" are needed in order to maintain the doctrinal purity of the covenant community, which is always either being influenced by or threatened from the infiltration of false teachers (e.g., Titus 1:5–16; 1 Tim. 1:3–7, 19–20).

The ecclesiastical authority structure also ensures that the Christian community is continuing in the truth and life of the kingdom. This positive element of mission is part of the larger positive role of the church in its responsibility of carrying out the original Adamic commission to subdue the ends of the earth and Israel's commission to be priests for, and a light of witness to, the world. Of course, Acts highlights this eschatological light-bearing mission of the new creation more than any other NT book (Acts 1:6–8; 2:17–3:26; 13:47; 26:16–18). In fact, the mention of deacons in Acts 6 and elders in Acts 20 is, at least in part, to indicate their role in intensifying

---

15. This section has been adapted from G. K. Beale, *A New Testament Biblical Theology: The Unfolding of the Old Testament in the New* (Grand Rapids: Baker Academic, 2011), 820–23.

the growth of the kingdom and encouraging elders to guard against false teaching.

The church existing in the latter days, when tribulation and kingdom overlap, contains some interesting implications. For example, one scholar has argued that the prohibitions in 1 Timothy 2:11–15 against women teaching authoritatively in the church at Ephesus are a response to women who had become influenced by rampant false teaching. Many argue that since this situation of false teaching was a local and unique problem to the church in Ephesus, Paul's prohibitions do not apply to other churches throughout the church age when this specific false teaching is absent.[16] But if false teaching is part of the inaugurated, end-time tribulation that continues throughout the whole epoch before Christ's second coming, then Paul's prohibitions are not to be restricted to a local situation. The Ephesian false teaching is an *expression* of the broader, end-time trial. Since the inaugurated latter-day trial means that the churches will be affected or at least threatened by false teaching and deception, Paul's prohibitions are always valid. Therefore, Paul's prohibitions are a part of eschatological ethics pertinent to the entire church age, during which the end-time tribulation of false teaching either is affecting churches or threatens to corrupt them.

The office of elder is not a response to occasional or temporarily unique conditions but rather owes its existence to the ongoing, uninterrupted eschatological tribulation of false teaching and deception. The office was established to guard the church's doctrine so that it will remain healthy as it conducts its mission to the world to expand the invisible boundaries of the new creation. Such an office is required until the consummation of the new creation.

In general, the office of elder in the church is the continuation of the position of elder in Israel. Whereas elders in Israel had both civil and religious authority, elders in the new covenant have full religious authority over the sphere of the new Israel, the church. Several observations point to this equivalence. Besides the use of the same word, "elders" (*presbyteroi*), the book of Acts repeatedly juxtaposes the phrase "rulers and elders" of Israel (4:5, 8) or "chief priests and elders" (4:23; 23:14; 25:15) or "elders and the scribes" (6:12) with "apostles and elders" of the church (15:2, 4, 6, 22, 23; 16:4). Just as the Jewish "rulers and elders and scribes gathered together in Jerusalem" to judge the validity of the emerging Christian

16. See, e.g., Gordon D. Fee, "Issues in Evangelical Hermeneutics, Part III: The Great Watershed—Intentionality and Particularity/Eternality: 1 Tim. 2:8–15 as a Test Case," *Crux* 26 (1990): 31–37. Fee shows that 1 Timothy is shot through with references to false teaching, which is an occasion that must control the interpretation of the epistle. Unfortunately, Fee assumes that such false teaching is evidence of a unique, local situation to which Paul's prohibition against women teaching in 1 Tim. 2:11–12 is partly a response. Accordingly, for Fee, this prohibition cannot be universalized for all times and places, since it is an ad hoc response to such a local and limited occasion.

movement (4:5–23), so too in "Jerusalem . . . the apostles and the elders were gathered together to consider this matter" about the Jewish-Christian teaching that new gentile converts had to keep the law of Moses (15:1–6). The function of the Jewish elders in Acts 4 and the Christian elders in Acts 15 appears virtually identical. Both are in an official position in their respective covenant communities to adjudicate whether a new theological teaching is valid.

The position of elder was created, at least partly, to help protect the church's theological health in the midst of an inaugurated, end-time tribulation. Preceding the Acts 15 account of the council at Jerusalem, Paul and Barnabas exhorted the believers "to continue in the faith," saying that "through many tribulations we must enter the kingdom of God" (14:22). And the very next verse asserts, "And when they had appointed elders for them in every church, with prayer and fasting they committed them to the Lord in whom they had believed" (14:23). This is the first reference to appointing elders outside Jerusalem, leading directly into the dispute needing judgment by the Jerusalem elders in Acts 15. Behind this dispute was a false teaching that, if allowed to continue, would destroy the emerging Christian movement. The connection of the elders in Acts 14 to "tribulations" and false teaching indicates their eschatological role to guide the church through the end-time theological threats (see Acts 20:27–32).

Implications

Faithful Proclamation of God's Word

Though only a few decades old, the early church faced severe testing on several fronts. From the very beginning, the apostles labored diligently to preserve the teachings of Jesus. False teachers often emerged from within the local congregations, and at other times the false teachers intruded from the outside. If the early church, a small community of devoted believers, struggled from the outset with latter-day false teaching, should it surprise us that heresy is rampant today, since we too live in the latter days?

In the face of widespread heresy, church leaders must herald God's truth crisply and effectively. In our postmodern climate, churches have alarmingly capitulated to the surrounding culture, which is an expression of end-time false teaching. The Bible's exclusive claims have been increasingly stymied and marginalized. David Wells rightly summarizes the church's current state in this regard:

> When we listen to the church today, at least in the West, we are often left with the impression that Christianity actually has very little to do with truth. Christianity

is only about feeling better about ourselves, about leaping over our difficulties, about being more satisfied, about having better relationships. . . . It is about everything except truth. And yet this truth, personally embodied in Christ, gives us a place to stand in order to deal with the complexities of life, such as broken relations, teenage rebellion, and job insecurities. . . . The church is, to put it charitably, very distracted right now. This may well explain why it is struggling for its very life in the West.[17]

The time has come for pastors and church leaders to stand up against the seemingly insurmountable tide of watered-down teaching and anemic doctrine. The church must cultivate theological education among its leadership and develop concrete ways to educate its congregations. Bible studies, small groups, and Sunday school are wonderful examples of how pastors can robustly educate their congregations. When doctrine is marginalized, churches will inevitably drift and fall prey to false teaching, since the spirit of the antichrist is always knocking at the door of churches (1 John 4:1–3).

One of the primary ways in which the NT combats the spread of false teaching is the establishment of church government.[18] Though all believers are end-time priests before God, elders are appointed as end-time priests in an official capacity to teach God's Word and guard against false teaching. False teaching, which began during Jesus's ministry, is a hallmark of the end-time tribulation (1 John 2:18–29). Since the eschatological tribulation continues in the present and will remain until Christ returns, false teaching will remain. Church elders must wage war against such deception. In 1 Timothy 4:1, Paul says, "In later times some will depart from the faith by devoting themselves to deceitful spirits and teachings of demons." A few verses later he encourages Timothy to instruct in light of the latter days: "If you put these things [the corrupt teachings in 4:2–3] before the brothers, you will be a good servant of Christ Jesus, being trained in the words of the faith and of the good doctrine that you have followed" (4:6). Therefore elders, as end-time harbingers of truth, must preserve and proclaim God's Word in earnest and without corruption.

Perseverance in the Face of Persecution

The covenant community has, from the very beginning, undergone severe persecution. We first discover this theme in Genesis 3:15: "I will put enmity between you [the serpent] and the woman, and between your offspring and

17. David F. Wells, *The Courage to Be Protestant: Truth-Lovers, Marketers, and Emergents in the Postmodern World* (Grand Rapids: Eerdmans, 2008), 88.
18. This paragraph is conceptually indebted to G. K. Beale, *New Testament Biblical Theology*, 820–23.

her offspring; he shall bruise your head, and you shall bruise his heel." From Genesis 3 to Revelation 20, the Bible bears witness to a "war of seeds" or "offspring" that culminated in Christ's work on the cross. The church now finds itself on the other side of the cross. Sin and death have been conquered, yet they still remain active.

Though defeated, the devil and his minions continue to assault the church. But as Christians, we can withstand these physical and spiritual attacks, since we are "sealed" by God (Rev. 7). Paul's words in Romans 8:35 remain deeply relevant: "Who shall separate us from the love of Christ? Shall tribulation, or distress, or persecution, or famine, or nakedness, or danger, or sword?" Since believers are spiritually resurrected, members of God's end-time kingdom, and part of the new heavens and earth, they have the power to overcome all forms of persecution. This is not "mind over matter," as commonly expressed in today's culture. This is a power fueled by God's Spirit, who binds believers to the future. The NT authors often encourage their churches to look beyond present affliction and lay hold of such power through faith (e.g., 1 Pet. 1:3–9).

One dimension that is commonly overlooked is ruling in the midst of persecution. Paradoxically, two realms coexist—those who belong to the kingdom and those who belong to the "evil one." The end-time kingdom, in a very real sense, has begun through Jesus, yet the presence of the end-time kingdom mysteriously involves suffering, persecution, and tribulation. On the cross, Jesus embodied the overlap of the ages, the arrival of the kingdom and the presence of the great tribulation. He was King at the moment of suffering and death. The Gospels encourage the reader to connect the dots by showing them how the fate of the Messiah is bound up with the presence of the kingdom and the tribulation, a truly ironic concept. The remainder of the NT is more explicit: just as Christ ruled over the kingdom in a veiled way through suffering in an end-time trial or tribulation, so do Christians. These twin themes, like protons and neutrons, are bound up with one another and will remain joined until the consummate establishment of the new heavens and earth.

Pastors and leaders are to respond to persecution by keeping both of these principles in mind. Persecution is not going away, since it is part of the "overlap of the ages," yet it is a demonstration of believers' royal triumph. But how does persecution relate to the believers' victory? Their victory is their perseverance as faithful witnesses amid suffering and defeat (as Christ himself did; cf. Rev. 1:5). Although they may be defeated physically, they reign spiritually with Christ. This is the irony of the cross, which finds its cruciform expression in the lives of Christ's followers (Rev. 14:4).

Though Jesus endured great suffering throughout his earthly ministry, he paradoxically began to rule in fulfillment of the royal Son of Man prophecy from Daniel 7—conquering the devil and demons, winning a victory through his death by redeeming people through it, and so on. In this same manner, his followers also spiritually rule over the devil, evil powers, and persecutors when they maintain their faith, a belief that identifies them with the present rule of Jesus in heaven. This end-time principle is expressed in Revelation 1:9: "I, John, your brother and fellow partaker in the tribulation and kingdom and perseverance which are in Jesus, was on the island called Patmos, because of the word of God and the testimony of Jesus" (NASB).

Practical Suggestions

1. *Study previous expressions of false teaching, beginning with those mentioned in Scripture.* False teaching is not abating, because the inaugurated great tribulation commences with Christ's first advent and concludes with his final coming. Church leaders, therefore, must strive to be students of Scripture if they genuinely believe that the devil and his antichrist are trying to infiltrate the covenant community. Daniel 8:25 predicts that the man of lawlessness will "destroy many while they are at ease" (NASB). Martin Luther wonderfully embodies a proper mind-set: "I have read through the Bible twice every year. If you picture the Bible to be a mighty tree and every word a little branch, I have shaken every one of these branches because I wanted to know what it was and what it meant."[19] When pastors are tempted to curb their weekly sermon preparation, they should remember that they are succumbing to the spirit of "this world" and of the antichrist, who tempts ministers to betray their commitment to feeding the flock through the vigilant study of God's Word (1 John 4:1–6). Jesus himself predicted that the inaugurated latter-day tribulation would be a time when "lawlessness will be increased, [and] the love of many will grow cold" (Matt. 24:12). This "coldness" affects one's devotion to God's Word (cf. Matt. 24:11). Jesus even claims, "The one who endures to the end will be saved" (Matt. 24:13). The enduring that Jesus describes is the proclamation of the "gospel of the kingdom" (Matt. 24:14).

All forms of heresy tend to have common denominators. When we study the NT conception of false teachers, several characteristics surface. False teachers tend to be (1) arrogant (Jude 16; Dan. 8:25 states that Israel's antagonist will "magnify himself" [NASB]), (2) gifted speakers and affable (2 Tim. 3:6–7; 2 Pet. 2:1; Jude 16), (3) divisive (2 Tim 3:2–3; Jude 19), and (4) promoters of fleshly desires (2 Pet. 2:2, 18; Jude 16). False teachers have the appearance of

19. Martin Luther, *Luther's Works*, ed. and trans. Theodore G. Tappert (Philadelphia: Fortress, 1967), 54:165.

orthodox teachers (2 Cor. 11:13–15), and it is not always easy to discern if someone is a false teacher or has simply succumbed to false teaching. This comports with Daniel's prediction of the great tribulation, when the antagonist and the false prophets will "by smooth words . . . turn to godlessness" many within the covenant community (Dan. 11:32 NASB).

Studying church history and historical theology is another way in which church leaders can be prepared for the onslaught of false teaching, since such teaching throughout the church is a concrete manifestation of latter-day tribulation. In a sense, ministers are studying the history of the great tribulation. We must be well acquainted with previous expressions of false teaching in the Bible, so that we can proactively deal with them when they surface. Again, Daniel 8:23–25 says that in the latter-day tribulation, Israel's end-time opponent will be "ambiguous [in] speech" (marg.), and "through his shrewdness he will cause deceit to succeed by his influence" (NASB). All churches either are faced with the threat of latter-day false teaching or are internally affected by it. This is one of the great redemptive-historical reasons why God appointed elders within the church—to guard it from false teaching.

2. *Discern the presence of false teaching.* In light of our technologically savvy world and the internet, the gospel can now reach billions of people with relative ease. Podcasts, blogs, and all forms of social media are now entrenched in our lives. But this technological blessing has a downside: false teaching can spread quickly. Recall again Daniel's prediction that the latter-day antichrist and his allies would be able to corrupt people "while they are at ease" (Dan. 8:25 NASB). False teaching is not marked as "spam" in our email inboxes or our Twitter feeds. It is given the same platform as orthodox teaching. The same can be said for blogs, Facebook, podcasts, and the like. The point is that congregations are beset by an unending supply of false teaching, and most consume it with little or no discernment.

As a homeowner, I (Ben) am responsible to maintain my landscaping weekly. Most homeowners can attest to the frustration of combating weeds in the garden and hedges. If I fail to spray for weeds even one week, I am shocked at how swiftly the weeds take hold. Despite their outward appearance, weeds also form a network of roots under plants and choke them from below. Likewise, false teaching tends to spread throughout congregations, little by little, and often is unrestrained. On the surface, false teaching may not manifest itself, yet it may grow in the subterranean depths. Over the course of time, false teaching takes root and wraps itself around unfortified hearts and minds. Without careful study of the Scriptures, individuals will inevitably fall prey to end-time, corrupt teaching. These individuals may not even realize that they have begun to be deceived.

How do leaders train their congregations to be vigilant and discerning within this technosaturated world? It may be a good idea for leaders to confront this issue directly and have very concrete discussions regarding social media and the internet. The pulpit is an excellent place where pastors can warn people and inoculate them against the disease of false teaching.

3. *Become aware of the persecuted church.* For a number of reasons, the evangelical church in the West struggles to empathize with the intensely persecuted church in the rest of the world. Certainly, the Western church is not immune to such persecution, but when it occurs, it is typically local and contained. Perhaps one of the most effective ways to deal with persecution is to become aware of the persecuted church in previous points in the church's history and currently in other parts of the world. Christians ought to have a bird's-eye view of church history, and a number of introductory books on church history are readily available. A rudimentary understanding of church history effectively puts our suffering into proper perspective.

In addition to grasping the past, Christians must understand the present. Several websites, such as Voice of the Martyrs (www.persecution.com), are dedicated to bringing an awareness of the global, persecuted church to the West. Even praying for the persecuted church in the worship service can raise awareness.

Suggested Reading

Allison, Gregg. *Historical Theology: An Introduction to Christian Doctrine.* Grand Rapids: Zondervan, 2011.

Ferguson, Everett. *From Christ to Pre-Reformation.* Vol. 1 of *Church History: The Rise and Growth of the Church in Its Cultural, Intellectual, and Political Context.* Grand Rapids: Zondervan, 2005.

Hendriksen, William. *More than Conquerors: An Interpretation of the Book of Revelation.* 1939. Reprint, Grand Rapids: Baker, 1998.

Riddlebarger, Kim. *Man of Sin: Uncovering the Truth about the Antichrist.* Grand Rapids: Baker Books, 2006.

Woodbridge, John, and Frank A. James III. *From Pre-Reformation to the Present Day.* Vol. 2 of *Church History: The Rise and Growth of the Church in Its Cultural, Intellectual, and Political Context.* Grand Rapids: Zondervan, 2013.

6

Guiding the Flock

With earnestness, first-century Jews anticipated the arrival of the messiah who would liberate them from Rome and usher in God's eternal kingdom. To some degree or another, everything the Jewish people did was bound up with this hope (their festivals, the Sabbath, the Mosaic law). Then it happened. Jesus brought Israel's (and humanity's) story to its long-awaited climax through his life, death, and resurrection. The gospel triggered the initial fulfillment of the OT's conception of the "latter days," drastically affecting how the NT saints and apostles ministered to their congregations. Eschatology not only affected their view of the local gathering of saints, but it also changed the way in which they led them. The apostles ministered to their congregations in accordance with the overlap of the ages.

After outlining how a biblical view of the latter days affects our preaching and how we combat false teaching and endure persecution, we now conclude this section on church leadership. In what follows, we will consider how the already–not yet bears upon leading by example, discipleship, and cultivating a vision for ministry. This last chapter is an attempt to round out our discussion on pastoral leadership by probing three often-discussed topics and nestling them in eschatology. Since the NT writers ministered to their congregations during the overlap of the ages, they led by example, treated one another as part of the new creation, and were mindful of God's end-time evaluation of their ministry.

Leading by Example

Imitating the Apostle John

The book of Revelation is often neglected as a resource for Christian leadership and Christian ethics in general. This is most likely tied to one's interpretation of the book as a whole. Do the events detailed within Revelation largely take place in the future? Are they merely a recollection of church history? We assume that Revelation largely concerns the fulfillment of end-time events, events that were initially fulfilled in the first century and will be consummately fulfilled at Christ's second coming.[1] Even if one takes the book's outlook as broadly describing only the future, Revelation certainly has some application for the church today. Keep in mind that the entire book circulated to the seven churches of Asia Minor (Rev. 2–3), and those churches must have benefited, at the very least, from the principles contained therein. G. K. Chesterton once remarked, "Though St. John the Evangelist saw many strange monsters in his vision, he saw no creatures so wild as one of his own commentators."[2] In avoiding such "monstrous" interpretations, our goal here is to answer two questions: What does the apostle John's leadership over the churches in Asia Minor look like, and are these churches, particularly their leaders, supposed to imitate John in this respect?

Testifying in the Face of Persecution

The book of Revelation opens with a chain of communication between God, Christ, an angel, and John: "The revelation of Jesus Christ, which God gave him to show to his servants the things that must soon take place. He made it known by sending his angel to his servant John, who bore witness to the word of God and to the testimony of Jesus Christ, even to all that he saw" (Rev. 1:1–2). God communicated the content of Revelation to Christ, who in turn communicated it to angels, who then gave it to John. John then "bore witness" to the "word of God," and he testified to the "testimony" of Jesus. This mode of communication ensured that the revelation was preserved and validated (cf. 22:16). John then delivered this testimony to the seven churches and their elders (Rev. 2–3), imploring them to testify to the world. However,

---

1. For scholars who espouse this view, see, e.g., G. K. Beale, *The Book of Revelation*, NIGTC (Grand Rapids: Eerdmans, 1999); William Hendriksen, *More than Conquerors: An Interpretation of the Book of Revelation* (1939; repr., Grand Rapids: Baker, 1998); and Dennis E. Johnson, *Triumph of the Lamb: A Commentary on Revelation* (Phillipsburg, NJ: P&R, 2001).

2. G. K. Chesterton, *Orthodoxy* (New York: John Lane, 1908; repr. San Francisco: Ignatius, 1995), 21–22.

one serious flaw of a few of the churches was their lack of testifying to the world around them (e.g., 2:4).

We learn that John is exiled on the island of Patmos and why he is there: "I, John, your brother and companion in the suffering and kingdom and patient endurance that are ours in Jesus, was on the island of Patmos because of the word of God and the testimony of Jesus" (Rev. 1:9 NIV). John is on Patmos because of his testimony to God's word. In other words, John is willing to be persecuted for his proclamation of the revelation. But John is not the only one who has been persecuted for testifying about Christ: "When he [the Lamb] opened the fifth seal, I saw under the altar the souls of those who had been slain because of the word of God and for testimony they had maintained" (6:9 NIV). Just as John suffered for his testimony, the deceased saints are martyred because of their testimony (cf. 11:7; 19:10; 20:4). Testifying about the risen Christ not only leads to persecution but also empowers believers, ironically, to be victorious over Satan. Revelation 12:11 succinctly states, "And they have conquered him by the blood of the Lamb and by the word of their testimony, for they loved not their lives even unto death." Here the saints conquer Satan by testifying to God and identifying with Christ (cf. 12:17). John, therefore, leads by example in testifying about Christ to a hostile world.

"Overcoming" the World

Revelation 1:9 claims that John is a "partner in the tribulation and kingdom." The ideas of "tribulation" and "kingdom," though discussed separately in the OT (esp. in Dan. 7), have been surprisingly merged into a unified, ironic concept in Revelation 1:9. Surprisingly, John participates in God's end-time kingdom by persevering through tribulation (1:6). John's behavior models Christ's actions on the cross; he likewise executed his rule in the midst of suffering (1 Cor. 1:18–2:16). Jesus labels his teaching in Matthew's Gospel as "mysteries of the kingdom." The latter-day kingdom is surprisingly fulfilled in two stages. The book of Daniel, perhaps more than any other OT book, demonstrates that the latter-day kingdom arrives after persecution and tribulation (e.g., Dan. 7:24–26; 12:1–3). Jesus's teaching on the kingdom differs in general from the latter-day conception of the kingdom in the OT and Judaism in that the kingdom and those within it coexist with pagan empires and wickedness.[3]

In a very real sense, while John is on Patmos suffering because of his resolved testimony for Christ, he is being "overcome" physically by the world. Physically, the world "overcomes" true believers, particularly John, yet true

---

3. For further discussion of this theme, see G. K. Beale and Benjamin L. Gladd, *Hidden but Now Revealed: A Biblical Theology of Mystery* (Downers Grove, IL: InterVarsity, 2014), 75–83.

believers spiritually "overcome" the world. John, while in exile on the island of Patmos and physically enduring "tribulation," rules and reigns in God's end-time kingdom, albeit in a spiritual manner. Outwardly, the apostle suffers intense persecution, but spiritually and invisibly he has triumphed over the devil and the world.

This behavior is ultimately modeled after Christ's conquering and overcoming Satan and the world through his death. Revelation 3:21 states, "He who overcomes, I will grant to him to sit down with Me on My throne, as I also overcame and sat down with My Father on His throne" (NASB; cf. Rev. 5:5–6). Later in Revelation, the beast is portrayed as overcoming the saints physically, but in reality they overcome him spiritually: "When they have finished their testimony, the beast that comes up out of the abyss will make war with them, and overcome them and kill them" (11:7 NASB; cf. 13:7). By suffering on Patmos and being "overcome" by the world physically, John the apostle triumphs over the world spiritually, thus modeling a genuine Christlike behavior for the seven churches of Asia Minor.

John is aware that the seven churches will look to him as an example of how to conduct oneself in testifying about Christ and in overcoming the world through physical suffering. The churches in Asia Minor, especially the churches' leadership, must imitate John, and John must imitate Christ. A central reason why John even penned the book of Revelation is to encourage the churches in Asia Minor to "overcome" or be "victorious" (2:7, 11, 17, 26; 3:5, 12, 21). Richard Bauckham rightly claims, "In a sense the whole book [of Revelation] is about the way the Christians of the seven churches may, by being victorious within the specific situations of their own churches, enter the new Jerusalem."[4] The Christian leaders of the churches in Asia Minor are admonished to overcome the world and teach their congregations to do the same. The seven churches must not give in to the political, social, and religious pressure.

Discipleship: Treating Christians as Part of the New Creation

Now that we have explored leading by example in Revelation, we turn to the topic of Christian leadership as it pertains to discipleship. Here we combine two distinct yet related issues—discipleship and counseling—under the umbrella of discipleship. We will unpack a few foundational truths that are related to discipleship in 2 Corinthians 5.

4. Richard Bauckham, *The Theology of the Book of Revelation*, NTT (Cambridge: Cambridge University Press, 1993), 14.

Paul's opponents in 2 Corinthians accuse him of being unsophisticated, weak in appearance, uncharismatic, and without the proper apostolic credentials. Paul responds by claiming that he is a genuine apostle because he identifies with the cross of Christ. He suffers, and God displays power through the apostle's weakness, just as the Father did through Christ. From 2:14 to 7:14, Paul describes various facets of his apostolic ministry. In 5:11–15, Paul explains what motivates him—"the love of Christ." The following section reveals the content of his message (5:16–6:2).

Because Paul is compelled by the love of Christ to preach the gospel, he "regard[s] no one from a worldly point of view" (5:16 NIV). Another way to translate this verse is "we regard no one according to the flesh" (ESV). The key phrase here is "according to the flesh" (*kata sarka*). It can simply mean "descendant" or a physical body (e.g., Gal. 4:23, 29; Eph. 6:5; Col. 3:22; Rom. 1:3). But, pertinently, this phrase often occurs in the context of discussions concerning the "old age" and behavior in accordance with it (e.g., Rom. 8:4–5, 12–13; 2 Cor. 1:17; 10:2–3). In light of this somewhat common Pauline phrase, the point could not be clearer: Paul and his associates have a different worldview, one that embraces the cross and its effects. Before Paul's conversion, he evaluated Christ according to the ethics of the "old age," which explains why he persecuted the church. But now that Paul has a different worldview, one that is in keeping with what God has done through Christ, he evaluates Christ (2 Cor. 5:16b) and believers differently.

After declaring that he now views Christ differently, Paul claims that anyone "in Christ" is a "new creation." In saying this, the apostle alludes to several key texts from the book of Isaiah (italics added):

2 Corinthians 5:17 NIV	Isaiah 43:18–19; 65:17 NIV
"If anyone is in Christ, the *new creation* has come: The *old* has gone, the *new* is here!"	"Forget the *former things*; do not dwell on the past. See, I am doing a *new thing*! Now it springs up; do you not perceive it? I am making a way in the wilderness and streams in the wasteland."
	"See, I will create *new heavens and a new earth*. The *former things* will not be remembered, nor will they come to mind." (cf. Isa. 66:22)

In their original contexts, these passages from Isaiah speak of Israel's restoration from exile, a second exodus of sorts from "Egypt," that is, Babylon. The prophet Isaiah calls this deliverance a "new creation," since the promised land will be a place of peace, righteousness, joy, the installation of God's kingdom, and so forth (see 65:18–25). Apparently, God will also perform a new-creational act by creating a new heavens and earth (65:17; 66:22). Just as God created the cosmos in Genesis 1–2, so too he will once again create a new heaven and earth. The Israelites are to forget their previous behavior, which brought them to the Babylonian exile (the "former things"), and embrace what God will be doing by re-creating Israel in the promised land!

Paul declares that an individual found in Christ is a "new creation" (lit., "there is new creation"). The promised restoration of Israel into the promised land is now being fulfilled through Christ. The same can be said for the long-awaited peace, forgiveness of sins, pouring out of the Spirit, return from "exile," joy, righteousness, and finally, new creation! By identifying with Christ through faith, believers partake of Christ's resurrection, an event that sparked the inauguration of the new creation (1 Cor. 15:20–28; Rev. 3:14). Believers are spiritually part of the inbreaking new creation and participate in the new heavens and earth.

Paul then goes on to describe how this restoration from exile takes place: God reconciles us through Christ (2 Cor. 5:18–21). Before conversion, individuals were spiritually "exiled" in Babylon, enemies of God, and enslaved to sin. But when individuals are joined to Christ through faith, God brings them into a right relationship with himself by creating them anew. These OT promises from Isaiah are now being fulfilled through Christ. "Paul understands both 'new creation' in Christ as well as 'reconciliation' in Christ (2 Cor. 5:18–20) as the fulfillment of Isaiah's promise of a new creation in which Israel would be restored into a peaceful relationship with Yahweh."[5]

We can now better appreciate Paul's exhortation in 2 Corinthians 5:16: "So from now on we regard no one *from a worldly point of view* [*kata sarka*]. Though we once regarded Christ in this way, we do so no longer" (NIV, italics added). Christ's work on the cross and his resurrection radically change Paul's understanding of the world around him. Paul's entire worldview has shifted—he more fully understands the OT, God's plan of redemption, the nature of sin, the grace of God, and so on. In 2 Corinthians 2:16 the apostle acknowledges that he treats people differently now that the new age has broken into history. Paul instructs the Corinthians to live in light of the new age by regarding others in accordance with the overlap of the ages. The Corinthians must realize that the world's values and ethics are completely different from God's.

Paul's teaching in 2 Corinthians 5 cuts two ways: the Christians at Corinth must treat each other as members of the new creation, individuals who have been spiritually released from Babylonian captivity and ushered into the

---

5. G. K. Beale, "The Old Testament Background of Reconciliation in 2 Corinthians 5–7 and Its Bearing on the Literary Problem of 2 Corinthians 6.14–7.1," *NTS* 35 (1989): 558.

promised land. But we must not forget that we have yet to arrive fully into the promised land. Though Christians are indeed a "new creation" and have an inheritance in the promised land (cf. Heb. 12:22), they are still coming out of "Babylonian exile" (what is often called "ongoing sanctification"). As Christians continue to emerge from exile and enter the promised land, they continue to shed their sinful baggage, which has weighed so heavily on them (Heb. 12:1). In addition, Christians must treat unbelievers in accordance with the overlap of the ages. The Corinthian church must understand that unbelievers are part of the "old age," people who are entrenched in sin and enslaved to a fallen world. The devil enslaves them and imprisons them in spiritual exile. These truths are foundational for how Christian leaders interact with unbelievers and disciple church members.

Vision: Ministering in Light of God's End-Time Evaluation

Christian leaders often struggle with determination, the passion to press on in the ministry.[6] It ebbs and flows. At times, ministers enjoy mountaintop experiences; it seems that nothing can unseat their love and passion for their congregation. Perhaps the pastor gave a good sermon or received an encouraging phone call from someone in the congregation. Inevitably, leaders descend from the mountain and battle immense discouragement. Perhaps the sermon series did not go as well as planned, a longtime friend abandoned the faith, or dissension has broken out within the church. This list goes on. Whatever the case may be, leaders endure a lifelong struggle with determination, and their faith is incessantly tested by fire.

The desire to persevere in the midst of difficult circumstances rests squarely upon what God has done in the past, what he's currently doing in the present, and what he will do in the future. The future aspect of pastoral ministry is bound up with the resurrection and the consummation of all things. By keeping an eye on what has already taken place *and* on what is yet to come, pastors have the ability to persevere under every conceivable difficulty. We will briefly examine one passage from 1 Corinthians 4, a text that is often overlooked in pastoral ministry. First Corinthians 4:1–5 concerns God's end-time evaluation of one's pastoral conduct.

Chapters 1–4 primarily address the problems of a divisive leadership and community. The members of Corinth are fleshly, since these divisions side

---

6. This section has been adapted from Benjamin L. Gladd, *Revealing the* Mysterion: *The Use of* Mystery *in Daniel and Second Temple Judaism with Its Bearing on First Corinthians*, BZNW 160 (Berlin: de Gruyter, 2008), 167–85.

with one leader over another (1:10–13; 3:1–4). Paul therefore attempts to remedy this situation by furnishing a series of examples for the Corinthians to imitate. Paul applies both agricultural (3:4–9) and architectural (3:10–11) metaphors to himself and Apollos to illustrate the collaboration between two church leaders; just as the field workers received their reward (3:8), so also builders receive theirs (3:12–15). Summarizing the entire argument from 1:10–2:16, Paul again underscores the need to boast only in Christ in 3:18–23 (cf. 1:17–18, 21, 23; 2:1–2). The leaders—Paul, Apollos, and Cephas—serve the church and not the reverse (3:22 [cf. 1:12; 3:4]).

After agricultural and architectural metaphors, Paul moves on to the third metaphor of serving the church as "servants of Christ" and "entrusted with the mysteries God has revealed":

> This, then, is how you ought to regard us: as *servants of Christ and as those entrusted with the mysteries God has revealed*. Now it is required that those who have been given a trust must prove faithful. I care very little if I am judged by you or by any human court; indeed, I do not even judge myself. My conscience is clear, but that does not make me innocent. It is the Lord who judges me. Therefore judge nothing before the appointed time; wait until the Lord comes. He will bring to light what is hidden in darkness and will expose the motives of the heart. At that time each will receive their praise from God. (1 Cor. 4:1–5 NIV, italics added)

How is Paul a "faithful" manager of "mysteries"? Paul considers himself to be in a mediatory position between God and the Corinthians. In other words, Paul consciously conducts himself as one who promulgates the message of the cross, a message that was revealed to him from God. In 1 Corinthians 2 Paul has clearly outlined a revelation that he has received: "For God has revealed them to us by his Spirit. . . . We have not received the spirit of the world but the Spirit who is from God, that we may understand what God has freely given us" (2:10–12 AT). This revelation is probably the unveiled mystery of the cross that Paul has just finished discussing in 2:1–9.

After mentioning the idea of faithfulness, Paul discusses his "examination" in 4:3–5. The beginning of verse 3 states that Paul is not concerned about being judged by the Corinthians, or by any human court for that matter, because Paul does not even judge himself. In 1 Corinthians 1:17, Paul declares that he was sent out by Christ not to preach the gospel "with wisdom and eloquence" (NIV; cf. 1 Cor. 2:1–4, 15). This verse boldly confronts a specific issue in the Corinthian church: Some members judged Paul because of his lack of persuasion and weak rhetorical delivery.[7] These Corinthians were examining him while he was proclaiming the revealed message of the cross.

In 4:3b–4, Paul extends this examination to himself, which corresponds to the immediate context of stewardship. Only the master is able to judge the servant, for he is answerable to no one but his lord. As an overseer of God's mysteries, Paul is under strict accountability to the Lord for his stewardship.

The climax of 4:1–4 is reached in verse 5 with the word "therefore." We could thus render Paul's words as "because the Lord is the judge in my life [4:3–4], *therefore* stop judging me before 'the Day.'" He then continues in 4:5b with the appearance of the Lord as the great judge and revealer. The event that Paul graphically describes here appears to be part of the general end-time judgment (cf. 2 Cor. 1:14; 1 Thess. 2:19; 3:13; 4:15; 5:2, 23), though for Paul, and for others sharing his pastoral office, the focus is on an end-time judgment concerning how they have conducted their stewardship of the message of the cross, the unveiled "mystery."

Paul's discussion in 3:10–15 strengthens this view.[8] Each time Paul employs an example of himself and Apollos engaging in ministry, he incorporates a specific end-time judgment.[9] The apostle speaks of field workers and builders receiving wages (3:8, 14). At the end-time judgment, God will evaluate the work of each church leader, whether a field worker or builder. Likewise here in 4:5, God appraises Paul's management of the mystery of the cross.

This judgment may explain a possible OT allusion in verse 5b. The verse may allude to a popular Greek translation of Daniel 2:22–23, a text that outlines the nature of the mystery (italics added).

1 Corinthians 4:5 NIV	Daniel 2:22–23 *NETS* [Theodotion]
"He will bring to *light* what is *hidden* in *darkness* and will expose the motives of the hearts. At that time each will receive their *praise* from God."	"He reveals deep and *hidden* things, knowing what is in the *darkness*, and the *light* is with him. You, O God of my ancestors, I acknowledge and *praise*, because you have given me wisdom and power, and you have made known to me what we petitioned from you, and you have made known to me the matter of the king."

7. Ben Witherington III, *Conflict and Community in Corinth: A Socio-Rhetorical Commentary on 1 and 2 Corinthians* (Grand Rapids: Eerdmans, 1995), 137.

8. Some view 3:8, 14–15 as a general judgment for *all* believers (Craig Blomberg, *1 Corinthians*, NIVAC [Grand Rapids: Zondervan, 1994], 74–82; Raymond Collins, *First Corinthians*, SP 7 [Collegeville, MN: Liturgical Press, 1999], 152–53). Though this language is similarly applied to all believers elsewhere in the NT (e.g., 2 Cor. 5:10), the immediate context argues against this position. Paul emphasizes church leaders and their responsibility to serve the church (3:23). The apostle is using himself and Apollos as examples not of general Christian behavior within the local church but of how *leaders* must conduct themselves by shepherding God's flock.

9. See F. M. Smit, "'What Is Apollos? What Is Paul?': In Search for the Coherence of First Corinthians 1:10–4:21," *NovT* 44 (2002): 238.

The combination of these words occurs only in the Greek translation of Daniel 2:22–23. The entire paragraph, Daniel 2:20–23, is a hymn of thanksgiving that encapsulates the nature of mystery. This passage speaks of God disclosing his wisdom to individuals. Wisdom, according to Daniel 2:20–23, comprises "deep and hidden things." Mystery in Daniel is God's revelation of this wisdom characterized by end-time events, particularly, the establishment of God's eternal kingdom. At the end of the hymn in 2:23, Daniel is thankful that God has revealed the mystery to him (see Dan. 2:19).

Ironically, in 1 Corinthians 4:5, God is not disclosing his wisdom to Paul; rather, God is unveiling the secrets of Paul's heart! The great revealer of mysteries now is laying bare the mysteries of the individual. The Lord brings to light the hidden things of darkness and divulges[10] the mysteries of Paul's and other leaders' hearts.

The context of Daniel 2:20–23 is insightful: Daniel venerates God because "wisdom and power" belong to him (Dan. 2:20; cf. 2:23). In 1 Corinthians 1:24 Paul designates Christ as the "power of God and the wisdom of God." In addition, Paul exhorts the church so that their faith may not rest on the "wisdom of men" but on the "power of God" (2:5; cf. 1:18–24, 30; 2:1, 4–8, 13; 4:20). In 4:5 God judges Paul *for his use of divine wisdom and power*, which were previously revealed to him as the message of the cross. The irony of this allusion from Daniel is that God employs his wisdom and power (Dan. 2:20; 1 Cor. 1:18, 21, 24, 30; 2:4–7) to evaluate Paul's *stewardship* of God's wisdom and power (the message of the cross) at the end-time judgment (Dan. 2:23; 1 Cor. 4:3–5).

Taking it one step further, Paul sustains the allusion to Daniel and delivers the result of this examination in 4:5c: "Finally, each one's praise will come from God." In Daniel 2:23 God receives praise for the revelation of the mystery, and now God himself praises the individual for his stewardship over the mystery. Paul therefore must take seriously his role as a keeper and guardian of divine wisdom (1 Cor. 4:2), for the Lord will appraise his conduct (4:3–5).[11]

---

10. In the Pauline corpus, the words "manifest"/"make known" (*phaneros/phaneroō*) are linked both to God trying an individual's heart (e.g., 1 Cor. 3:13; 14:25; 2 Cor. 5:10) and to a disclosure of hidden mysteries (Rom. 16:26; Col. 1:26; 1 Tim. 3:16).

11. Some commentators understand this judgment as applicable to everyone because of the clause "each will receive their praise from God" in 1 Cor. 4:5 (NIV) (Alan F. Johnson, *1 Corinthians*, IVPNT [Downers Grove, IL: InterVarsity, 2004], 79; Collins, *First Corinthians*, 171). Apparently the word "each" (*hekastos*) has led to the confusion. All the metaphors are parallel to one another (3:6–15; 4:1–5), and each metaphor contains a latter-day judgment (3:8, 13–15; 4:5). This consistency is confirmed with the word "each" in 3:8 and 3:13. In these passages, "each" (*hekastos*) refers not to everybody but to each *leader*—the field workers (3:6–8), builders (3:10–15), and stewards (4:1–5). Therefore, Paul consistently applies these metaphors to the leaders of the church and not to the congregation (see Gordon Fee, *First Epistle to the Corinthians*, NICNT [Grand Rapids: Eerdmans, 1987], 136).

Paul's ministry, particularly his preaching the message of the cross, is done in anticipation of what is to come. Paul knows that the Lord will one day hold him accountable, at the very end of history, for preaching a gospel that is free from deceit and error. With an eye on Christ's end-time evaluation of his ministry, Paul's desire is that he be found "faithful" in the proclamation of the crucified Christ (4:2). These Corinthian leaders must not be characterized by rhetoric (1:17), which causes fractures to the unity at Corinth, but by humble service (2:1–5). Like Paul, these leaders are responsible for their proclamation of the gospel; one day God will evaluate the integrity of their message. They must "imitate" Paul by anticipating the future evaluation of their own ministry (4:16).

Implications

Christian Leaders Must Lead by Example in Their Embodiment of the Cross

As demonstrated in the book of Revelation, proclaiming the gospel inexorably leads to eschatological suffering, the same suffering that the OT prophets predict will occur in the latter days (e.g., Ezek. 38; Dan. 7). Revelation 11 symbolically depicts the "two witnesses" and the "two lampstands" (i.e., the church; Rev. 1:12, 20) as faithfully proclaiming truth to the world in the latter days. Consequently, the "beast," in fulfillment of Daniel 7, attacks and kills these faithful witnesses (Rev. 11:7–10), who are resurrected at the very end of the age (11:11–12). The two witnesses represent the saints as they faithfully proclaim God's Word between the first and second comings of Christ. Revelation 11 is a blueprint for church leaders: ministers of the gospel are to proclaim truth, knowing that end-time hostility will inevitably grow and lead to death. The more Christian leaders testify about the crucified Christ, the more the world grows hostile.

Patterning one's life after Christ's work on the cross, that is, his spiritual triumph in the midst of physical defeat, is all encompassing. At the very moment Christ endured latter-day tribulation on the cross, he, as the cosmic King, vanquished the devil and began to establish the eternal kingdom. The established pattern of the cross applies to all facets of life, resisting a piecemeal application. We should not look to Christ's pattern of suffering only when we encounter end-time suffering; rather, we must apply this pattern to all of life. The ethics of the cross are eschatological to the core, and therefore our embodiment of them is likewise eschatological. The ethics of the cross revolutionizes our entire worldview. When we likewise suffer end-time affliction, we can be confident that we are participating in God's kingdom and ruling over the devil. Additionally, when Christian leaders embody the message of the cross, they become an example to others. Church congregations inevitably look to their leaders for direction. Leaders must consciously conduct themselves in light of this ever-present, end-time reality.

Discipleship Should Be Practiced in Accordance with the Overlap of the Ages

One crucial dimension of the inbreaking of the new age through Christ's death and resurrection is the way in which Christians treat one another. Recall Paul's conclusion that each believer is a "new creation" (2 Cor. 5:17) and that Isaiah's prophecies concerning the restoration of all things in the new heavens and earth have initially been fulfilled in the life of the believer (Isa. 65:17; 66:22). The physical and spiritual restoration of God's people and creation that Isaiah saw at the very end of the age has been applied to the saints, albeit in a partial manner. Believers are not only forgiven through faith in Christ; they are also created anew by God's end-time Spirit. When we interact with each other, privately and corporately, we are required to do so in light of the dawning of the new age.

On the other hand, believers still possess indwelling sin and corrupt bodies and continue to live in the old age (though their identity is in the new age). Believers will inevitably sin, but they will not be mastered by sin. John states that "no one who is born of God will continue to sin, because God's seed remains in them; they cannot go on sinning, because they have been born of God" (1 John 3:9 NIV; cf. Rom. 6:18). This has considerable bearing upon how we counsel and disciple one another. If a person confesses Christ and demonstrates that faith through works, Christian leaders must treat that individual as though he or she inextricably belongs to the long-awaited new heavens and earth. The person has, as John so dramatically says, "passed out of death into life" (1 John 3:14). Those who have joined themselves to Christ through faith belong to the new heavens and earth, the realm of righteousness, peace, mercy, and so on. Those who counsel and disciple others must have a firm grasp of this truth since they nurture the faith of other believers.

Preach and Teach in Light of God's End-Time Judgment

Church leaders should tremble at James's words: "Not many of you should become teachers, my brothers, for you know that *we who teach will*

be judged with greater strictness" (3:1, italics added). These words from
James and other NT writers ought to shape how Christian leaders conduct
their ministry, particularly proclaiming Christ crucified. As we saw above,
the same God who reveals the end-time mystery of the cross will likewise
reveal the end-time "purposes" of the minister's heart (1 Cor. 4:5). Leaders
must ensure that their message and conduct are faithful and in keeping with
Scripture (1 Cor. 4:6). The latter-day evaluation affects the aims and goals of
each church leader; it plays no small role in the leaders' vision of ministry.
Though the Corinthians are not in a position to judge the apostle Paul, the
Lord certainly is (4:3–5). The book of Daniel predicts that in the latter days
the "wise," those who truly possess insight into God's wisdom, will "make
many understand" (Dan. 11:33). That is, the wise are teachers within the
covenant community who instruct others in God's truth. But Daniel goes
on to prophesy that "many shall join themselves to them [the "wise"] with
flattery" (11:34). Apparently, false teachers will come alongside and masquer-
ade as the "wise" teachers and deceive. What separates these two groups is
one's commitment to the truth and perseverance amid intense persecution
(11:33b–35). Church leaders fulfill Daniel's prophecy of "wise ones" when
they faithfully preach and minister. We ought to ask, weekly, whether or not
our Sunday messages stand up to the scrutiny of God, the great revealer of
mysteries of the heart (see 1 Cor. 14:25).

Practical Suggestions

1. *Do a study of "overcomer"/"overcoming" in the book of Revelation.* Read
through the book of Revelation, making note of all the occurrences of the word
"overcomer"/"overcoming" in the book. The OT pattern is that eschatological persecution/tribulation precedes end-time restoration. This is particularly
the case in Daniel 12:1–2 (NIV): "There will be a time of distress such as
has not happened from the beginning of nations until then. But at that time
your people—everyone whose name is found written in the book—will be
delivered. Multitudes who sleep in the dust of the earth will awake: some to
everlasting life, others to shame and everlasting contempt" (cf. Dan. 7:23–27).
These two eschatological concepts, though sequentially arranged in the OT,
have been fused together at the cross (Rev. 5:5–6). Study the book of Revelation and take note of how each occurrence of "overcomer"/"overcoming"
is applied and to whom. These twin concepts are thoroughly eschatological
and play an integral part in our Christian life. Believers must recognize that
their spiritual and physical sufferings are part of the end-time tribulation and

the establishment of God's eternal kingdom. Listing specific examples, how does the believer overcome the world spiritually? How does Satan overcome believers physically?

2. *List several ways in which the already–not yet shapes how church leaders counsel and disciple.* How does the already–not yet affect counseling those who struggle with habitual sin? As mentioned above, how does the inbreaking of Isaiah's new creation affect premarital counseling? If believing husbands and wives recognize that their partner has initially come out of exile and entered the new creation, then they can expect that over time each should be growing in new-creational unity with Christ and thus producing the fruit of love toward one another. Though couples have yet to arrive fully into the new creation, this inaugurated stage of restoration drastically affects marital expectations and conduct. But both husband and wife are also not completely out of exile; they bear some of the old sinful baggage of their exile. Consequently, they must be patient, bear with one another, and forgive one another, fully appreciating that neither is yet a perfected human being. Recall how Paul in Ephesians 5:8–14 first describes how believers are part of the end-time people of God and then proceeds to work out the implications for their relationships (Eph. 5:15–6:20). Few ministers, though, connect eschatology with discipleship and counseling, and fewer implement it. Christian leaders must first understand these eschatological concepts and then make these connections in counseling. It will be a tremendous help to meeting the needs of the congregation.

3. *Orient your ministry to pass the test of God's end-time evaluation.* With our emphasis on what God has done in the past, we sometimes lose sight of what God will do in the future. As mentioned above, Paul's sketch of the minister's end-time evaluation in 1 Corinthians 3–4 is the fullest description of this eschatological event in the NT. Paul describes ministers of the gospel with the OT metaphor of temple building. Ministers are instruments of God, who play a key role in the church's growth as the end-time temple (cf. 1 Cor. 3:16–17; 1 Pet. 2:4–10). If church leaders "build" this latter-day temple consisting of God's people with integrity and faithfully proclaim God's Word, then they will receive a "reward" (1 Cor. 3:14). But if they "build" with dishonesty and selfishness, then "the builder will suffer loss [of some or many in the congregation] but yet will be saved" (3:15 NIV). Evaluate the key components of your ministry (preaching, counseling, discipleship, etc.) and ensure that they will stand the test of God's end-time judgment so that those to whom you minister will have the mettle to pass through the end-time judgment.

Suggested Reading

Carson, D. A. *The Cross and Christian Ministry: An Exposition of Passages from 1 Corinthians*. Grand Rapids: Baker, 1993.

Keller, Timothy. *Walking with God through Pain and Suffering*. New York: Penguin Group, 2013.

Mohler, Albert. *The Conviction to Lead: 25 Principles for Leadership That Matters*. Minneapolis: Bethany House, 2012.

Patrick, Darrin. *Church Planter: The Man, the Message, the Mission*. Wheaton: Crossway, 2010.

Stott, John R. W. *Basic Christian Leadership: Biblical Models of Church, Gospel, and Ministry*. Downers Grove, IL: InterVarsity, 2002.

Part 3

End-Time Ministry

Service in the Latter-Day Temple of God

Up to this point, we have established the theological framework in part 1 (chaps. 1–3) and applied this already–not yet framework to Christian leadership (chaps. 4–6). Now in this third and final part we address three often-discussed facets of ministry within the end-time temple of God: worship, prayer, and missions. Eschatology not only enriches how pastors lead their churches; it also energizes and informs how the church interacts with God and the world around us.

The chapter on worship (chap. 7) reflects on the covenantal nature of corporate worship and ties it to what God has accomplished in the "latter days" through the work of his Son. Chapter 8 reminds us that prayer plays a vital role in the establishment of God's end-time kingdom. We round out our project in chapter 9 by linking missions to the grand narrative of the Bible, in particular how missions is tethered to the expansion of God's end-time temple and the new creation.

7

Worship

Celebrating the Inaugurated New Covenant

One of the most sobering things about parenting is watching your children begin to imitate you. When one of my (Matt's) sons was two years old, he began sitting in my favorite chair with a book and a highlighter. He would take the highlighter and pretend to run it over the pages, just as he had seen me do countless times. Cute and harmless, right?

Sometimes, however, the imitation was not a good thing. With very few exceptions, I consider vegetables to be at best a necessary evil. As my sons grew older, they began to notice that often I would not put any vegetables on my plate at dinner. One night, after my wife had insisted they put some vegetables on their plate and eat them, my son replied, "Why is it that Daddy doesn't have to eat vegetables, but I do?" Busted. I had no good response. My sons wanted to imitate my refusal to eat vegetables, which in the long run would prove harmful to them.

By our very nature we as human beings imitate and reflect whom and what we admire. Whether it is our favorite athlete, musician, actor, relative, or someone else, over time we begin to emulate the way they speak, think, act, dress, and live. That is no accident; God created us in his image so that we would reflect his character. We are hardwired this way by God himself, so that "what people revere, they resemble, either for ruin or restoration."[1] As we worship God, we reflect his beauty through the way we think, feel, speak, and act.

---

1. G. K. Beale, *We Become What We Worship: A Biblical Theology of Idolatry* (Downers Grove, IL: InterVarsity, 2008), 16. The statement quoted here is the main thesis of the book.

The problem is that because we enter this world as rebels against God, our default is to worship something in creation rather than the Creator himself (Rom. 1:21–25). But through the proclamation of the gospel, the Spirit opens peoples' eyes "to give the light of the knowledge of the glory of God in the face of Jesus Christ" (2 Cor. 4:6). Because the Spirit removes the veil from our hearts, "we all, with unveiled face, beholding the glory of the Lord, are being transformed into the same image from one degree of glory to another" (2 Cor. 3:18). Because Christ has come, those who repent and believe in Christ are able to "worship the Father in spirit and truth, for the Father is seeking such people to worship him" (John 4:23).

But God does not redeem us so that we are isolated followers of Christ. He saves us into the church, the assembly of the eschatological people of God.[2] As believers we are members of the body of Christ, each with our own distinctive gifts (1 Cor. 12:1–31). God has reconciled both Jew and gentile alike to himself through the cross, making us fellow citizens with the saints and members of the household of God (Eph. 2:12–22). When we gather to worship the Lord, we display the "manifold wisdom of God . . . to the rulers and authorities in the heavenly places" (Eph. 3:10). God's glory is seen more clearly when individuals with diverse gifts, abilities, languages, ethnicities, and socioeconomic backgrounds unite to worship Jesus Christ.

So while it is absolutely true that we are called to live our individual lives as an act of worship before God (Rom. 12:1–2), the focus of this chapter will be the *corporate gathering* of God's people. Indeed, there is something unique about the church assembling to worship God, something that cannot truly be duplicated in other contexts. That something is the corporate experience of what God has already done for us in Christ as we await the consummation of all that God has promised us. To see how this reality works itself out in the corporate gathering of God's people, we first need to define what we mean by worship.

What Is Worship?

Defining the term "worship" can be challenging because of the various ways it is used. Allen Ross offers this helpful definition:

> True worship is the celebration of being in covenant fellowship with the sovereign and holy triune God, by means of [1] the reverent adoration and spontaneous

---

2. The Greek word for church (*ekklēsia*) in its most basic sense means "assembly," and it is the most common Greek word used in the LXX to refer to the assembly of God's people gathered in worship.

praise of God's nature and works, [2] the expressed commitment of trust and obedience to the covenant responsibilities, and [3] the memorial reenactment of entering into covenant through ritual acts, *all with the confident anticipation of the fulfillment of the covenant promises in glory.*[3]

Before we dig into the specifics of this definition, notice how Ross rightly captures the already–not yet nature of worship. After describing the various means of celebrating the nature and work of God, he emphasizes that all of worship is carried out "with the confident anticipation of the fulfillment of the covenant promises in glory." So as we expand on Ross's definition of worship, we will explain how the already–not yet is central to each element.

The Starting Point of Worship

Celebration of the Covenant Relationship

The starting point for worship is a covenant relationship with the Triune God. A covenant is "an elected relationship of obligation established under divine sanction and indicated by an oath—commitment (often with cursings for disobedience and blessings for obedience)."[4] When God makes a covenant, it is rooted in who he is and what he has already done. Yet covenants also contain promises and threats as to what will happen if the covenant obligations are or are not met. Thus embedded within every covenant relationship is the already of who God is and what he has done, along with the not yet of what God promises or threatens to do depending on whether the covenant obligations are met.

The proper response to making a covenant is celebration expressed in worship.[5] After God first announced his covenant with Abram (Gen. 12:1–3), Abram and his family journeyed into Canaan (12:4–9). Twice during that journey Abram built an altar to worship Yahweh as an expression of trust in Yahweh and his promises (12:7–8). When God finished making the covenant with Israel at Mount Sinai (Exod. 19:1–23:33), he summoned Moses and the people of Israel to worship (24:1–11). David's immediate response to God promising an eternal kingdom to his descendants (2 Sam. 7:8–17) was to go

---

3. Allen P. Ross, *Recalling the Hope of Glory: Biblical Worship from the Garden to the New Creation* (Grand Rapids: Kregel, 2006), 67–68, italics added.

4. G. K. Beale, *A New Testament Biblical Theology: The Unfolding of the Old Testament in the New* (Grand Rapids: Baker Academic, 2011), 42n39. Beale's definition is based on the Westminster Confession of Faith, §7.2.

5. As Ross notes, "Describing worship as celebration does not nullify the fact that it is a service or that there are solemn and serious aspects to it" (*Recalling the Hope of Glory*, 68). In this context, "celebrate" overlaps in meaning with "commemorate," which often carries a more solemn sense.

and sit before Yahweh and praise him in prayer (7:18–29). Jesus announced the new covenant during a Passover celebration (Matt. 26:26–29), which concluded with those present singing a hymn (26:30).

These examples make it clear that the proper response to being in a covenant with God is celebrating that relationship in worship. Now let's look at *how* we celebrate.

Three Means of Worship

According to Ross, we celebrate our covenant relationship with God in three primary ways. The first is "reverent adoration and spontaneous praise of God's nature and works." The starting point for worship is a proper understanding of who God is. The Ten Commandments begin with God identifying himself as "the LORD your God, who brought you out of the land of Egypt, out of the house of slavery" (Exod. 20:2). God's identity is inseparably connected to the redemption of his people. Because that is who Yahweh is, worshiping other gods or making an image of him is strictly forbidden (20:3–4). This prohibition is further grounded with the following assertion: "For I the LORD your God am a jealous God, visiting the iniquity of the fathers on the children to the third and the fourth generation of those who hate me, but showing steadfast love to thousands of those who love me and keep my commandments" (20:5b–6). Unless we understand who God truly is, we cannot worship him in the way he deserves to be worshiped.

Of course, we need more than an intellectual grasp of God's attributes. There must be a heart-level delight in who God is. Jonathan Edwards describes this well in his sermon "A Divine and Supernatural Light" (1734):

> There is a difference between having an opinion that God is holy and gracious, and having a sense of the loveliness and beauty of that holiness and grace. There is a difference between having a rational judgment that honey is sweet, and having a sense of its sweetness. A man may have the former, that knows not how honey tastes; but a man can't have the latter, unless he has an idea of the taste of honey in his mind. So there is a difference between believing that a person is beautiful, and having a sense of his beauty. . . . The former rests only in the head, speculation only is concerned in it; but the heart is concerned in the latter. When the heart is sensible of the beauty and amiableness of a thing, it necessarily feels pleasure in the apprehension. It is implied in a person's being heartily sensible of the loveliness of a thing, that the idea of it is sweet and pleasant to his soul; which is a far different thing from having a rational opinion that it is excellent.[6]

6. Jonathan Edwards, *The Sermons of Jonathan Edwards: A Reader* (New Haven: Yale University Press, 1999), 127–28.

When the eschatological Spirit opens our eyes to the beauty of God in the face of Jesus Christ (2 Cor. 4:6), we are compelled to reverently adore and spontaneously praise God for who he is and what he has already done for us.

The second means of celebrating our covenant relationship with God is "the expressed commitment of trust and obedience to the covenant responsibilities." A clear vision of who God is and what he has done for us demands a response. At the heart of that response is repentance for our sin and faith in the person and work of Jesus Christ. One of the clearest examples of this reality is found in Isaiah 6.

> In the year that King Uzziah died I saw the Lord sitting upon a throne, high and lifted up; and the train of his robe filled the temple. Above him stood the seraphim. Each had six wings: with two he covered his face, and with two he covered his feet, and with two he flew. And one called to another and said: "Holy, holy, holy is the LORD of hosts; the whole earth is full of his glory!" And the foundations of the thresholds shook at the voice of him who called, and the house was filled with smoke. (6:1–4)

Confronted with this overwhelming vision of who God is, Isaiah responds, "Woe is me! For I am lost; for I am a man of unclean lips, and I dwell in the midst of a people of unclean lips; for my eyes have seen the King, the LORD of hosts!" (6:5). Seeing the Lord in his glory led Isaiah to turn away from his sin. By faith he received God's provision of atonement (6:6–7). Because of his repentance and faith, Isaiah was ready to respond when God asked "Whom shall I send, and who will go for us?" (6:8).

The Gospel of John sheds further light on this encounter. Despite the many signs that Jesus performed, many refused to believe in him (John 12:36–37). To explain why so many did not believe, John quotes from Isaiah 53:1 and Isaiah 6:10 (John 12:38–40). Then comes the punch line: "Isaiah said these things because he saw his glory and spoke of him" (John 12:41). The one whom Isaiah saw "sitting upon a throne, high and lifted up" (Isa. 6:1) was none other than the Lord Jesus Christ.

When the church gathers to worship, by faith we see the same Lord Jesus Christ. Paul vividly describes this in 2 Corinthians 3:18: "And we all, with unveiled face, beholding the glory of the Lord, are being transformed into the same image from one degree of glory to another. For this comes from the Lord who is the Spirit." As the Word is preached, songs of worship sung, ordinances celebrated, prayers offered, and possessions freely given to the Lord, we see the glory of God. When we encounter God, he summons us to continual repentance and faith as tangible ways to celebrate our covenant relationship with him.

The third way we celebrate our covenant relationship with God is "memorial reenactment of entering into covenant through ritual acts." These ritual acts of worship picture the spiritual realities that establish and sustain our covenant relationship with God. In the new covenant, God has given baptism and the Lord's Supper. As we shall see, both have already–not yet dynamics.

The Lord's Supper originates in Jesus celebrating the Passover with his disciples on the night he was betrayed. In the old covenant, Passover commemorated God delivering Israel from slavery in Egypt (Exod. 11–12). By the time of Jesus, the Passover festival had taken on additional significance, as the Jewish people languished under Roman rule. They looked forward to the day when God would lead his people in a new exodus through one who was greater than Moses.[7] The prophets often spoke of this new exodus as the renewal of creation itself (Isa. 43:14–21; 51:1–11; Hosea 2:14–23; Amos 9:11–15).

Little wonder, then, that on that fateful night with his disciples, Jesus tells them, "I have earnestly desired to eat this Passover with you before I suffer" (Luke 22:15). The reason for his eagerness is that the new exodus has finally come. Jesus reveals the true significance of the Passover elements by identifying the bread as his body, given as a sacrifice for his people (22:19). The cup "that is poured out for you is the new covenant in my blood" (22:20). What the prophets promised (Isa. 54:1–17; Jer. 31:31–34) long ago was now being inaugurated with the death of the ultimate Passover lamb, Jesus Christ (1 Cor. 5:7). His resurrection as the last Adam would signal the dawning of the new-creational kingdom. When Jesus promises "I will not drink again of this fruit of the vine until that day when I drink it new with you in my Father's kingdom" (Matt. 26:29), he initially fulfills that promise in his resurrection appearances (see Acts 10:41) in anticipation of its consummation in the new heavens and new earth.[8]

Within the celebration of the Lord's Supper, we see the already–not yet. Jesus instructs his disciples, "Do this in remembrance of me" (Luke 22:19). As his followers, we commemorate what Jesus has already done for us through his sacrificial death on the cross for our sins. But we also look forward to the day when we will eat and drink with Jesus when the kingdom is consummated (Luke 22:16, 18; Rev. 19:6–9). Paul beautifully brings the already–not yet together when he states, "For as often as you eat this bread and drink the cup, you proclaim the Lord's death until he comes" (1 Cor. 11:26). Because of the eschatological nature of the Lord's Supper, it is necessary for us to examine

7. See further Craig S. Keener, *The Gospel of John: A Commentary*, 2 vols. (Peabody, MA: Hendrickson, 2003), 1:669–71.

8. See further G. K. Beale, "The Eschatological Conception of New Testament Theology," in *"The Reader Must Understand": Eschatology in Bible and Theology*, ed. K. E. Brower and M. W. Elliott (Leicester, UK: Apollos, 1997), 46–48.

ourselves to make sure we do not partake "in an unworthy manner" and thus "be guilty concerning the body and blood of the Lord" (1 Cor. 11:27). Thus "the Supper contains in itself a beginning form of the Last Judgment, which will be consummated at the end of time."[9]

Our first introduction to baptism in the NT is with the ministry of John, who was "proclaiming a baptism of repentance for the forgiveness of sins" (Luke 3:3). His ministry signaled the inauguration of the new exodus (Isa. 40:3–5, quoted in Luke 3:4–6; cf. Matt. 3:3; Mark 1:3). Because that new exodus promises wrath upon God's enemies, all—even Abraham's descendants—must repent to see God's salvation (Luke 3:7–9). But John's baptism anticipated the even greater baptism that the Messiah would bring, a baptism in the Spirit (Luke 3:16–17). After his resurrection, Jesus then commissions his people to "make disciples of all nations, baptizing them in the name of the Father and of the Son and of the Holy Spirit, teaching them to observe all that I have commanded you" (Matt. 28:19–20). Baptizing believers in the name of the Triune God will signify their identification as the eschatological people of God.

When the promise of the Spirit was fulfilled at Pentecost (Acts 2:1–41), baptism took on even more significance. First, it was a visible sign of the cleansing that the Spirit brings at conversion in the new covenant (Ezek. 36:24–27). Paul makes this clear in Titus 3:5 when he refers to "the washing of regeneration and renewal of the Holy Spirit." Both regeneration (*palingenesia*) and renewal (*anakainōsis*) are new-creation terminology, referring not only to our individual experience of new creation (Rom. 12:1–2) but also to the transformation of creation itself (Matt. 19:28). Furthermore, baptism represents our visible identification with the eschatological people of God, as Paul notes in 1 Corinthians 12:13: "For in one Spirit we were all baptized into one body—Jews or Greeks, slaves or free—and all were made to drink of one Spirit." Water baptism also reminds us that God has given the Spirit to his people to empower us as witnesses of his saving acts through the Messiah, Jesus Christ (Acts 1:4–8).

Second, baptism pictures our union with Christ (Rom. 6:1–11).[10] Being "baptized into Christ Jesus" means that we share in his death and burial (6:3–4). Paul goes on to explain that baptism signifies that "our old self was crucified with him in order that the body of sin might be brought to nothing, so that we would no longer be enslaved to sin" (6:6). Baptism further signifies that we share in Christ's resurrection, which means that we can walk in newness of life now (6:4, 7) in anticipation of our future bodily resurrection (6:5, 8).

9. Ibid., 47.
10. The description of baptism here holds true regardless of whether one holds to pedobaptism or believer's baptism, an issue on which we as authors disagree (Gladd affirms pedobaptism, and Harmon does not).

Thus in baptism we see the already–not yet of our covenant relationship with God. It portrays that we have already shared in Christ's death and have been given the Holy Spirit to mark us off as the eschatological people of God, who walk in newness of life. It visibly demarcates us as those who have begun to experience God's work of new creation. Yet it also anticipates our future bodily resurrection, which is the culmination of redemption (Rom. 8:23).

Conclusion

As we have worked our way through Allen Ross's helpful definition of worship, we have seen the already–not yet nature of our corporate worship. Ross himself draws these realities out even further:

> So our worship must be eschatological. It should not only prepare us to live and serve in this world in view of the coming of the Lord, but it should also celebrate victory over the world. . . . It has been this hope of glory that has inspired the worship of God from the very beginning. . . . All our worship looks back and recalls the biblical and historical events that have shaped our tradition; but in recalling the principles and practices of those earlier stages in the household of faith, we also recall their inspiration for worship—the hope of glory. . . . Our worship after all is a celebration of the great works of our glorious Lord, especially his saving deeds, with a view to their fulfillment in glory. And if the aspects of the order of our worship form a reenactment of and response to God's plan of redemption, they are at the same time a foreshadowing and rehearsal for that time when we shall worship in the heavenly sanctuary with the angelic choirs.[11]

This reference to worship in the heavenly sanctuary provides a natural transition for us explore how God designed our earthly worship to reflect the worship he receives in heaven.

Earthly Worship Patterned after Heavenly Worship

From the very beginning God designed worship here on earth after the pattern of worship in heaven. We see this most clearly in the design of his earthly sanctuary. Indeed, multiple OT passages, along with other Jewish writings, indicate that the three-part structure of the tabernacle/temple reflected the structure of the cosmos.[12] Psalm 78:69 is perhaps the clearest text: "He built his

11. Ross, *Recalling the Hope of Glory*, 71–72.
12. G. K. Beale, *The Temple and the Church's Mission: A Biblical Theology of the Dwelling Place of God*, NSBT 17 (Downers Grove, IL: InterVarsity, 2004), 31–50.

sanctuary like the high heavens, like the earth, which he has founded forever." Understood this way, the outer court represented the habitable world where humanity dwelt, the Holy Place stood for the visible heavens and their lights, and the Most Holy Place represented the invisible heavens where God and his hosts dwelt. In other words, heaven and earth are not separated by a great gulf, never to be crossed, but are united through God's tabernacle/temple on earth.

The Bible develops this connection in several ways; two of the most prominent are in the descriptions of the garden of Eden and the tabernacle.

The Garden of Eden

The garden of Eden was designed by God to be his sanctuary here on earth, the place where he dwelt with his people.[13] There God is described "walking" (*mithallēk*) in the garden with Adam and Eve (Gen. 3:8), just as God "walks" (*mithallēk*) among his people by dwelling in the tabernacle (Deut. 23:14; Lev. 26:12; 2 Sam. 7:6–7). Adam was put in the garden "to work" (*'ābad*) and "keep" (*šāmar*) it just as the priests were charged to "minister"/"serve" (*'ābad*) in the tabernacle and "guard" (*šāmar*) its purity (Gen. 2:15; Num. 3:7–8). The cherubim placed in the garden to protect its purity after Adam sinned (Gen. 3:24) reappear in the tabernacle (Exod. 25:18–19) and the temple (1 Kings 8:6–7) as guardians of God's presence in the Most Holy Place. Ezekiel 28:11–19 further confirms that Eden was a temple where God's presence dwelt with Adam. Later Jewish literature, such as *Jubilees* 8.19, makes the identification even clearer: "And he [Noah] knew that the garden of Eden was the holy of holies and the dwelling of the LORD."[14]

The Tabernacle

The Bible is even more explicit in describing the tabernacle as being made as a "copy" of the heavenly sanctuary. After describing the contributions that the people were to give (Exod. 25:1–7), God instructs Moses, "Let them make me a sanctuary, that I may dwell in their midst. Exactly as I show you concerning the pattern of the tabernacle, and of all its furniture, so you shall make it" (25:8–9). It was so important to the Lord that his earthly sanctuary be made according to the pattern God showed Moses that this command is repeated four more times (25:40; 26:30; 27:8; Num. 8:4).

13. This section depends heavily on ibid., 66–80; see also Ross, *Recalling the Hope of Glory*, 90–116.

14. O. S. Wintermute, trans., "Jubilees," in *The Old Testament Pseudepigrapha*, ed. J. H. Charlesworth (Garden City, NY: Doubleday, 1983–85), 2:73.

The author of Hebrews builds on this foundation when explaining the superiority of Christ as our high priest. As the "one who is seated at the right hand of the throne of the Majesty in heaven" (Heb. 8:1), he is also "a minister in the holy places, in the true tent that the Lord set up, not man" (8:2). By contrast, the levitical priests "serve a copy and shadow of the heavenly things" (8:5), an assertion supported by quoting Exodus 25:40. As our high priest, Jesus passed "through the greater and more perfect tent (not made with hands, that is, not of this creation)" to offer his own blood for our sins (9:11). The comparison culminates in 9:23–24, "Thus it was necessary for the copies of the heavenly things to be purified with these rites, but the heavenly things themselves with better sacrifices than these. For Christ has entered, not into holy places made with hands, which are copies of the true things, but into heaven itself, now to appear in the presence of God on our behalf." While the main point is the superiority of Christ as our high priest and the new covenant that he inaugurated, the author of Hebrews clearly affirms that the earthly tabernacle was a pattern of the true heavenly sanctuary.

Present-Day Worship as Participation in Heavenly Worship

Whereas in the previous section the point was that God designed his earthly sanctuary according to the pattern of his heavenly one, here the point is that when we worship here on earth, we are actually participating in heavenly worship. We will look at two of the clearest passages that teach this: Revelation 4:1–5:14 and Hebrews 12:18–29.

Revelation 4:1–5:14

Revelation begins with a prologue (1:1–20) and the letters to the seven churches (2:1–3:22). After this, the Spirit transports John into heaven, where he is given a vision of God's throne room (4:1–5:14).[15] That vision divides into two parts—the worship of God (4:1–11) and the worship of Christ (5:1–14).[16] The parallels between the two demonstrate that Christ as the Lion and the Lamb who redeems his people is worthy of the praise that belongs to God alone.

15. The structure of this entire vision is based on Dan. 7; see G. K. Beale, *The Use of Daniel in Jewish Apocalyptic Literature and in the Revelation of St. John* (Lanham, MD: University Press of America, 1984), 181–228; and G. K. Beale, *The Book of Revelation: A Commentary on the Greek Text*, NIGTC (Grand Rapids: Eerdmans, 1999), 313–16.
16. For a helpful comparison of these two chapters, see James M. Hamilton, *Revelation: The Spirit Speaks to the Churches*, Preaching the Word (Wheaton: Crossway, 2011), 134–35.

John begins with a description of God sitting on his throne (4:2–3) and the scene around him (4:4–8a). Day and night the various beings around the throne worship God for his work of creation (4:8b–11). The four living creatures cry out, "Holy, holy, holy, is the Lord God Almighty, who was and is and is to come!" (4:8). In response, the twenty-four elders fall down in worship (4:9–10), singing "Worthy are you, our Lord and God, to receive glory and honor and power, for you created all things, and by your will they existed and were created" (4:11). Thus the focus of their worship is God's role as Creator and sovereign ruler of the universe, a role he has had from the dawn of creation.

In chapter 5 the scene shifts to "a scroll written within and on the back, sealed with seven seals" and held by the one sitting on the throne (5:1).[17] Although initially no one is able to open it (5:2–4), one of the elders tells John, "Behold, the Lion of the tribe of Judah, the Root of David, has conquered, so that he can open the scroll and its seven seals" (5:5). In response to the Lamb taking the scroll, the four living creatures and the twenty-four elders fall before him in worship (5:6–8). They sing this song: "Worthy are you to take the scroll and to open its seals, for you were slain, and by your blood you ransomed people for God from every tribe and language and people and nation, and you have made them a kingdom and priests to our God, and they shall reign on the earth" (5:9–10). Countless angels then join with the four living creatures and the twenty-four elders to cry out together, "Worthy is the Lamb who was slain, to receive power and wealth and wisdom and might and honor and glory and blessing!" (5:12). But the worship of the Lamb is not limited to these heavenly beings:

> And I heard every creature in heaven and on earth and under the earth and in the sea, and all that is in them, saying, "To him who sits on the throne and to the Lamb be blessing and honor and glory and might forever and ever!" And the four living creatures said, "Amen!" and the elders fell down and worshiped. (5:13–14)

The worship directed toward the Lamb focuses on his sacrificial death, which accomplishes the redemption of his people, who are drawn "from every tribe and language and people and nation" (5:9).

There are at least two textual clues indicating that the worship described in Revelation 4:1–5:14 is a present reality in which believers now participate.

---

17. Although scholars have debated the nature of this scroll, it seems best to see it as a covenantal promise of inheritance that "in a comprehensive manner . . . includes God's plan of redemption and judgment formulated throughout the OT, a plan that encompasses the development of all sacred history, especially from the cross to the new creation" (Beale, *Revelation*, 341; see 339–48).

First, there are several echoes of throne-room visions from the OT. The vision of one seated on the throne (4:2, 9–10), the presence of the six-winged living creatures (4:8), and the refrain of "Holy, holy, holy, is the Lord God Almighty" (4:8) echo the language of Isaiah 6:1–7. Imagery from Ezekiel 1–2 is even more prominent throughout Revelation 4:1–5:1. Such imagery signals that the worship of the sovereign Lord that John sees in heaven is a present continuation of the worship witnessed by various prophets in the OT.

Second, the four living creatures and the twenty-four elders are described as "each holding a harp, and golden bowls full of incense, which are the prayers of the saints" (5:8). The prayers of praise, confession, thanksgiving, and supplication offered by God's people are a fragrant aroma that fills his heavenly throne room.[18] John's vision shows that what the psalmist prayed ("Let my prayer be counted as incense before you," Ps. 141:2) is a reality.

Although not explicit in the text, two additional factors suggest that believers participate in the heavenly worship of the Lamb. First, a number of commentators have noted a close relationship between the elders, the angels, and the church here on earth. G. K. Beale provides a helpful summary:

> As in chapters 1–3, the church is pictured in angelic guise to remind its members that already a dimension of their existence is heavenly, that their real home is not with the unbelieving "earth-dwellers," and that they have heavenly help and protection in their struggle to obtain their reward and not be conformed to their pagan environment. One of the purposes of the church meeting on earth in its weekly gatherings (as in 1:3, 9) is to be reminded of its heavenly existence and identity by modeling its worship and liturgy on the angels' and the heavenly church's worship of the exalted lamb, as vividly portrayed in chapters 4–5. This is why scenes of heavenly liturgy are woven throughout the Apocalypse.[19]

Second, some scholars have argued that the worship described here follows a pattern similar to that of the early church.[20] As Allen Ross notes, "This should not come as a surprise because the church was following the patterns of worship that had been developed down through history, patterns that were inspired

18. Beale (ibid., 357–58) notes that within the larger context, the prayers in view here are the cries of the martyrs crying out to God to vindicate his justice by judging his enemies (see 6:9–11 and 8:4). Even if this is the primary focus of these prayers, the context of Ps. 141:2 certainly allows for a broader reference to prayers in general.

19. Ibid., 323.

20. See, e.g., Allen Cabaniss, "Note on the Liturgy of the Apocalypse," *Int* 7 (1953): 78–86. Others have noted similarities to a synagogue liturgy; see, e.g., Pierre Prigent, *Apocalypse et liturgie*, CahT 52 (Neuchâtel, Switzerland: Delachaux & Niestlé, 1964), 46–79. A common trend among such studies is to claim that John consciously patterned his description of the throne room after one of these liturgies, but as we will note, this gets the relationship exactly backward.

by the revelation from heaven."[21] Thus John is not "shaping" his description of the throne room around existing Jewish or Christian patterns of worship; rather, his description reveals that the already existing patterns of worship in the early church reflected the worship that presently takes place in heaven.

Hebrews 12:18–29

Having just called for perseverance in the face of hostility and the dangers of immorality (12:3–17), the author of Hebrews reminds us that we are already part of the heavenly assembly. After describing Israel's experience at Sinai (12:18–21), he contrasts it with our experience as believers under the new covenant:

> But you have come to Mount Zion and to the city of the living God, the heavenly Jerusalem, and to innumerable angels in festal gathering, and to the assembly of the firstborn who are enrolled in heaven, and to God, the judge of all, and to the spirits of the righteous made perfect, and to Jesus, the mediator of a new covenant, and to the sprinkled blood that speaks a better word than the blood of Abel. (12:22–24)

The perfect tense of the verb translated "have come" (*proselēlythate*) indicates that this is the status of believers in the present. We are already citizens of the heavenly Jerusalem, and when we assemble for corporate worship, we are gathering with countless angels to celebrate the new covenant. As the assembly of the firstborn, we join together with God's people who have already died—the great cloud of witnesses who have gone before us (Heb. 12:1)—to appear before God, the judge of all creation. At the same time we are appearing before our Savior Jesus Christ, who through his blood inaugurated the new covenant. Yet because our redemption is not yet consummated, we must listen to God's voice (12:25). There still remains a future day when God will shake the earth in judgment (12:26–27). Therefore our proper response is to "offer to God acceptable worship, with reverence and awe, for our God is a consuming fire" (12:28–29).

Implications

Our Corporate Worship Should Reflect Both the Already and the Not Yet

When we gather to worship, we are celebrating our covenant relationship with God. The foundation of that covenant is the person and work of Jesus

21. Ross, *Recalling the Hope of Glory*, 481n21.

Christ, who redeemed us from our sin. He has ushered in the last days and marked us off as his people by pouring out the eschatological Spirit on us. So the content of our songs, prayers, and sermons should repeatedly explain the mighty works of God in a way that displays their greatness and reminds us that we are in the latter days. Special focus should rest on Jesus's death and resurrection as eschatological events and their significance for us. Recalling the saving acts of God provokes wonder and gratitude in our hearts. At the same time, our singing, praying, and preaching should draw attention to the culmination of our redemption in a new heavens and new earth. We should use our sanctified imagination to portray the glories of God dwelling with us in the new creation, where every last stain of the fall has been removed. Pointing to the glory that awaits us motivates us to pursue Christlikeness and stirs deeper affection for Christ our King.

Our Corporate Worship Should Be Patterned after Heavenly Worship

From Genesis to Revelation, earthly worship is patterned after heavenly worship. Why should our corporate worship today be any different? Because God's latter-day presence has descended on his people through the outpouring of the Spirit, God's heavenly temple has extended down to earth and encompassed his eschatological people. Obviously Scripture does not provide a detailed liturgy for our corporate worship, but it does indicate various elements that should be included. We should corporately confess the attributes of God, such as his holiness (Isa. 6:3; Rev. 4:8) and his power as the Creator (Rev. 4:10–11). Our songs should proclaim the worthiness of Christ as the Redeemer-King who has purchased people from every tribe and language and people to be a kingdom of priests (Rev. 5:9–10). The preaching of God's redemptive plan as revealed in Scripture should be the focal point of our corporate gathering as the eschatological people of God (see Rev. 5:1–14). Our corporate worship should be marked by fervent prayer so that God's heavenly throne room is filled with the sweet aroma of incense (Rev. 5:8; 8:3–5). Thus Scripture itself, whether through an explicit command or a necessary implication of a biblical text, should govern our corporate worship.[22] God abundantly demonstrates that he cares how his people worship him in both the old and new covenants (Exod. 20:4; 32:1–10; Lev. 10:1–20; John 4:19–24; 1 Cor. 11:2–34; 14:1–40; 1 Tim. 2:8–15; 4:13–16). We would be wise, then, to allow God's revelation in Scripture to determine the content, intent, and tenor of our worship.

22. This is sometimes referred to as the "regulative principle." For a helpful explanation and application, see Mark Dever and Paul Alexander, *The Deliberate Church: Building Your Ministry on the Gospel* (Wheaton: Crossway, 2005), 77–88.

Our Corporate Worship Should Reflect Our Participation in Heavenly Worship

Entering the presence of God is an overwhelming experience. Because of our union with Christ, God "raised us up with him and seated us with him in the heavenly places in Christ Jesus" (Eph. 2:6). God has already made us a new creation by spiritually raising us from the dead. Because we are seated with Christ in the heavenly places, we are commanded, "Set your minds on things that are above, not on things that are on earth" (Col. 3:2). This general command for our everyday lives should be all the more applicable to our corporate worship. There should be a tangible solemnity to our corporate gatherings, as the author of Hebrews teaches (12:28–29). As the latter-day people of God, we have access to the throne of God to "receive mercy and find grace to help in time of need" (Heb. 4:16). As we raise our voices in song, we join the chorus of angels and the saints who have gone before us, singing "Salvation belongs to our God who sits on the throne, and to the Lamb" (Rev. 7:10).

Practical Suggestions

1. *Study the snapshots of worship in the Bible*. Numerous passages in Scripture describe or portray God's people worshiping. A good place to start is by reading through Revelation. As you encounter passages that portray worship, study them, meditate on them, even pray through them. Take notes on what you observe, paying special attention to how the already–not yet shapes heavenly worship. Brainstorm ways to help your congregation understand that when they gather together they are participating in heavenly worship. Consider specific ways to apply these truths in your own congregation. Evaluate your corporate worship service in light of what you learn. What changes do you need to make to help your church celebrate their identity as the latter-day people of God?

2. *Strive to raise people's view of God*. A central goal of corporate worship is to raise our view of God. So all the elements (preaching, singing, praying, giving, reading Scripture, etc.) should regularly deepen our awe and wonder toward the God we are worshiping. Remind the congregation that because of what Jesus has done for them, they are able to worship in the power of the eschatological Spirit. Select songs and read passages of Scripture that portray the beauty, power, and majesty of God. As you prepare your sermons, look for strategic opportunities to highlight God's faithfulness to fulfill his promises. Take advantage of opportunities to highlight the work of each person of the Trinity in our redemption: the Father, who determined to sum up all things in Christ in the fullness of times (Eph. 1:10); the Son, who redeemed us by

inaugurating the new creation (Eph. 1:7, 11); and the eschatological Spirit, who mediates to us our inheritance now in anticipation of our full possession of it on the last day (Eph. 1:13–14).

3. *Regularly celebrate the ordinances.* Since the ordinances are "memorial reenactments" of our covenant relationship with God, they should be a regular feature of our corporate worship. When you baptize someone, highlight that it is a picture of the new resurrection life we have because we are united with Christ. When you celebrate the Lord's Supper, remind the congregation that Jesus has accomplished the new exodus to free us from our sins and that he promises to one day consummate his kingdom in a new heavens and new earth. Make the ordinances a clear reflection of the reality that we live between the inauguration of the latter days and their future consummation.

Suggested Reading

Beale, G. K. *The Temple and the Church's Mission: A Biblical Theology of the Dwelling Place of God.* NSBT 17. Downers Grove, IL: InterVarsity, 2004.

———. *We Become What We Worship: A Biblical Theology of Idolatry.* Downers Grove, IL: InterVarsity, 2008.

Chapell, Bryan. *Christ-Centered Worship: Letting the Gospel Shape Our Practice.* Grand Rapids: Baker Academic, 2009.

Dever, Mark, and Paul Alexander. *The Deliberate Church: Building Your Ministry on the Gospel.* Wheaton: Crossway, 2005.

Ross, Allen P. *Recalling the Hope of Glory: Biblical Worship from the Garden to the New Creation.* Grand Rapids: Kregel, 2006.

8

Prayer

Pleading for the Consummation of the New-Creational Kingdom

Since this is a chapter on prayer, I (Matt) will begin with a confession. I am not very handy around the house. So several years ago when I wanted to put hardwood floors in my house, I turned to my friend Nate. Nate is one of those guys who seems to know how to do just about anything. But in addition to his general overall competence, he had put in hardwood floors before. So, based on his proven track record of expertise and experience, I asked him to help me put in my hardwood flooring. The results were amazing.

We use this sort of logic all the time. When we find ourselves in need, we look for someone who we think can deliver. Our level of confidence in someone's being able to deliver on what they promise is directly tied to their character and past performance.

Yet when it comes to prayer, we fail to apply that logic. But what difference might it make in our prayer lives if we embraced the reality of what God has *already* done for us in Christ as the foundation for trusting him for what is *yet to come*? To find out, we will need to explore what the Bible says about prayer, and what better place to begin than with Jesus?

Jesus's Teaching on Prayer

Jesus both modeled and taught prayer. Even in our increasingly biblically illiterate culture, the words of the Lord's Prayer are still widely recognized.

133

Both Matthew (6:9–13) and Luke (11:2–4) record it, albeit in slightly different forms. As we walk through Matthew's version, we will see how much the already–not yet, eschatological dynamic runs through it. First, though, we need to understand the context.

After John baptized Jesus (Matt. 3:13–17), the Spirit led him into the wilderness to be tempted by Satan (4:1–11). Unlike Adam, who disobeyed when tempted by Satan, Jesus obeys. Unlike the nation of Israel, who disobeyed when tempted in the wilderness by Satan, Jesus obeys. He is the true, obedient Son of God, who defeats Satan. Soon after his forty days in the wilderness, Jesus learns of John's arrest (4:12). Returning to Galilee in fulfillment of OT prophecy, Jesus begins his public ministry (4:13–17). Matthew summarizes Jesus's message as "Repent, for the kingdom of heaven is at hand" (4:17). Because Jesus, the long-promised messianic King, is here, the end-time kingdom of heaven is here. He continues his ministry by calling his first disciples (4:18–22) and traveling throughout Galilee, preaching the gospel of the kingdom and healing (4:23–24). Large crowds from the surrounding regions begin to follow him (4:25), and seeing these crowds, Jesus ascends the mountain to teach (5:1).

What follows is the Sermon on the Mount (5:2–7:27), which is a vision of what life in the kingdom is supposed to look like. It portrays how a person who has already entered the kingdom of heaven through repentance and faith should live. Thus it is not a list of things to do in order to get into the kingdom but guidelines for those who are already in the kingdom. This instruction is necessary precisely because those who have already entered the kingdom by faith do not yet live in a new heavens and new earth (Rev. 21–22), but rather in a world that remains under the effects of the fall and the curse.

It is against this backdrop that Jesus instructs his followers how to pray (6:5–14). Unlike the hypocrites, who love to be seen when they pray, we are to pray privately (6:5–6). Unlike the gentiles, we are not to multiply empty words and phrases to gain a hearing before God, but rather trust that God already knows what we need before we ask (6:7–8). The model of how we are to pray is given in 6:9–13, which for the sake of convenience can be divided into two sections: prayer based on God's character and purposes (6:9–10) and prayer for our needs (6:11–13). As we walk through both these sections line by line, we will see the already–not yet, end-time dynamic of prayer emerge clearly.

Prayer Based on God's Character (Matt. 6:9–10)

Jesus begins by addressing God as "our Father in heaven" (6:9). Contrary to popular culture and twentieth-century Protestant liberalism, God is not the Father of all humanity. Rather, he is the Father of those who have been born again by the Spirit of God (John 1:12; 3:1–8) and adopted into God's family because they are identified by faith with Jesus, the Son of God (Gal. 4:1–7). Because of his special relationship with the Father, Jesus called God "Abba" (Mark 14:36). Although not quite equivalent to the English term "Daddy," it communicates a combination of intimacy, warmth, trust, and affection that was uncharacteristic of Jewish prayers in Jesus's day.[1] Because we are already united to Christ by faith, the Spirit of Christ inside of us prompts us to cry out to God, "Abba! Father!" (Rom. 8:15; Gal. 4:6). As our Father who is "in heaven," he is the transcendent and sovereign ruler of the universe who is able not only to hear our prayers but also to respond to them.

The first request in the prayer comes in the next line: "Hallowed be your name." The word "hallowed" is not used much in everyday conversation and is likely to be confused for "hollowed" by most people. To "hallow" is to treat something as holy, as set apart for a special purpose or use.[2] In biblical times, a name was more than simply a label or a title; it was an expression of who the person actually was. Thus when Moses asks God for his name at the burning bush (Exod. 3:13), he is asking God to reveal himself more fully. When God commands Israel not to take his name in vain (Exod. 20:7), he is forbidding them from treating him as anything less than the righteous and holy God that he is. Thus to "hallow" the name of our Father in heaven is to show reverence to him, to treat him as worthy of our ultimate devotion and allegiance. It means recognizing the ultimate greatness of God and our comparative small-ness. That is why the angels around the throne of God continuously cry out "Holy, holy, holy is the Lord God Almighty!" (Isa. 6:3; Rev. 4:8).

As part of his promise to usher in the new creation, God had promised that "the earth shall be full of the knowledge of the LORD as the waters cover the sea" (Isa. 11:9). As we speak, God is directing all of human history to the day when "every knee [will] bow and every tongue confess that Jesus Christ is Lord to the glory of God the Father" (Phil. 2:10–11). On that day God's name will be hallowed to the fullest extent. We who believe in Jesus Christ have already confessed Christ as Lord, but we live in a world that remains in rebellion against God. So when we pray for God to hallow his name, we are asking him to make his greatness more widely known. We are asking him to demonstrate the present reality of his greatness in and through our lives, as we await the day when all of creation will recognize and confess it.

---

1. The groundbreaking study was by Joachim Jeremias, published in German in 1966. It was subsequently translated into English and published as *The Prayers of Jesus*, SBT 6 (Naperville, IL: Allenson, 1967), 11–65.

2. The Greek verb used here is *hagiazō*, which comes from the same word family as *hagios* ("holy"). See BDAG 9–10.

The second request is "Your kingdom come" (6:10). In the OT, the establishment of God's eschatological kingdom was specifically connected to the latter days. Before he explains the king's vision, Daniel says that God "has made known to King Nebuchadnezzar what will be in the latter days" (Dan. 2:28). He concludes his explanation by stating, "In the days of those kings the God of heaven will set up a kingdom that shall never be destroyed, nor shall the kingdom be left to another people. It shall break in pieces all these kingdoms and bring them to an end, and it shall stand forever" (2:44). The dawn of God's kingdom is inseparably linked to the latter days.

So when Matthew refers to the kingdom, he does so against this backdrop, so that the beginning of the kingdom is the beginning of the latter days. To this point in Matthew, John the Baptist and Jesus have both announced that "the kingdom of heaven is at hand" (3:2; 4:17). Jesus has already been traveling throughout Galilee "proclaiming the gospel of the kingdom" (4:23). He has already stated that the kingdom belongs to "the poor in spirit" (5:3) and "those who are persecuted for righteousness' sake" (5:10). So if the kingdom is already at hand, why do Jesus's followers need to pray for it to come?

The answer is that although the kingdom has already broken into this fallen world in the person and work of Jesus Christ, it has not yet been consummated in all its fullness. In the meantime, God intends the church to be an outpost of his kingdom in this fallen world. Our lives individually and corporately should tangibly demonstrate that the sovereign rule of God in and through Jesus Christ has broken into this world.

By praying for God's kingdom to come, we are asking God to rule over every area of our lives. We are asking him to subdue the remnants of sin in our lives as we await the day when all of God's enemies are confined to the lake of fire (Rev. 20:7–15). Yet we are also asking him to turn us away from pursuing our own kingdoms of career, wealth, influence, prestige, family, and so on, so that we may seek first his kingdom and his righteousness (Matt. 6:33).

The third request is "Your will be done" (6:10). This request is closely related to the previous one, but with a slightly different emphasis. By praying this, the Christian is asking three things.[3] First, we are asking that God's will (which includes his righteous demands and his purposes in human history) be done *now* on earth as it is in heaven. As D. A. Carson notes, "This prayer corresponds to asking for the present extension of the messianic kingdom."[4]

---

3. Adapted from D. A. Carson, "Matthew," in *The Expositor's Bible Commentary*, ed. Frank E. Gaebelein (Grand Rapids: Zondervan, 1994), 8:170–71.
4. Ibid., 170.

Through our prayers God extends the present reach of his kingdom in both its scope (as more people enter the kingdom through repentance and faith) and its depth (as God's people surrender greater control of their lives to King Jesus). Second, we are asking for God's will to *one day* be fully accomplished. In other words, "this prayer corresponds to asking for the consummation of the messianic kingdom."[5] As we continue to live in this present evil age, our yearning for the full realization of the kingdom should increasingly intensify. Third, we are asking that God's will be done here on earth *in the same way* that it is now done in heaven. Carson helpfully summarizes:

> In the consummated kingdom it will not be necessary to discuss superior righteousness (5:20–48) as antithetical to lust, hate, retaliatory face-slapping, divorce, and the like; for then God's will, construed now as his demands for righteousness, will be done as it is now done in heaven: freely, openly, spontaneously, and without the need to set it over against evil.[6]

Thus each one of the three requests in this first half of the Lord's Prayer is set within the framework of the inaugurated last days. Praying that God's name would be hallowed expresses our recognition that although he is transcendently majestic, many in this world do not yet see that reality. Although the kingdom has broken into this world, we pray for it to come in all its fullness because it has not yet been consummated. So we pray for God's will to be done on earth as it is in heaven, which is a plea for God to manifest his kingdom rule now in the life of his people as we await the complete realization of all that God has ordained.

Prayer for Our Needs (Matt. 6:11–13)

The already–not yet, eschatological dynamic is not left behind once the transition is made to prayer for our needs; it remains the framework within which these requests are made. Strictly speaking, there are four distinct requests, but the last two are a pair that will be treated together.

First, we are to pray "Give us this day our daily bread" (6:11). On the surface this appears to be nothing more than a request for our most basic physical need. But there is far more than first meets the eye. Several times the NT uses the imagery of a great banquet to describe the consummation of God's purposes (Matt. 22:1–14; Luke 14:15–24; Rev. 19:6–9). Such imagery is taken from the OT, from passages like Isaiah 25:6–9 (italics added):

5. Ibid.
6. Ibid.

On this mountain the LORD of hosts will make for all peoples *a feast of rich food, a feast of well-aged wine, of rich food full of marrow, of aged wine well refined*. And he will swallow up on this mountain the covering that is cast over all peoples, the veil that is spread over all nations. He will swallow up death forever; and the Lord GOD will wipe away tears from all faces, and the reproach of his people he will take away from all the earth, for the LORD has spoken. It will be said on that day, "Behold, this is our God; we have waited for him, that he might save us. This is the LORD; we have waited for him; let us be glad and rejoice in his salvation."

In light of this background, it should not be surprising that the first sign Jesus performs is turning water into wine at the wedding feast in Cana (John 2:1–11).[7] God promised that when he restored "the booth of David that is fallen, . . . the mountains shall drip sweet wine, and all the hills shall flow with it" (Amos 9:11–15). Joel prophesied that when the day of the Lord came, "the mountains shall drip sweet wine" (Joel 3:18). So by transforming the water into wine, Jesus is announcing that, as the Bridegroom of God's people, he has come to usher in the latter-day messianic age.[8]

To further demonstrate his identity as the Bridegroom, Jesus miraculously feeds large numbers of people (Mark 6:30–44; 8:1–10) and even shares meals with sinners (Matt. 11:19; Luke 5:27–32). The night before his death, while sharing the Passover meal with his disciples, Jesus points forward to that great banquet when he says to his disciples, "I have earnestly desired to eat this Passover with you before I suffer. For I tell you I will not eat it until it is fulfilled in the kingdom of God" (Luke 22:15–16). Thus when Jesus turns water into wine at a wedding, provides food for the masses, eats with sinners, and institutes the celebration of the Lord's Supper, it is a preview of the messianic banquet anticipated in passages like Isaiah 25:6–9.

But although there is a sense in which believers have tasted the first course of the messianic banquet, the full meal remains a future hope rather than a present reality. So in the meantime we must pray for God to give us each day our daily bread. In doing so we acknowledge our dependence on God for our most basic needs, as well as express our trust in his provision based on his past

7. By calling it the "first of his signs" (John 2:11), John may be indicating more than simple chronology. He may also be saying that this particular sign is primary "because it points to the new dispensation of grace and fulfillment that Jesus is inaugurating"; see D. A. Carson, *The Gospel according to John*, PNTC (Grand Rapids: Eerdmans, 1991), 175.

8. Elsewhere in the Gospels, bridegroom imagery is applied to Jesus (Mark 2:18–20; John 3:29), and wedding imagery is applied to the consummation of the messianic age (Matt. 22:1–14; 25:1–13). But notice that within John 2:1–11 the already–not yet tension is present. Jesus performs the miracle to signal that the messianic age has begun but emphasizes that his hour (i.e., his death and resurrection) has not yet come.

faithfulness to us. After all, not only has God provided physically for his people throughout history (Exod. 16:1–36), but he has also given the living bread that has come down from heaven in the person of Jesus Christ (John 6:50–51).

Second, we are to pray "Forgive us our debts" (Matt. 6:12). Although it is possible that Jesus has in view literal or physical debts, the parallel in Luke 11:4 ("forgive us our sins") makes clear that he means sins.[9] Our sins are thus framed as our failure to pay God the ultimate obedience that he deserves; as a result we are indebted to him well beyond our ability to pay. Consequently, we are subject to his judicial wrath, condemned to an eternity apart from God in hell. But thanks to Jesus's life of perfect obedience and sacrificial death on the cross for our sins, all who trust in him as their substitute before God have their sins/debts pardoned.

Why then is it necessary for us to ask God to forgive our sins? Forgiveness itself is an end-time reality that has been brought forward into the present. In the ultimate sense, forgiveness is something that happens on judgment day; when believers appear before God, he will announce for all the world to see that our sins have been dealt with at the cross. It is a public declaration of what has occurred in the past. But it is possible to experience forgiveness now, in the present, because of the work of Jesus (Mark 2:1–12; Luke 18:9–14; Rom. 3:21–4:25). In fact, the moment a person believes in Christ, all that person's sins—past, present, future—are forgiven.

So when we as believers pray "Forgive us our debts," we are not praying for God to forgive sins in the legal/judicial sense of the term, but rather are asking for God to restore our relationship with him. But this request to restore our relationship with him when we have sinned is rooted in the fact that God has already forgiven our sins at the cross. For believers, their final judgment has been pushed back to the cross and placed on Jesus, so that he suffered their final judgment in their place. Thus believers will not have to face that judgment at the very end of the age.

The reality of being forgiven by God works itself out in a very tangible and practical way: "as we also have forgiven our debtors" (Matt. 6:12). The point here is not that God forgives us because we forgive others; it is in fact the opposite. We are able to forgive others because God has first forgiven us. This point is so important that right after finishing the Lord's Prayer, Jesus emphasizes that those who do not forgive others show that they themselves have not truly experienced God's forgiveness (6:14–15; cf. Matt. 18:21–35; Luke 7:36–50). Paul puts it succinctly: "Be kind to one another, tenderhearted, forgiving one another, as God in Christ forgave you" (Eph. 4:32).

9. See the discussion in Carson, "Matthew," 172.

Finally, we are to pray "Lead us not into temptation, but deliver us from evil" (Matt. 6:13). The word translated "temptation" ranges in meaning from "test" or "trial" to "temptation."[10] Although it can have the general sense of temptation that believers experience in everyday life (James 1:12–15), it is also used to refer to the final time of testing that precedes the consummation of God's kingdom (1 Pet. 4:12; Rev. 3:10). So is Jesus instructing us to pray that we not be led into everyday temptations or that we be spared from the final testing that will come at the end of this present evil age?

The answer is both. Jesus and the early church believed that the entire period between the first and second comings of Jesus would be marked by tribulation (Matt. 24:9–14). Near the end of this period a final great tribulation will take place, which will be greater than any previous tribulation in human history (Matt. 24:21–28). Thus even the regular testing and temptations that believers face in our everyday lives belong to the same category as this final testing at the end of the present evil age.[11]

So when we pray to not be led into temptation, we are acknowledging that we live in an age where we experience "the desires of the flesh and the desires of the eyes and pride in possessions" (1 John 2:16 marg.). We are caught in the warfare between the desires of the flesh and the desires of the Spirit, which wage war in our souls (Gal. 5:16–26). Although our old self was crucified with Christ and our slavery to sin has ended (Rom. 6:1–11), we are still tempted to offer ourselves to sin as instruments of unrighteousness (Rom. 6:12–23). Therefore we pray not to be led into temptation as we await the day when every remnant of sin and the curse are gone (Rev. 22:3).

The second part of the verse complements this emphasis: "Deliver us from evil" (Matt. 6:13). Instead of a request to be delivered from evil in the general sense, Jesus likely means "deliver us from the evil one" (NIV).[12] Although Jesus defeated Satan initially in the wilderness (Matt. 4:1–13) and decisively through his death and resurrection (Col. 2:13–15; Heb. 2:14–18), God has not yet cast him into the lake of fire for all eternity (Rev. 20:10). As he awaits his ultimate doom, Satan "prowls around like a roaring lion, seeking someone

10. See BDAG 793. While it might seem odd to pray that God would not lead us into temptation, this request is best understood as an example of litotes, a figure of speech that expresses an idea by negating its opposite. Thus the sense is not merely "Lead us not into temptation" but "Lead us into righteousness"; see D. A. Carson, *Jesus' Sermon on the Mount and His Confrontation with the World: An Exposition of Matthew 5–10* (Grand Rapids: Baker, 1999), 75–76.

11. For a detailed explanation of this view, see Brant Pitre, *Jesus, the Tribulation, and the End of the Exile: Restoration Eschatology and the Origin of the Atonement*, WUNT 204 (Tübingen: Mohr Siebeck, 2005), 146–53.

12. Both the grammar and the context suggest this; see Carson, "Matthew," 174; R. T. France, *The Gospel of Matthew*, NICNT (Grand Rapids: Eerdmans, 2007), 251.

to devour" (1 Pet. 5:8). Therefore, we must resist him by submitting ourselves to God (1 Pet. 5:9; James 4:7). We do so by praying that God would deliver us from him and by wearing the armor that he has given us to stand against Satan's schemes (Eph. 6:11).

By now it should be clear that every request in the Lord's Prayer is decisively shaped by the dawn of the latter days. It is a model for how we should pray as those who have experienced the initial blessings of God's kingdom but await its final consummation. We pray this prayer in the confidence that God has already begun his good work of redemption in us and in the confident hope that he will complete every aspect of that work on the day of Christ Jesus (Phil. 1:6).

Jesus's eschatological understanding of prayer is further evident in what he says about the purpose of the temple. Defending his cleansing of the temple, Jesus quotes the last line of Isaiah 56:7: "My house shall be called a house of prayer for all peoples" (Mark 11:17). The immediate context of Isaiah 56:6–7 speaks of "foreigners who join themselves to the LORD, to minister to him, to love the name of the LORD, and to be his servants" and whose "burnt offerings and . . . sacrifices will be accepted on my altar." Isaiah foresees the eschatological people of God (including gentiles!) serving as priests in an end-time temple, a conclusion confirmed in 66:21, "And some of them [from among the gentiles] also I will take for priests and for Levites, says the LORD." Thus by quoting Isaiah 56:7 Jesus is signaling that the days of the physical earthly temple are numbered because the eschatological temple will soon descend when the Spirit is poured out at Pentecost (Acts 2:1–41). Believers serve as priests (1 Pet. 2:9) in this eschatological temple, offering prayers that ascend into heaven as incense offerings before the Lord (Rev. 5:8; 8:3–5).[13]

Paul's Teaching on Prayer

But is this already–not yet, end-time dynamic present in other passages that deal with prayer? After all, it is certainly possible that the Lord's Prayer is the exception rather than the rule. To determine whether what we have seen with the Lord's Prayer is a consistent feature of prayer elsewhere in the NT, we turn now to explore Paul's prayers. Since there are so many places in Paul's Letters where he describes how he prays for his fellow believers, we will focus our attention on those prayers where the already–not yet dynamic is most apparent.

13. See further G. K. Beale, *The Temple and the Church's Mission: A Biblical Theology of the Dwelling Place of God*, NSBT 17 (Downers Grove, IL: InterVarsity, 2004), 397–99.

Ephesians 1:15–23

Paul begins his letter with a stirring blessing in which he highlights many of the spiritual benefits that God has given to us in Christ (1:3–14). We were chosen before the foundation of the world to be holy and blameless (1:4) and predestined for adoption into his family (1:5) so that God's grace would be praised (1:6). We were redeemed by the riches of his grace as part of his eternal plan to sum up all things in Christ in the fullness of time (1:7–10). Since we have been predestined according to God's purpose, we have an inheritance awaiting us to the praise of God's glory (1:11–12). These realities are ours because we believed the gospel and have been sealed with the eschatological Spirit as a guarantee that God will one day give us our entire inheritance, again to the praise of God's glory (1:13–14).

Based on everything that God has done for his people (described in 1:3–14), Paul now lays out how he prays for the Ephesians (1:15–23). This paragraph can be divided into three sections: thanksgiving (1:15–16a), intercession (1:16b–19), and praise (1:20–23).[14] Paul has continually thanked God "ever since I heard about your faith in the Lord Jesus and your love for all God's people" (1:15 NIV). This constant thanksgiving takes place as he remembers the Ephesians in his prayers (1:16).

In 1:17–19 Paul states the content of his prayer for the Ephesians. What at first seems like a jumble of different requests is actually one main request with several explanatory phrases. The main request is "that the God of our Lord Jesus Christ, the glorious Father, may give you the Spirit of wisdom and revelation" (1:17 NIV).[15] In other words, Paul wants believers to experience fresh manifestations of the Spirit, who gives wisdom and revelation "so that you may know him better" (1:17 NIV). This is necessary even though as believers we have already had the eyes of our hearts enlightened (1:18). The ultimate purpose of God giving fresh manifestations of the Spirit is so that believers may know three things: (1) the hope to which God has called his people; (2) the riches of God's inheritance in his people; and (3) the immeasurable greatness of God's power toward his people (1:18–19). Peter O'Brien summarizes Paul's thought here:

> Here in the intercession of verses 17–19, the apostle's prayer to God is that the
> Spirit, who had been given to the readers at their conversion (cf. v. 13), might

---

14. Peter T. O'Brien, *The Letter to the Ephesians*, PNTC (Grand Rapids: Eerdmans, 1999), 125.

15. Some translations (e.g., ESV, NASB, KJV) do not capitalize the word "spirit," in which case "spirit" would refer to the human spirit. But a better case can be made for understanding "spirit" here as a reference to the Holy Spirit; see Harold W. Hoehner, *Ephesians: An Exegetical Commentary* (Grand Rapids: Baker Academic, 2002), 256–58.

impart wisdom and revelation to them so that they might understand more fully God's saving plan and live in the light of it. The mystery had already been made known in Christ (vv. 9–10), but the readers needed to grasp its full significance, not least of all their own place within it. And as the Spirit worked in their midst, giving them insights and revealing God's purposes in Christ, so they would grow in the knowledge of God.[16]

God does all of this for his people according to the same great power that he used to raise Christ from the dead and seat him at his right hand in the heavenly places (1:19b–20). Because Christ is there, he is sovereign over "all rule and authority and power and dominion, and above every name that is named, not only in this age but also in the one to come" (1:21). In fulfillment of Psalm 8:6, this rule extends over all things, including the church, which is his body (1:22–23).

The already–not yet runs through this prayer as an undercurrent, surfacing in several places. First, Paul's prayer to know God and his ways better (1:15–23) is based on what God has already done for believers (1:3–14). Because Paul knows what God has already done for his people, he is compelled to pray for a growing experience of those realities, recognizing that for all we have already experienced, we have not yet plumbed the depths of what awaits us in the consummation.

Second, the expression "the hope to which he has called you" (1:18) points forward to the consummation of all God's purposes in Christ in the fullness of time (Eph. 1:10). Paul elsewhere expresses the content of that hope as the revelation of the children of God with their resurrected bodies in a new heavens and new earth (Rom. 8:18–25; 1 Cor. 15:51–56). It is nothing less than sharing in the glory of God (Rom. 5:2), the full realization of eternal life with God (Titus 1:2; 3:7). Such hope is only possible because Christ is in us (Col. 1:27). But hope itself is rooted in what God has already done for us as we anticipate what is yet to come. "For in this hope we were saved. Now hope that is seen is not hope. For who hopes for what he sees? But if we hope for what we do not see, we wait for it with patience" (Rom. 8:24–25).

Third, the phrase "the riches of his glorious inheritance in the saints" (1:18) directs our attention to the future day when God takes full and final possession of his inheritance, his redeemed people. We are already his people, redeemed by Christ and sealed with the Holy Spirit (1:3–14). But our redemption will not be truly complete until we as the bride of Christ celebrate the wedding supper of the Lamb with God in a new heavens and new earth (Rev. 19:6–8).

16. O'Brien, *Ephesians*, 132.

Only then will God take full and final possession of us as his sinless people. As we await that day, we pray for God to give us a greater grasp of these realities so that they will shape our lives in this present evil age.

Fourth, the prayer culminates with a breathtaking description of Christ's supremacy over all creation. As the risen Lord, he has dominion "above every name that is named, not only in this age but also in the one to come" (1:21). Here is the most explicit mention of the already–not yet, eschatological dynamic in this passage. Because of the resurrection and ascension, Jesus already has complete authority over all creation, but he has not yet completely destroyed every enemy for good. In this present age we pray with the confidence that Christ has ultimate authority, even when our circumstances might tempt us to think otherwise. Our confidence in the power of Christ in the present rests both on what God has already done (raised Christ from the dead and seated him at God's right hand) and in eager anticipation of what he will one day do (completely destroy every enemy).

In short, we can summarize Ephesians 1:15–23 as Paul's prayer that believers will experience in greater measure everything God has already done for us as we eagerly wait for God to bring to completion all that he has promised us. In prayer, we express our gratitude for the already while expressing our yearning for and hope in the not yet.

1 Corinthians 1:4–9

Despite the numerous challenges Paul dealt with in the church at Corinth, his love and concern for them never wavered. Even though Paul writes very sharply to this church, he begins this letter by expressing his constant gratitude to God for them "because of the grace of God that was given you in Christ Jesus" (1:4). The Corinthians have already experienced the grace of God that forgives sin, and that grace came to them because they are in Christ Jesus. But the grace of God does more than simply forgive our sins; Paul explains that because of it "in every way you were enriched in him in all speech and all knowledge" (1:5).[17] The riches of God's grace in Christ Jesus are so dynamic that it begins to transform the way we speak and think,[18] although, as the rest of 1 Corinthians makes clear, this is still a work in progress. This transformation

---

17. While it is common for Paul to speak of God's riches (e.g., Eph. 1:7–8; 2:4–7; Col. 1:27), here the emphasis is on believers becoming rich in Christ. Of course, such riches come through Christ's poverty (2 Cor. 8:9); see Roy E. Ciampa and Brian S. Rosner, *The First Letter to the Corinthians*, PNTC (Grand Rapids: Eerdmans, 2010), 63–64; Gordon D. Fee, *The First Epistle to the Corinthians*, NICNT (Grand Rapids: Eerdmans, 1987), 38–39.

18. Although the combination of "speech and knowledge" anticipates the discussion of spiritual gifts in chaps. 12–14 (these same two words occur together in 12:8), the usage here in

confirms that the gospel message about Jesus Christ is true (1:6). As a result, the Corinthians did not lack any spiritual gift (1:7a). Indeed, their problem was not a lack of spiritual gifts but a lack of wisdom to know how to use them (see 1 Cor. 12–14)!

Believers experience the realities of what God has done for them (1:3–7a) "as you eagerly wait for our Lord Jesus Christ to be revealed" (1:7b NIV). As great as what God has already done for his people is, there is still much more to come. But in the meantime, as we wait for Christ to be revealed, he "will sustain you to the end, guiltless in the day of our Lord Jesus Christ" (1:8).[19] The same grace that first saved the Corinthians is also the means by which Christ sustains his people in the present as they await the day of Christ. On that day believers will be guiltless because God's work of redemption will be completed. As if to reassure the Corinthians that they can base their lives on these mind-boggling realities, Paul reminds them, "God is faithful, by whom you were called into the fellowship of his Son, Jesus Christ our Lord" (1:9). In other words, God can be trusted to fulfill his promises in the future because he has proved himself faithful to his promises in the past. The evidence of his past faithfulness is that the Corinthians have been called into fellowship with Christ and each other through the gospel message.

Perhaps the best way to summarize how the already–not yet shapes this prayer is to look at past, present, and future.[20] Paul begins by thanking God for several things that he has already done. He has shown believers grace in Christ Jesus by forgiving our sins and giving us his Holy Spirit to dwell in us (1:4). He has enriched us in all speech and knowledge so that the way we speak and think is now different (1:5). Furthermore, he has called us into fellowship with Jesus Christ and each other (1:9). On top of that he has given us every spiritual gift to build up his people for faithful service to Christ (1:7). All of this is rooted in God's faithfulness to his promises in the gospel (1:9).

With God's faithfulness in the past as our foundation, in the present we "eagerly wait" for Christ to be revealed in the day of Christ (1:7–8 NIV). Paul uses this rare Greek verb only to refer to the eager anticipation and expectation

---

1:5 is likely broader, including speech and knowledge in general; see Ciampa and Rosner, *First Letter to the Corinthians*, 63–64.

19. The verb translated "sustain" (*bebaiōsei*) is the same one rendered "confirmed" (*ebebaiōthē*) in verse 6. The repetition of this word continues the legal metaphor of 1:6. So the point is that just as God confirmed the testimony about Christ by giving believers spiritual gifts, so God will also confirm his faithfulness by sustaining believers until the end; see Fee, *1 Corinthians*, 43.

20. This progression of past, present, and future is helpfully brought out by Ciampa and Rosner, *First Letter to the Corinthians*, 66.

the believers have for God to consummate all his promises.[21] We see this clearly in Romans 8:23–25, where he uses it twice:

> And not only the creation, but we ourselves, who have the firstfruits of the Spirit, groan inwardly as we *wait eagerly* for adoption as sons, the redemption of our bodies. For in this hope we were saved. Now hope that is seen is not hope. For who hopes for what he sees? But if we hope for what we do not see, we *wait* for it with patience. (italics added)

It is because we have already tasted the firstfruits of our redemption (the gift of the Spirit) that we groan for its fullness to come as soon as possible.

Thus as believers our ultimate hope is in the future, fixed on "the revealing of our Lord Jesus Christ" (1:7) on "the day of our Lord Jesus Christ" (1:8). On that day we will be guiltless in his presence. Thankfully we are not left to our own resources to make it from our present state of waiting to the consummation of God's purposes. God is the one "who will sustain you to the end" (1:8).

For Paul, prayer grows out of our gratitude for God's past faithfulness, erupts from our eager anticipation of Christ's return, and orients us to our eternal destiny.

Philippians 1:3–11

Paul experienced a special bond with the Philippians. Several times they had partnered with Paul in his ministry through both their prayers and financial gifts. In response to their latest gift, Paul writes the church to thank them for their generosity and update them on the progress of the gospel through his circumstances as a prisoner in Rome. His gratitude for the Philippians breaks forth into joyful prayer for them because of their fellowship in the gospel (1:3–5). Such joyful prayer is rooted in the confidence "that he who began a good work in you will bring it to completion at the day of Jesus Christ" (1:6). Combined with this confidence is Paul's deep affection for the Philippians, forged in their partnership in the defense and confirmation of the gospel (1:7–8). In light of what God has already done for the Philippians, a sense of joy pervades this section, as does an eager expectation of what God has yet to do in the future.

When Paul turns to the content of his prayer for them, the latter-day dynamic becomes even more pronounced. The main request is "that your love may abound more and more, with knowledge and all discernment" (1:9).

---

21. The verb is *apekdechomai*, and it occurs just eight times in the NT: Rom. 8:19, 23, 25; 1 Cor. 1:7; Gal. 5:5; Phil. 3:20; Heb. 9:28; 1 Pet. 3:20.

Convinced that they already love God and others, Paul prays for this love to overflow like a river bursting over its banks. Such love abounds in the knowledge of Christ (which surpasses everything else; see 3:7–14) and the ability to discern the path of wisdom in a world full of folly.

But love overflowing with knowledge and all discernment is not an end in itself. The purpose of this overflowing love is so that they "may approve what is excellent" (1:10a). Because life has many situations where it is challenging to know what to do, believers need a deepening knowledge of Christ and all discernment in order to make the best choices. In addition, such a prayer to be able to approve what is excellent "spells the death of entrenched mediocrity, of smug self-satisfaction, of contentment with our own excuses."[22] True biblical love penetrates every area of our lives so that we cannot remain content with just getting by in our spiritual lives.

As a result of approving what is excellent, believers will be "pure and blameless for the day of Christ" (Phil. 1:10b). While perfect obedience to God is impossible in this life (3:12–15), the genuine follower of Christ is marked by the desire to grow in godliness. Being pure and blameless demands more than behavior modification; it also requires the transformation of our thoughts, beliefs, intentions, attitudes, and dispositions. This progressive transformation is in anticipation of the day of Christ, when he "will transform our lowly body to be like his glorious body, by the power that enables him even to subject all things to himself" (3:21).

To make sure we understand what Paul means by pure and blameless, he further describes it as being "filled with the fruit of righteousness that comes through Jesus Christ, to the glory and praise of God" (Phil. 1:11). The righteousness of Jesus Christ that God gives to his people inevitably produces the tangible fruit of a changed life as the Spirit transforms us to reflect Jesus Christ (Rom. 8:29; Gal. 5:22–24).[23] Such a radical transformation will be so evident to all on the day of Christ that glory and praise will be given to God.

The importance of the already–not yet is evident in at least two important ways. First, our confidence in what God has yet to do is based on remembering what God has already done for us. When we reflect on the evidence of God's grace in the lives of other people around us, it prompts not only gratitude but also a confident expectation that God will one day complete the work of

---

22. D. A. Carson, *Praying with Paul: A Call to Spiritual Reformation*, 2nd ed. (Grand Rapids: Baker Academic, 2014), 105. For sustained reflection on the implications of this prayer for pastoral ministry, see esp. 110–12.

23. For further explanation of this verse, see Matthew S. Harmon, *Philippians*, Mentor Commentary (Fearn, Ross-shire, Scotland: Christian Focus, 2015), 103–6.

making us like his Son, Jesus. One prominent way this confident expectation expresses itself is joyful prayer for others.

Second, our growth in godliness contains already–not yet, eschatological elements. We have already experienced God's love at work in our lives, but this love must continually be growing. So we pray that this love would fuel our knowledge of Christ and enable us to grow in our ability to approve what is excellent. We cry out to God to make us pure and blameless in this life as we long for the day of Christ, when God will consummate his work of new creation in our lives. We plead for God to fill us with the fruit of righteousness, which was promised as an end-time gift in the OT, and which he has already given us in his Son, Jesus Christ. And we look forward to the day when our remarkable transformation from slaves to sons calls forth praise to God from all creation.

So here in Philippians 1:3–11 Paul prays for ongoing growth in godliness based on what God has already done for his people and in confident expectation that he will complete that work on the day of Christ. Paul builds on what he knows to be already true as a foundation for asking God for what is not yet fully realized.

Implications

We Approach God on the Basis of Who He Is and What He Has Already Done

Since God's character does not change (Ps. 102:25–27; Heb. 13:5), we need not fear that today he will be different than he was in biblical times. Stop to consider all that God has already done for us. He chose us before the foundation of the world and sent his Son to accomplish our salvation (Eph. 1:3–14). He has ushered in the promised latter days (Acts 2:14–21). He has resurrected us spiritually and transferred us from the kingdom of darkness into the kingdom of his Son (Eph. 2:1–10; Col. 1:13–14). He forgave our sins (Col. 3:13). He adopted us into his family as sons and daughters in anticipation of our final resurrection on the last day (Rom. 8:23; Gal. 4:1–7), when we will be fully consummated children of God (Rom. 8:16–23). He sealed us with the end-time Holy Spirit (Eph. 1:13–14). He called us into fellowship with him and each other (1 John 1:1–3). He gave us spiritual gifts to serve others and produce eschatological fruit in our lives (Gal. 5:22–23; 1 Pet. 4:10–11), fruit that was promised to appear in the end-time new creation (Isa. 32:15–18; 57:14–19).[24] The list goes on,

24. See further Matthew S. Harmon, *She Must and Shall Go Free: Paul's Isaianic Gospel in Galatians*, BZNW 168 (Berlin: de Gruyter, 2010), 214–21.

but the point should be clear: God has already done astonishing things for us to make us his people.

On top of that, God has already done remarkable things in our lives. Each of us can identify things that God has done through our circumstances or others to show us his love—the job opportunity that came at just the right time, the words of a friend in a time of need, the sermon that hit us right where we were at, the mercy of a neighbor who forgave us, the shoulder to cry on when grieving, and so on. The story of our lives is filled with things that God has already done for us.

We Confidently Ask God for What He Has Promised to Do

Because of who God is and his proven track record, we should confidently ask him to do what he has promised. God's priority is the display of his glory through the establishment of his eschatological kingdom; our prayers should be oriented toward this same goal. Yet how often do our prayers transcend our own personal circumstances to beg God to extend the fame of his name to the ends of the earth? Because God's kingdom has already broken into this world through the work of Jesus, we can pray with confidence that he will work to extend that kingdom until the earth is "filled with the knowledge of the glory of the LORD as the waters cover the sea" (Hab. 2:14).

But we cannot honestly pray for God's kingdom to be fully realized without at the same time praying for God to transform us so that our lives reflect more consistently in the present what we will be in the eschatological future—"pure and blameless for the day of Christ" (Phil. 1:10). The apostle John makes the connection between our current, latter-day identity as God's children and how we live today in light of Christ's return: "Beloved, we are God's children now, and what we will be has not yet appeared; but we know that when he appears we shall be like him, because we shall see him as he is. And everyone who thus hopes in him purifies himself as he is pure" (1 John 3:2–3).

Because God has provided for our greatest need in forgiving our sins, we can confidently ask him to meet our ongoing needs, even the most basic ones. Besides, "your Father knows what you need before you ask him" (Matt. 6:8). As his children, we are able to ask him to bring those who are still in darkness into "the kingdom of his beloved Son" (Col. 1:13). For our brothers and sisters in Christ, we can pray that they will grow in their knowledge of the Lord and experience the power of Christ in their lives (Eph. 1:15–23). Based on our confidence that God has an eschatological inheritance waiting for us, we can pray for God to sustain fellow believers so that they can rejoice in the midst of trials (1 Pet. 1:3–9). As heirs of God and partakers of the promise in Christ Jesus, we can pray for God to display his manifold wisdom to all of creation through the church (Eph. 3:6, 10). When we intentionally ground our prayers for what we want God to do in the rock-solid foundation of who he is and what he has already done, we will experience the confidence that God will answer our prayers (1 John 5:14–15).

Practical Suggestions

1. *Study and pray the prayers of others.* The place to begin is with Scripture; what better place to learn to pray than the inspired words of God himself? In addition to the passages mentioned in this chapter, an excellent place to begin is with the Psalms. Pay special attention to how the already–not yet shapes the prayers themselves. Make note of what aspects of God's character and his previous actions form the basis of the biblical author's prayer. Identify what God is being asked to do in the prayer. For example, when you read the Lord saying in Psalm 2:6, "As for me, I have set my King on Zion, my holy hill," praise God for the fact he has already installed his promised King, Jesus, through his crucifixion and resurrection and has inaugurated the last days. As you read the Lord's words to the anointed king, "Ask of me, and I will make the nations your heritage, and the ends of the earth your possession" (Ps. 2:8), pray for God to hasten the day when this promise will be fully realized in a new heavens and new earth. While not on the same level as Scripture, there are collections of written prayers that can stimulate our own praying. An excellent resource is *The Valley of Vision*,[25] which is a collection of Puritan prayers. As we immerse ourselves in how other saints have prayed through the years, with an eye to the already–not yet, we will find our own prayers taking up the language of the Bible and shaping the way we pray, both privately and in corporate settings.

2. *Write out your prayers.* The value of writing out your prayers is that it forces you to slow down and think about what you are praying. It also provides an opportunity to more intentionally shape your prayers so that they align with Scripture. Identify specific ways that you, your family, and your congregation are experiencing the blessings of the last days, such as ways the eschatological Spirit has given comfort or power in specific situations. Try to verbalize why these blessings are eschatological in nature. Thank the Lord for his grace shown to you. From that foundation, ask the Lord to bring to full realization the promises he has made to you and the people you lead. This practice can

25. Arthur Bennett, ed., *The Valley of Vision: A Collection of Puritan Prayers & Devotions* (Carlisle, PA: Banner of Truth, 2002).

be especially valuable to help you model prayer for others when you pray in the corporate worship service.

3. *Keep a record of God's faithfulness.* All throughout Scripture we see God commanding his people to do something as a memorial of what he has done (e.g., Josh. 4:1–24; 1 Cor. 11:23–26). One simple way of doing this is keeping a prayer journal. In it you can record what God has already done for you in Christ as a way of prompting grateful worship and humble confidence while you also ask God for what is yet to come. Make note of specific ways you have experienced the joy that comes from the forgiveness of your sins and the presence and power of the end-time Spirit in your life. You can also record specific prayer requests and note answers when they happen. Record specific examples of how you have prayed for God to advance his latter-days kingdom here on this earth and the ways that God has answered. Try to articulate how these prayers and answers to them are essentially eschatological in nature. That way, when you are tempted to doubt God's faithfulness, you can look not only at the Scriptures but also at his proven track record in your own life.

Suggested Reading

Bennett, Arthur, ed. *The Valley of Vision: A Collection of Puritan Prayers & Devotions.* Carlisle, PA: Banner of Truth, 2002.

Carson, D. A. *Jesus' Sermon on the Mount and His Confrontation with the World: An Exposition of Matthew 5–10.* Grand Rapids: Baker, 1999.

———. *Praying with Paul: A Call to Spiritual Reformation.* 2nd ed. Grand Rapids: Baker Academic, 2014.

Keller, Timothy. *Prayer: Experiencing Awe and Intimacy with God.* New York: Dutton, 2014.

Piper, John. "Prayer: The Power of Christian Hedonism." Chap. 6 in *Desiring God: Meditations of a Christian Hedonist.* 25th anniversary reference ed. Colorado Springs: Multnomah, 2011.

9

Missions

Extending God's Eschatological Presence to the Ends of the Earth

Nearly every organization in today's world has a mission statement. These statements attempt to encapsulate in a short but memorable way the reason why an organization exists. Take, for example, the mission statement of Apple: "Apple is committed to bringing the best personal computing experience to students, educators, creative professionals and consumers around the world through its innovative hardware, software and Internet offerings."[1] Nonprofit organizations, such as the American Heart Association, also use mission statements: "To build healthier lives, free of cardiovascular diseases and stroke."[2]

While nowhere in the Bible is there an explicit mission statement like these, there are a number of statements that indicate what God's mission in this world is. Understanding what God is doing in the world and how we as human beings fit into that mission is the foundation for how we approach missions in the church. The place to begin is with God's creation of humanity in Genesis 1.[3]

1. See http://www.specimentemplates.org/mission-statements/apple-computer-mission-statement.htm.
2. See http://topnonprofits.com/examples/nonprofit-mission-statements/.
3. While there are texts that ground God's mission in the world in eternity past (e.g., John 17:1–25; Eph. 1:3–10; 2 Tim. 1:8–10; Rev. 13:8), the biblical starting point must be Gen. 1 to understand these references.

God's Mission Revealed in the Old Testament

God creating humankind is the pinnacle of Genesis 1. What distinguishes human-ity from the rest of creation is that we are made in the image of God. This fact is so important that the text specifically mentions it three times (1:26–27). Just as in the ancient Near East victorious kings would set up images of themselves in territories they ruled to reflect their glory and their presence, so too the Lord places his image in the garden of Eden to represent him and rule over the earth under his authority.[4] The text explicitly connects humanity being created in God's image with our mission in the verse that immediately follows (Gen. 1:28): "And God blessed them. And God said to them, 'Be fruitful and multiply and fill the earth and subdue it, and have dominion over the fish of the sea and over the birds of the heavens and over every living thing that moves on the earth.'"

As G. K. Beale aptly summarizes, "Genesis 1:27 provides the means by which the commission and goal of verse 28 was to be accomplished: human-ity will fulfill the commission by means of being in God's image."[5] As God's vice-regent, Adam was given the mission of expanding the boundaries of the garden (God's temple) until the entire earth was filled with the glory of God. This commission is further explained in Genesis 2:15: "The LORD God took the man and put him in the garden of Eden to work it and keep it." As we noted in chapter 7, the verbs "work" (*'ābad*) and "keep" (*šāmar*) are used together elsewhere for the role of priests who serve God in the tabernacle (e.g., Num. 3:7). This, along with several other features of Genesis 1–2, indicates that Adam is not merely a gardener, but a priest serving in God's garden sanctuary. Beale summarizes well the picture that emerges from Genesis 1–2:

> The intention seems to be that Adam was to widen the boundaries of the Gar-den in ever increasing circles by extending the order of the garden sanctuary into the inhospitable outer spaces. The outward expansion would include the goal of spreading the glorious presence of God. This would occur especially by Adam's progeny born in his image and thus reflecting God's image and the light of his presence, as they continued to obey the mandate given to their parents and went out to subdue the outer country.[6]

Thus the combined picture that emerges from Genesis 1–2 shows that Adam was a priest-king commissioned to protect the purity of God's garden sanctu-ary and expand its borders until it extended over the entire earth.

4. See further G. K. Beale, *The Temple and the Church's Mission: A Biblical Theology of the Dwelling Place of God*, NSBT 17 (Downers Grove, IL: InterVarsity, 2004), 81–87.
5. Ibid., 81.
6. Ibid., 85.

God's commission for Adam had an inherently eschatological nature. Had Adam faithfully obeyed, "he would have experienced even greater blessing than he had before his sin."[7] Ruling over and subduing the entire earth required defeating the serpent in the garden as the starting point of Adam's eventual worldwide dominion. Filling the earth with image-bearing offspring, especially understood in light of its interpretation in Psalm 8, was the means by which God's glory would fill the earth. Once he had fulfilled God's commission, Adam would have eaten decisively from the tree of life and entered into a heightened state of eschatological rest in which his physical and spiritual state would have been permanently protected from death and corruption. The blessings he already experienced in part would have been intensified and consummated if Adam had obeyed.

But Adam failed in his commission. Instead of protecting the purity of the garden sanctuary and subduing the serpent, Adam rebels against God when tempted (Gen. 3:1–13). While passing judgment (3:14–19), however, God sounds a note of promise—a descendant of the woman will one day crush the serpent. In the meantime, God exiles Adam and his wife from the garden, placing "the cherubim and a flaming sword that turned every way to guard the way to the tree of life" (3:24).

After judging the world through the flood, God reissues the commission to Noah once he emerges from the ark. Twice God tells Noah, "Be fruitful and multiply and fill the earth" (Gen. 9:1, 7). By repeating the language of Adam's commission, God indicates that Noah and his descendants are to carry out what Adam failed to do. Because the Lord remains committed to his mission of filling the earth with his glory through his people, he makes a covenant to never again destroy creation with a flood (9:8–17). But the ominous reminder that even after the flood "the intention of man's heart is evil from his youth" (8:21) foreshadows that Noah will fare no better than Adam in fulfilling his role in God's mission. That foreshadowing is confirmed when Noah's descendants join together to reject God's purpose and try to make a name for themselves through building the tower of Babel. Once again God brings judgment (11:1–9).

God's plan for fulfilling his mission takes further shape when he calls Abram (Gen. 12:1–3). Just as God blessed Adam, gave him land, and called him to extend God's blessing to the ends of the earth (1:28–30), so now God blesses Abram, promises him land, and expresses his intention to bless all the families of the earth through him (12:1–3). But whereas the commissions to Adam

---

7. G. K. Beale, *A New Testament Biblical Theology: The Unfolding of the Old Testament in the New* (Grand Rapids: Baker Academic, 2011), 33–34. What follows is adapted from 33–46.

(1:28–30) and Noah (9:1–7) are expressed as commands, beginning here with Abram, God's commission is spoken as a promise.[8] God formalizes this promise through making a covenant with Abram, even changing his name to Abraham (15:1–21; 17:1–27). Throughout the course of Abraham's life, God expands the scope of this promise to include more descendants than can be numbered (13:16; 15:5; 22:17), a multitude of nations (17:5), kings coming forth from him (17:6), possessing the gates of his enemies (22:17), and having the Lord as their God (15:1; 17:8). This promise would find initial fulfillment in the singular descendant Isaac (17:15–21; 26:3–5) and be passed down through Jacob (27:26–29; 28:13–15) to his twelve sons (49:1–27).

As the book of Exodus opens, Jacob and his descendants had been "fruitful and increased greatly; they multiplied and grew exceedingly strong, so that the land was filled with them" (Exod. 1:7). By echoing the language of the commission to Adam and the promise to Abraham, Moses shows that God's mission is moving forward. God responds to Israel's groaning under their slavery by raising up Moses to deliver them (3:1–4:17) and further advance God's covenant with "Abraham, Isaac, and Jacob" (2:24; 6:6–8). After redeeming Israel from their slavery in Egypt, God brings them to Mount Sinai to make a covenant with them. He says to them:

> You yourselves have seen what I did to the Egyptians, and how I bore you on eagles' wings and brought you to myself. Now therefore, if you will indeed obey my voice and keep my covenant, you shall be my treasured possession among all peoples, for all the earth is mine; and you shall be to me a kingdom of priests and a holy nation. These are the words that you shall speak to the people of Israel. (Exod. 19:4–6)

By referring to Israel as a "kingdom of priests and a holy nation," Moses signals that they, like Adam, have both a royal and a priestly role within God's redemptive plan. As a nation they are a "corporate Adam," entering the promised land to establish a new sanctuary for the Lord to dwell in. Through their holy lives, God will draw the surrounding nations to see the glory of the Lord and come under his saving rule. But like both Adam and Noah before them, Israel does not take long to fail. The incident with the golden calf (Exod. 32:1–34:35) begins a pattern of failure that runs through Israel's forty years in the wilderness and continues through the period of the judges and the reign of Israel's first king, Saul.

But a new note of hope sounds forth when David becomes king. Once God has granted him rest from his enemies, David desires to build a house (i.e.,

---

8. See further ibid., 52–58.

temple) for the Lord. Instead, the Lord asserts that he will build a house (i.e., a dynasty) for David (2 Sam. 7:1–29). The heart of God's promise is found in 2 Samuel 7:12–16:

> When your days are fulfilled and you lie down with your fathers, I will raise up your offspring after you, who shall come from your body, and I will establish his kingdom. He shall build a house for my name, and I will establish the throne of his kingdom forever. I will be to him a father, and he shall be to me a son. When he commits iniquity, I will discipline him with the rod of men, with the stripes of the sons of men, but my steadfast love will not depart from him, as I took it from Saul, whom I put away from before you. And your house and your kingdom shall be made sure forever before me. Your throne shall be established forever.

David is promised a descendant who will rule over an eternal kingdom and build a sanctuary in which God can dwell with his people. God is making it clear that he is still pursuing his mission of ruling over creation through a vice-regent who will build a place for God's glory to dwell. This promise finds initial and partial fulfillment in David's son Solomon, who extends his kingdom beyond the borders of Israel and builds a temple for the Lord to dwell in. But just as all before him, Solomon also fails, pursuing the gods of his foreign wives. Yet the promise remained of a descendant of David who would fulfill the commission that Adam, Noah, Israel, and Solomon were never able to carry out.

Psalm 8 demonstrates that David himself understood this connection between the promise God made to him and the commission given to Adam. The psalm begins, "O Lord, our Lord, how majestic is your name in all the earth! You have set your glory above the heavens" (8:1). The parallelism between "name" and "glory" indicates that they are roughly synonymous, while "earth" and "heavens" are paired to express totality. Magnifying the name of the Lord is the means by which God's glory is manifested in all creation. David frames the entire poem by repeating the first part of this refrain. After noting God's power over his enemies (Ps. 8:2), David marvels at God's commission to Adam in the verses that follow.

> When I look at your heavens, the work of your fingers,
>   the moon and the stars, which you have set in place,
> what is man that you are mindful of him,
>   and the son of man that you care for him?
> Yet you have made him a little lower than the heavenly beings
>   and crowned him with glory and honor.
> You have given him dominion over the works of your hands;
>   you have put all things under his feet,

all sheep and oxen,
    and also the beasts of the field,
the birds of the heavens, and the fish of the sea,
    whatever passes along the paths of the seas. (Ps. 8:3–8)

Given David's wonder that God appointed Adam to rule over creation in Genesis 1, it seems likely that he would have seen God's promise to him in 2 Samuel 7 as an extension of that very same dominion. It would be one of his descendants who would finally exercise humanity's rightful rule over creation under the authority of the Lord himself.

Through the prophets God expands on this promise. Isaiah 11:1–9 is an excellent example of this. Echoing the promise of 2 Samuel 7, Isaiah declares that God will raise up a Spirit-anointed descendant of David (Isa. 11:1–2). His rule over humanity will be marked by righteousness and faithfulness (11:3–5). But this rule will not be limited to humanity; it will entail the transformation of creation itself (11:6–8). The culmination of the passage reveals the ultimate goal of God's work through this Spirit-anointed Davidic king: "They shall not hurt or destroy in all my holy mountain, for the earth shall be full of the knowledge of the LORD as the waters cover the sea" (11:9).

The "holy mountain" is another way of referring to the temple (compare the expression "the mountain of the house of the LORD" in Isa. 2:2). The picture of the earth being filled with the knowledge of the Lord recalls God's commission to Adam to expand the boundaries of God's garden sanctuary so that his glorious presence would one day extend to all of creation. As part of this restoration, God will bring together Jew and gentile alike to form the eschatological people of God (11:10–16).

A second key prophetic passage is Daniel 7:1–27. Daniel sees a vision of four beasts (7:1–8), followed by the scene in heaven where the "Ancient of Days" sits on his throne ruling over human history (7:9–12). Notice what happens next (7:13–14):

I saw in the night visions,
and behold, with the clouds of heaven
    there came one like a son of man,
and he came to the Ancient of Days
    and was presented before him.
And to him was given dominion
    and glory and a kingdom,
that all peoples, nations, and languages
    should serve him;

> his dominion is an everlasting dominion,
>> which shall not pass away,
> and his kingdom one
>> that shall not be destroyed.

The "one like a son of man" receiving an eternal kingdom over "all peoples, nations, and languages" echoes both the commission given to Adam and the promise made to David. When Daniel asks for the interpretation, he is told that four beasts represent four kings (7:15–17) but that "the saints of the Most High shall receive the kingdom and possess the kingdom forever, forever and ever" (7:18). So the "son of man" is identified with "the saints of the Most High." After Daniel asks for further explanation of the fourth beast (7:19–26), the vision concludes as follows: "And the kingdom and the dominion and the greatness of the kingdoms under the whole heaven shall be given to the people of the saints of the Most High; his kingdom shall be an everlasting kingdom, and all dominions shall serve and obey him" (7:27).

So while the "one like a son of man" in 7:13–14 appears to be an individual who receives an eternal kingdom, in 7:18 and 7:27 it is "the saints of the Most High" who inherit the kingdom. But this is not a contradiction! The son of man is both an Adamic and Davidic figure who exercises the dominion that both ultimately failed to exercise. All who are identified with the son of man share in the eternal kingdom that he receives.[9] Thus in the latter days God will usher in a kingdom over all creation and manifest his glorious presence through his redeemed people.

From this very brief survey of the OT, we see that despite the failure of Adam, Noah, Israel, and Solomon, God remained profoundly committed to seeing the fulfillment of his commission to Adam. God will establish his rule over creation through his human vice-regent and fill the earth with his glorious presence. But as the OT closes, the question remains: Who is the seed of the woman, the descendant of David, who will obey where all others failed, crush the serpent, fulfill Adam's commission, and rule over an eternal kingdom that encompasses a renewed creation where God's glorious presence is manifested? And when will he come?

God's Mission Fulfilled in Jesus Christ

As we noted in chapter 2, the NT makes clear that Jesus comes to fulfill the commission that Adam and Israel failed to accomplish. The Gospel writers

9. See further ibid., 191–94.

portray Jesus as "recapitulating" both Adam's and Israel's experiences, but obeying where they had failed. In his descent into and return from Egypt, his baptism in the Jordan, and his wilderness temptation, Jesus begins to fulfill the eschatological commission that Adam and Israel failed to complete.[10] As part of obeying where Adam and Israel had failed, Jesus fulfills this commission in four primary ways.[11]

First, he begins to multiply his people by proclaiming the good news of the kingdom of God. After his wilderness temptation, Jesus settles in Galilee and begins to preach, "The time is fulfilled, and the kingdom of God is at hand; repent and believe in the gospel" (Mark 1:15; cf. Matt. 4:12–17). The latter days in which God's kingdom would be realized have broken into this fallen world, and God is beginning to fulfill his promises! The one for whom John the Baptist prepared the way as a voice crying in the wilderness (Matt. 3:1–12) has finally come. The eschatological people of God are brought into existence as Jesus begins calling disciples to follow him (Matt. 4:18–22). As Jesus travels throughout Galilee teaching and preaching, large crowds begin following him, and word about him spreads throughout the surrounding region (Matt. 4:23–25). In response to Peter informing Jesus that everyone in Capernaum is looking for him, Jesus answers, "Let us go on to the next towns, that I may preach there also, for that is why I came out" (Mark 1:38). Jesus will let nothing deter him from "multiplying" his people through the preaching and teaching of the kingdom of God. He is the last Adam, being fruitful and multiplying and beginning to fill the earth with his people so that Adam's eschatological commission will be fulfilled.

Over time Jesus even begins to involve his people in preaching the good news. He gives his twelve disciples authority to engage in the same kind of ministry as Jesus himself and sends them out to the villages of Israel to announce the arrival of the kingdom (Matt. 10:1–11:1). Shortly after Jesus resolutely sets his face toward Jerusalem (Luke 9:51), he commissions an even larger group of seventy-two to go into the villages ahead of him to announce the arrival of God's kingdom (10:1–20). By involving his followers in the preaching of the gospel, Jesus is preparing them for the day when he will carry out his mission through them. These eschatological image-bearers are beginning to fill the earth with God's glorious presence, thus carrying out the end-time commission given to Adam in Genesis 1:28.

Second, Jesus exercises authority over creation. Along with preaching and teaching the good news of the kingdom, he further validates his message by healing various sicknesses and diseases. When disciples of John the Baptist

---

10. See further the discussion in chap. 2 above.
11. For a much fuller unpacking of this, see Beale, *New Testament Biblical Theology*, 385–437.

approach Jesus to ask him if he is the promised one, Jesus responds, "Go and tell John what you hear and see: the blind receive their sight and the lame walk, lepers are cleansed and the deaf hear, and the dead are raised up, and the poor have good news preached to them" (Matt. 11:4–5).

Jesus takes these words from Isaiah 35:5–6, a passage that foresaw a day when God would transform creation itself for his redeemed people to dwell in. Through his healing, Jesus is exercising his authority over creation in anticipation of its total transformation on the last day. As the last Adam, Jesus Christ "became a life-giving spirit" (1 Cor. 15:45)[12] and exercises the dominion Adam was supposed to exercise but did not. As the son of David, Jesus demonstrates he is the true Shepherd-King over an eternal kingdom by healing those who cry out to him for mercy (Matt. 20:29–34).[13] These healings point forward to Jesus's own resurrection as the firstfruits of the resurrection of God's end-time people to the state of heightened eschatological blessing promised to Adam. Put differently, these healings are temporary reversals of the curse on Adam and humanity and a signal that Jesus is exercising the eschatological dominion over creation that Adam was commissioned to implement but failed to do.

Jesus's dominion over creation extends to authority over the demonic realm as well. Unlike Adam, who failed to defeat the serpent in the garden and protect the purity of God's sanctuary, Jesus triumphs over Satan in the wilderness (Matt. 4:1–11). He is the son of David who has entered the house of the strong man, bound him, and ransomed his people from Satan's power (12:22–32). In sending out his followers to further his mission, Jesus even delegates his authority over the demonic realm to them (Luke 10:17). In response to their excitement, Jesus says, "I saw Satan fall like lightning from heaven. Behold, I have given you authority to tread on serpents and scorpions, and over all the power of the enemy, and nothing shall hurt you" (10:18–19). As the serpent crusher, Jesus not only exercises authority over the demonic realm but also shares that authority with his people.

12. For a helpful discussion of this challenging text, see ibid., 262–63. Beale summarizes: "The apparent point is that the first human was created to reach the goal of such a glorious, imperishable body, *if* he had obeyed God and been faithful in reflecting God's image and carrying out the mandate of Gen. 1:28. . . . In contrast to the first Adam, who failed because of faithless disobedience, Christ has subdued and obeyed in the way his progenitor should have. Consequently, Christ has inherited that for which humanity was originally destined but failed to reach" (ibid.).

13. The connection between Jesus's identity as the son of David and his authority to heal may come from Ezek. 34. After condemning the false shepherds of Ezekiel's day (34:1–10), the Lord promises a day when he himself will shepherd his people through his servant David (34:11–24). He will establish a covenant of peace with them that involves the transformation of creation itself (34:25–31). Through his shepherd David, God will bring healing to his people (34:16).

162

Even the inanimate created order is subject to Jesus. On at least two separate occasions, he feeds several thousand people with a very small amount of food (Mark 6:30–44; 8:1–10). After sending his disciples ahead of him across the Sea of Galilee, Jesus walks across the water to join them (6:45–52). Amid a storm that threatens to sink their boat, Jesus calms the winds and the waves with a simple word of rebuke (4:35–41). No wonder his disciples exclaim, "Who then is this, that even the wind and the sea obey him?" (4:41).

Third, Jesus takes upon himself the curse that Adam, Israel, and all humanity brought upon themselves through their rebellion against God. The angel informs Joseph that the son Mary will bear will be named Jesus, "for he will save his people from their sins" (Matt. 1:21). To explain the nature of greatness in the kingdom, Jesus points to his own example: "The Son of Man came not to be served but to serve, and to give his life as a ransom for many" (Matt. 20:28). Jesus builds on this statement when, during the Passover with his disciples, he offers the cup to them and explains, "This is my blood of the covenant, which is poured out for many for the forgiveness of sins" (Matt. 26:28). By echoing the language of Isaiah 53 in these two passages, Jesus identifies himself as the Suffering Servant who bears the curse for the sins of Adam, Israel, and humanity.[14]

Fourth, through his resurrection from the dead, Jesus attains the glorious state that both Adam and Israel failed to reach. As the "firstborn from the dead" (Col. 1:18), Jesus experiences the resurrection of God's people that Ezekiel 37:1–14 foresaw. Even more fundamentally, the resurrected Jesus inaugurates the kingdom rule that Adam never achieved. Paul explains this in 1 Corinthians 15:21–28:

> For as by a man came death, by a man has come also the resurrection of the dead. For as in Adam all die, so also in Christ shall all be made alive. But each in his own order: Christ the firstfruits, then at his coming those who belong to Christ. Then comes the end, when he delivers the kingdom to God the Father after destroying every rule and every authority and power. For he must reign until he has put all his enemies under his feet. The last enemy to be destroyed is death. For "God has put all things in subjection under his feet." But when it says, "all things are put in subjection," it is plain that he is excepted who put all things in subjection under him. When all things are subjected to him, then the Son himself will also be subjected to him who put all things in subjection under him, that God may be all in all.

14. See further Matthew S. Harmon, "For the Glory of the Father and the Salvation of His People: Definite Atonement in the Synoptics and Johannine Literature," in *From Heaven He Came and Sought Her: Definite Atonement in Historical, Biblical, Theological, and Pastoral Perspective*, ed. David Gibson and Jonathan Gibson (Wheaton: Crossway, 2013), 275–77.

Jesus is the firstfruits of the resurrection, and when he comes again, his people will also be physically raised from the dead. As the last Adam, he is presently "destroying every rule and every authority and power" (1 Cor. 15:24). His present reign will continue "until he has put all his enemies under his feet" (15:25), including death as the last enemy. What Adam failed to do, the resurrected Jesus will bring to fruition.

After his death and resurrection, Jesus exercises his authority as the last Adam and the Son of Man to commission his followers to carry his mission forward by preaching the good news of what he has done: "And Jesus came and said to them, 'All authority in heaven and on earth has been given to me. Go therefore and make disciples of all nations, baptizing them in the name of the Father and of the Son and of the Holy Spirit, teaching them to observe all that I have commanded you. And behold, I am with you always, to the end of the age'" (Matt. 28:18–20). Jesus's claim to have all authority in heaven and on earth echoes the language of both Daniel 7:13–14 and Genesis 1:28–31. Based on his authority, Jesus commissions his followers to "make disciples of all nations." As the son of Abraham who inherits the promises, he multiplies his followers among all the nations through the preaching and teaching of his people.

So through his life of perfect obedience, Jesus obeys where Adam, Israel, and all humanity failed. Through his sacrificial death on the cross, Jesus pays the penalty that Adam, Israel, and all humanity deserved for their sinful rebellion against God. Through his resurrection, Jesus attains the glorified state that Adam, Israel, and all of humanity failed to attain.[15] Before ascending to heaven, he commissioned his followers to participate in his mission through their proclamation of the gospel. We see that worked out most clearly in the book of Acts.

God's Mission Carried Out through His Spirit-Indwelt People

Luke introduces Acts by stating that his gospel account "dealt with all that Jesus began to do and teach" (Acts 1:1). By phrasing it this way, Luke indicates that this second book will cover what Jesus is continuing to do and teach. As Alan Thompson suggests, one could rightly title the book "the Acts of the Lord Jesus, through his people, by the Holy Spirit, for the accomplishment of God's purposes."[16] Through the Holy Spirit, the risen Jesus continues his mission through his people preaching the gospel.

15. On the unexpected nature of how Jesus fulfills the OT expectations, see chap. 2 above.
16. Alan J. Thompson, *The Acts of the Risen Lord Jesus: Luke's Account of God's Unfolding Plan*, NSBT 27 (Downers Grove, IL: InterVarsity, 2011), 49.

This is apparent from the beginning of Acts. Jesus instructs his followers to remain in Jerusalem until they receive the promised Holy Spirit (Acts 1:4–5). In response to the disciples asking whether the time has come for him to "restore the kingdom to Israel" (1:6), Jesus responds, "It is not for you to know times or seasons that the Father has fixed by his own authority. But you will receive power when the Holy Spirit has come upon you, and you will be my witnesses in Jerusalem and in all Judea and Samaria, and to the end of the earth" (1:7–8).

Because Jesus had been raised from the dead, it was natural for the disciples to conclude that the consummation of God's kingdom was at hand. After all, that is a reasonable conclusion from several OT passages, which link resurrection with the end-time judgment and new creation (e.g., Isa. 26:1–21; Ezek. 37:1–14; Dan. 12:1–3).[17] But Jesus's answer to their question reflects an already–not yet dynamic. Yes, through his life, death, and resurrection Jesus has inaugurated the last days when God's promises will be fulfilled. But by stressing that it is not for the disciples to know "times or seasons that the Father has fixed by his own authority," Jesus indicates that the full realization of those promises remains for a future day. As they live between the already of what Jesus has done and the not yet of what the Father will do, Jesus explains how he will continue his mission. God will send the Holy Spirit to empower them to be his witnesses to the ends of the earth.

As David Pao has argued, the promise of being Spirit-empowered witnesses to the ends of the earth signals the initial fulfillment of several texts in Isaiah.[18] In Isaiah 32:15–20 the pouring out of the eschatological Spirit signals the restoration of God's people. The Spirit transforms nature and God's people so they both bear the marks of new creation. This restoration is accomplished by a Spirit-anointed Servant who will be a light for the nations so that the Lord's salvation will extend to the ends of the earth (Isa. 42:1; 49:6). Those redeemed by the work of the Servant become witnesses who declare the mighty works of the Lord (43:10–12; 54:17). By echoing the language of these texts, Jesus signals that the long-promised restoration of God's people has begun, though its fullness awaits a future day.

Less than two weeks later, God's promise is initially fulfilled by the pouring out of the Holy Spirit on the day of Pentecost (Acts 2:1–4). Jesus's disciples begin proclaiming the mighty works of God in different languages so that those gathered from around the Mediterranean world can understand them (2:5–13). Peter explains to the crowd that they are witnessing the outpouring

17. On the various elements of the OT hope, see chap. 1 above.
18. David W. Pao, *Acts and the Isaianic New Exodus* (Grand Rapids: Baker Academic, 2002), 91–96.

of the Spirit promised in the latter days and then proceeds to proclaim the good news of what Jesus has done (2:14–36). In response, about three thousand people repent and believe (2:37–41). Through his life-giving, eschatological Spirit, the risen Lord Jesus is continuing his mission of proclaiming the good news of the kingdom through his people. Jesus is being fruitful and multiplying his people by raising the spiritually dead to eternal life through the life-giving Holy Spirit. By filling them with his Spirit, he is expanding the latter-day earthly sanctuary where God dwells.

The rest of Acts shows how God's glory in his people begins to expand out toward the ends of the earth as they preach the gospel. Despite opposition, the risen Lord continues to multiply his people through the proclamation of the good news—first in Jerusalem, then in Judea, Samaria, and ultimately to the ends of the earth. Along the way Luke provides a series of summary statements about the progress of the word of God, such as the one found in Acts 6:7: "And the word of God continued to *increase*, and the number of the disciples *multiplied* greatly in Jerusalem, and a great many of the priests became obedient to the faith" (italics added; see also 2:41, 47; 5:14; 12:24; 19:20; 28:30–31). By using the language of "increase" and "multiply," Luke echoes God's commission to Adam in Genesis 1:28, the promise to Abram in Genesis 12:1–3, and the growth of the Israelites while in Egypt in Exodus 1:7. As David Peterson has noted, "The language of the creation mandate (Gen. 1:22, 28; 8:17; 9:1, 7) becomes the basis for the promise that God will grow and multiply his chosen people (Gen. 28:3; 35:11; 47:27; 48:4; Exod. 1:7; Lev. 26:9; Jer. 3:16; 23:3)."[19] The risen Lord Jesus continues his mission of multiplying his people through the faithful preaching of the gospel.

In at least one other passage, Luke makes clear that Jesus the Servant continues his mission through his people.[20] While in Pisidian Antioch, Paul preaches the gospel in a synagogue where it is well received by Jews and gentiles alike (Acts 13:13–43). But the next Sabbath, when even greater crowds gather to hear Paul and Barnabas, some of the Jews argue with them (13:44–45). Paul responds, "It was necessary that the word of God be spoken first to you. Since you thrust it aside and judge yourselves unworthy of eternal life, behold, we are turning to the Gentiles. For so the Lord has commanded us, saying, 'I have made you a light for the Gentiles, that you may bring salvation to the ends

19. David Peterson, *The Acts of the Apostles*, PNTC (Grand Rapids: Eerdmans, 2009), 33n142; see also Jerome Kodell, "The Word of God Grew: The Ecclesial Tendency of Logos in Acts 6,7; 12,24; 19,20," *Bib* 55 (1974): 505–19.

20. For further discussion of Acts 13:13–52, see Matthew S. Harmon, *She Must and Shall Go Free: Paul's Isaianic Gospel in Galatians*, BZNW 168 (Berlin: de Gruyter, 2010), 111–14; and Pao, *Acts and the Isaianic New Exodus*, 96–101.

of the earth'" (Acts 13:46–47). Paul explains his preaching the gospel to the
gentiles by quoting from Isaiah 49:6, the very same text echoed in Acts 1:8.
The risen Lord Jesus is fulfilling the mission of the Servant to be a light to the
gentiles so that salvation may go to the ends of the earth.

Paul confirms this conclusion in his Letter to the Galatians.[21] In describing
his conversion, he writes, "But when he who had set me apart before I was born,
and who called me by his grace, was pleased to reveal his Son to me, in order
that I might preach him among the Gentiles, I did not immediately consult with
anyone; nor did I go up to Jerusalem to those who were apostles before me, but
I went away into Arabia, and returned again to Damascus" (Gal. 1:15–17). Paul
echoes the language of Isaiah 49:1–6 to indicate that his apostolic ministry is
the fulfillment of the Servant's mission. Yet at several other points in the letter,
Paul uses the language of Isaiah 52:13–53:12 to identify Jesus as the Suffering
Servant (Gal. 1:4; 2:20; 3:13; 4:4–5). The two themes come together in Galatians
2:20 when Paul writes, "I have been crucified with Christ. It is no longer I who
live, but Christ who lives in me. And the life I now live in the flesh I live by faith
in the Son of God, who loved me and gave himself for me."

In his conversion, the old Paul was crucified with Christ, who then raised
him to new life and came to dwell inside him by the Spirit. The Suffering
Servant Jesus Christ now lives in Paul to carry out the mission of the Servant
to be a light to the nations, as described in Isaiah 49. Since we as believers are
indwelt by the Spirit, we are the conduit through which the risen Lord Jesus
continues the mission of the Servant to be a light to the nations so that his
salvation may extend to the ends of the earth.

Peter speaks of this same reality from a different perspective when he describes believers as a holy priesthood (1 Pet. 2:4–10). When we come to Jesus
Christ, the chosen and precious living stone, we become living stones being
built into a spiritual house (2:4–5a). The purpose behind this is "to be a holy
priesthood, to offer spiritual sacrifices acceptable to God through Jesus Christ"
(2:5b). After using a series of OT texts (Isa. 28:16; Ps. 118:22; Isa. 8:14) to
identify Jesus as the chosen stone (1 Pet. 2:6–8), Peter returns to priesthood
language in describing our identity as believers: "But you are a chosen race,
a royal priesthood, a holy nation, a people for his own possession, that you
may proclaim the excellencies of him who called you out of darkness into his
marvelous light. Once you were not a people, but now you are God's people;
once you had not received mercy, but now you have received mercy" (1 Pet.
2:9–10). Among the OT texts that Peter draws from is Exodus 19:6, where

21. Here we are summarizing what is argued in much greater detail in Harmon, *She Must
and Shall Go Free*, 103–22.

God describes Israel as a royal priesthood. By echoing this language, Peter signals that believers, through their identification with Jesus Christ, are priests mediating the presence of God in the world. We do this by proclaiming the good news of who Jesus is and what he has done. What Adam and Israel failed to do, Jesus now does through his royal priesthood of believers.

That is the task that God has given us as his people. As we wait for Jesus's return, we are priests who mediate God's presence to the world by proclaiming the good news of the kingdom of Jesus Christ. Through us Jesus is being fruitful and multiplying his people so that the earth will be filled with his glory.

God's Mission Consummated in a New Heavens and New Earth

The final consummation of God's mission in this world is described in Revelation 21–22. In these two chapters John describes the new heavens and new earth as a city-temple where God's glorious presence dwells in its fullness with humanity.[22] After describing the city in language borrowed from several OT passages (Rev. 21:9–21), John continues:

> And I saw no temple in the city, for its temple is the Lord God the Almighty and the Lamb. And the city has no need of sun or moon to shine on it, for the glory of God gives it light, and its lamp is the Lamb. By its light will the nations walk, and the kings of the earth will bring their glory into it, and its gates will never be shut by day—and there will be no night there. They will bring into it the glory and the honor of the nations. But nothing unclean will ever enter it, nor anyone who does what is detestable or false, but only those who are written in the Lamb's book of life.
>
> Then the angel showed me the river of the water of life, bright as crystal, flowing from the throne of God and of the Lamb through the middle of the street of the city; also, on either side of the river, the tree of life with its twelve kinds of fruit, yielding its fruit each month. The leaves of the tree were for the healing of the nations. No longer will there be anything accursed, but the throne of God and of the Lamb will be in it, and his servants will worship him. They will see his face, and his name will be on their foreheads. And night will be no more. They will need no light of lamp or sun, for the Lord God will be their light, and they will reign forever and ever. (Rev. 21:22–22:5)

The glorious presence of God now fills the entire created order to such a degree that the sun and moon are no longer necessary to give their light. Nations

---

22. See Beale, *Temple and the Church's Mission*, 365–73; and in much greater detail G. K. Beale, *The Book of Revelation: A Commentary on the Greek Text*, NIGTC (Grand Rapids: Eerdmans, 1999), 1039–1121.

and kings reflect to God his own glory as they worship the Lamb who sits on the throne. God's redeemed people serve as priest-kings who rule over a renewed creation as they were originally intended to do. Every impure thing and every last stain from the curse is gone. God's original mission in Genesis 1–2 is finally and completely realized!

Implications

God's Mission Advances through the Proclamation of the Gospel

The primary way that Jesus carries out his eschatological, Adamic mission in this world is through his people proclaiming the good news of the kingdom. We are Spirit-empowered witnesses who testify to what God has already done in the latter days through his Son, who is the last Adam. Because we still live in this present evil age, we will face opposition as we preach the good news. These are the birth pangs of God advancing his new creation kingdom. In the midst of war, famine, earthquakes, persecution, and even false prophets, Jesus promises that "this gospel of the kingdom will be proclaimed throughout the whole world as a testimony to all nations, and then the end will come" (Matt. 24:14). Therefore, as Kevin DeYoung and Greg Gilbert summarize, "The mission of the church is to go into the world and make disciples by declaring the gospel of Jesus Christ in the power of the Spirit and gathering these disciples into churches, that they might worship the Lord and obey his commands now and in eternity to the glory of God the Father."[23] If the central focus of the church, then, is to proclaim the gospel, everything that the church does should in some way be related to that mission, a mission that is eschatological at its core.

God's Mission Accelerates through Our Presence in the World

Prioritizing the proclamation of the gospel does not in any way diminish the value or importance of the many other good things that the church can and does do. As end-time priests who offer ourselves as living sacrifices, we are extending the boundaries of the eschatological temple. "God's presence grows among his priestly people by their knowing his word, believing it and obeying it, and then they spread that presence to others by living their lives faithfully and prayerfully in the world."[24] Running a homeless shelter, providing job training, or building a crisis pregnancy center are among the many tangible

---

23. Kevin DeYoung and Greg Gilbert, *What Is the Mission of the Church? Making Sense of Social Justice, Shalom, and the Great Commission* (Wheaton: Crossway, 2011), 62.
24. Beale, *Temple and the Church's Mission*, 400.

ways to bring just a taste of the blessings of God's new-creational kingdom into this fallen world. But without hearing the gospel message and responding in repentance and faith, no matter how much good a person experiences through such good works, that person will never enter the kingdom of God. Everything that the church does should in some way facilitate the sharing of the gospel. As we do these various good things such as meeting physical needs, alleviating human suffering, or even making our communities a better place to live, our lives bear witness to the truthfulness of the gospel we preach.[25]

God's Mission Involves All His People

While not every believer is called to go into vocational ministry or go to a foreign land to preach the gospel, all Christians are called to be involved in Jesus's continuing mission of being a light of salvation to the ends of the earth. God's latter-day promise to fill the earth with his glory "as the waters cover the sea" (Hab. 2:14) is being fulfilled through us because we are the eschatological people of God who proclaim his excellencies (Isa. 43:21; 1 Pet. 2:9). Therefore, at a minimum, believers should be giving generously and praying for those directly involved in spreading the gospel to the ends of the earth. Wherever God has placed us, he commands us, "Keep your conduct among the Gentiles honorable, so that when they speak against you as evildoers, they may see your good deeds and glorify God on the day of visitation" (1 Pet. 2:12). We should always be ready "to make a defense to anyone who asks you for a reason for the hope that is in you; yet do it with gentleness and respect" (1 Pet. 3:15). The early church grew as a result of "ordinary" believers sharing the gospel with friends, family, neighbors, and coworkers wherever they went (Acts 8:4). As those who have already experienced the eschatological blessings of God's kingdom, we bear witness through our words and our lives to the reality of who Jesus is and what he has done in the latter days. Pastors are called to equip all of God's people to share the good news of Jesus Christ within the overlap of the ages (Eph. 4:11–16).

Practical Suggestions

1. *Evaluate the various ministries of the church in light of their relationship to the mission of the church.* While not every ministry of the church involves

---

25. An important distinction should also be made between what the church as an organization/institution *must* do and what individual Christians *can* and/or *should* do. On this, see further DeYoung and Gilbert, *What Is the Mission of the Church?*, 223–39.

direct proclamation of the gospel, every ministry should in some way be connected to it. Try to articulate how that ministry manifests the presence of
God through his eschatological people. Reflect on how God's end-time reign
through Christ and his people is expressed through this ministry. If you cannot explain how a particular ministry at least indirectly facilitates the spread
of the gospel, you may need to rethink it.

2. *Preach/teach to mobilize the church for its mission.* The preaching and
teaching ministry of the church should regularly articulate God's mission in
the world and motivate his people to participate in it. Remind your hearers of
their identification with Christ, the last Adam, who through us is multiplying
his people and exercising an increasing dominion over the earth in fulfillment
of the original eschatological Adamic commission in Genesis 1:28. Highlight
examples of God's end-time kingdom advancing around the world, especially
through the ministry of those whom your church supports. Consider preaching a series on key texts that articulate God's mission in the world and our
role in that mission.

3. *Pray for God to raise up laborers.* Jesus himself commands us to pray
for God to raise up laborers (Matt. 9:37–38). As the good shepherd who lays
down his life for the sheep (John 10:10, 14), Jesus is working through the
church to gather his remaining sheep (Ezek. 34:11–24; John 10:16). God is
raising up "fishers of men" to gather together his eschatological people (Jer.
16:16; Mark 1:17). Therefore, asking God to move in the hearts of his people
to send them out to the ends of the earth should be a regular feature of the
church's prayer life. We should also be praying consistently for unbelievers in
our lives, both as individual believers and as a corporate body.

Suggested Reading

Beale, G. K. *The Temple and the Church's Mission: A Biblical Theology of the Dwelling Place of God.* NSBT 17. Downers Grove, IL: InterVarsity, 2004.

DeYoung, Kevin, and Greg Gilbert. *What Is the Mission of the Church? Making Sense
of Social Justice, Shalom, and the Great Commission.* Wheaton: Crossway, 2011.

Piper, John. *Let the Nations Be Glad! The Supremacy of God in Missions.* 3rd ed.
Grand Rapids: Baker Academic, 2010.

Conclusion

By now it should be clear how pervasive and significant the already–not yet is for understanding the life and ministry of the church, but let us take a look back at how each chapter bears this out.

Part 1: Theological Foundation: *Grasping the Already–Not Yet*

Chapter 1: The End Starts at the Beginning

In chapter 1 G. K. Beale articulates the theological landscape of the book and builds the framework for this entire project. He argues that eschatology does not merely pertain to future events but is highly relevant for the present. The apostles understood that they were already living in the "latter days," and they understood their present salvation and other key doctrines as end-time realities.

Dr. Beale lays out the basic story line of the OT. The grand story line is the story of God, who progressively reestablishes out of chaos his eschatological, new-creational kingdom over a sinful people by his Word and Spirit through promise, covenant, and redemption, resulting in worldwide commission to the faithful to advance this kingdom and in judgment (defeat or exile) for the unfaithful, unto his glory. This story begins in Genesis 1–3 and flows through all subsequent portions of the OT, from Adam to Noah, the patriarchs, and then Israel. The discrete time period known as the "latter days" is the final phase of God's story line and signals the final fulfillment of his promises to Israel and creation.

The NT continues this identical story line with Christ at the center: Jesus's life of covenantal obedience, trials, death for sinners, and resurrection by the

Spirit has launched the fulfillment of the eschatological, already–not yet, new-creation reign, bestowed by grace through faith and resulting in worldwide commission to the faithful to advance this kingdom and in judgment for the unfaithful, unto God's glory. All that the OT foresaw would occur in the end times has begun already in the first century and continues on until the final coming of Christ. Unexpectedly, believers live in the "overlap of the ages." On the one hand, believers partially enjoy the blessings of the long-awaited kingdom of God, the pouring out of the Spirit, the defeat of Satan, and so on. Yet the kingdom has not arrived in its fullness, the Spirit has yet to dwell consummately with the covenant community, and Satan remains active.

Chapter 2: The Nature of the End-Time Church

The second chapter sketches the nature of the church by first articulating the OT conception of the people of God, from Adam and Eve to restored Israel in the "latter days." We noticed how one of the most consistent themes of the OT is God's people failing to keep God's covenant. Yet in the midst of Israel's repeated failure and downward spiral into further rebellion, God promises to enable his people to obey him fully. This perfect obedience was achieved through the person and work of Jesus. The story of Jesus is the story of Israel. Jesus repeats Israel's steps by going into exile in Egypt (Matt. 2:15) and being tempted in the wilderness for forty days by the devil (4:1–11). Christ achieves what Adam and Eve, the patriarchs, and Israel should have achieved. Since the Spirit unites the church to Christ, what is true of Christ is true of the church (1 Cor. 1:30). By identifying ourselves with Christ, we are the restored, end-time people of God (Acts 2). Regardless of ethnicity, Jews and gentiles stand on equal ground and inherit the long-awaited covenant blessings (Eph. 3; Gal. 3:14).

Understanding the church as the latter-day people of God is crucial for the remainder of the project. Like spokes protruding from a wheel, the subsequent chapters detail how the NT authors ministered to their congregations as the end-time people of God.

Chapter 3: Life in the Overlap of the Ages

Our next chapter is meant to situate believers, as the end-time people of God, within the overlap of the ages. Since all believers equally participate in the kingdom, we are now bound to a set of latter-day "kingdom ethics" (Matt. 5–7). All Christians belong to the new age and are required to live accordingly. This principle is fleshed out in Jesus's teaching on the "love command" (Matt.

22:36–38) and on ministering to the poor (Luke 14:7–24). We also discussed Jesus's teaching on the resurrection in John 5. The "hour" or timing of the resurrection has now begun in the ministry of Christ, especially in his resurrection (Dan. 12:1–3; John 5:25). Jesus's teaching on the already–not yet aspect of resurrection entails a radical new way of viewing the Christian life. At present, Christians are enjoying their resurrected state, albeit in a spiritual manner. We rounded out our chapter with a discussion of the importance of the Spirit's work in the believer's life. All believers, but especially pastors, must understand that living in light of the kingdom and our present spiritual resurrection is central to the Christian life. Eschatology is highly relevant and immensely practical.

Part 2: Pastoral Leadership: *Leading God's End-Time Flock in the Already–Not Yet*

Chapter 4: Feeding the Flock

Chapter 4 kicks off a three-part series on Christian leadership. A principal part of a minister's job is preaching to the local congregation. We argued that preaching itself is embedded within the already–not yet. Peter's sermon in Acts 2 is rife with eschatological language (e.g., 2:17). The central thrust of Peter's message is that the outpouring of the Spirit proves that the last days have dawned in the life, death, and resurrection of Jesus, and therefore his audience must repent and receive forgiveness (2:37–39). The Spirit is God's end-time agent of renewal, who raised Jesus from the dead and incorporated those believing Israelites at Pentecost into God's end-time temple. The Spirit installed believers into this temple as priests, who worship and mediate God's presence to the nations.

In 1 Corinthians 1–2, we noticed that the apostle Paul's preaching ministry centers on communicating the unveiled mystery of what God has already done in Christ (2:1–16). Through Paul's preaching, God manifests his power through the work of the Spirit, who was given to God's people to signal that the age to come had dawned in and through the work of Jesus Christ. As the eschatological people of God, we have received the Spirit of God to enable us to understand God's wisdom in the cross (2:12). According to Daniel 11–12, the righteous Israelites (the "wise ones") will be privy to revelation in the "latter days" (11:33; 12:3–4, 10). Paul claims that the Spirit's work in the life of Corinthian believers is nothing short of this eschatological reality, which was prophesied in Daniel. God imparts this end-time wisdom through the proclamation of the gospel, empowered by the Spirit (1 Cor. 2:13). Paul makes a similar point in Colossians 1:24–2:5, where he proclaims the revealed mystery that pertains to God's redemptive plan in the person and work of Christ. Paul exhorts the Colossians to pursue Christlikeness in the present as they anticipate appearing before God on the last day fully mature in Christ. Pastors and church leaders must preach and teach in accordance with the overlap of the ages and call their people to live in light of their position in the "latter days."

Chapter 5: Guarding the Flock

The second aspect of pastoral leadership stresses the importance of protecting the flock from satanic assaults. We examined how the NT authors draw a direct correlation between the latter days and the onslaught of false teaching and persecution. In 2 Thessalonians 2:3 Paul claims that the "man of lawlessness" described in Daniel has not yet arrived on the scene, but, alarmingly, there is a sense in which the end-time oppressor is already on the scene. The end-time tribulation began with Christ's first advent and continues into the church age. The tribulation will continue and grow more intense, particularly preceding Christ's second coming. Central to the present tribulation is false teaching. Although the latter-day foe has not yet come in bodily form, the antagonist inspires the false teachers at Thessalonica, who deceive and persecute the church. We learned that other portions of the NT closely resemble Paul's claim (e.g., Matt. 24:5; 1 John 2:18–23). The Thessalonians must continue to stand firm in the faith in the midst of grave persecution. The book of Jude offers advice on how to deal with end-time false teachers. Jude commands his congregation to expect false teachers to operate within the church and to engage them accordingly (vv. 17–18). Prayer and careful meditation on God's Word are essential for battling false teaching (vv. 20–21). Christians ought to extend a hand of mercy to those who have succumbed to false teaching and make an attempt to preserve them in the gospel (vv. 22–23). As the global church continues to be persecuted throughout the world, pastors must continue to comfort their flock and encourage them to stand fast during the present tribulation. Even when it does not seem apparent, false teachers are alive and well in the modern-day church, and pastors and leaders must discern their presence and engage them.

Chapter 6: Guiding the Flock

The third and final part of our series on Christian leadership is devoted to three broad topics—leading by example, discipleship, and cultivating a vision. The churches in Asia Minor must imitate John, and John must imitate

Christ. We saw how the apostle John uses himself as an example of testifying to the risen Christ (Rev. 1:1–2) and experiencing victory through inaugurated, eschatological tribulation (1:9). We delved into the topic of discipleship through the lens of 2 Corinthians 5, where we learned that the Corinthians must treat each other as members of the end-time new creation, and they must also treat unbelievers in accordance with the overlap of the ages in which the latter-day, eternal new creation overlaps with the old age that is passing away. The Corinthian church must understand that unbelievers are part of the "old age," entrenched in sin and enslaved to a fallen world. Lastly, our discussion of a pastor's vision looks toward the future. With an eye on Christ's end-time evaluation of his ministry, Paul desires that he be found "faithful" in the proclamation of the crucified Christ (1 Cor. 4:2). Christian leaders must imitate Paul's exemplary behavior, treat Christians as though they are part of God's new creation, and conduct their ministry in light of God's end-time judgment.

Part 3: End-Time Ministry: *Service in the Latter-Day Temple of God*

Chapter 7: Worship: *Celebrating the Inaugurated New Covenant*

Although we are called to live all of life as an act of worship, there is something unique about the corporate gathering of God's people to worship. The already–not yet has a profound impact on how our corporate worship is expressed. Being rooted in the covenant with the Triune God, the church celebrates that intimate relationship (Matt. 26:26–29). Covenant worship is ultimately patterned after heavenly worship (Rev. 4:1–5:14). The worship directed toward Christ, the Lamb, focuses on his sacrificial death, which accomplishes the redemption of his people, who are drawn "from every tribe and language and people and nation" (5:9). We learned that Israel's tabernacle/temple was a model of a heavenly, cosmic reality (Heb. 9:23–24) and that the church is the end-time temple of God. Pastors and worship leaders ought to celebrate the church's covenant relationship with God by focusing on what God has accomplished in his Son. Leaders should communicate the glories of God dwelling with us in the new creation through singing, praying, preaching, and celebrating the ordinances.

Chapter 8: Prayer: *Pleading for the Consummation of the New-Creational Kingdom*

One aspect of the Christian life that is incredibly eschatological is the topic of prayer. We examined how the Lord's Prayer (Matt. 6:9–13), which is tied to the already–not yet, focuses on God's character and purposes and on our needs. Praying that God's name will be "hallowed" expresses our recognition that although he is transcendently majestic and glorious, many in this world do not yet see that reality. Although the kingdom has broken into this world, our prayer is that it will arrive in its fullness. We also plead with God to manifest his kingdom rule now in the life of his people, while we await the complete realization of all that God has ordained. Paul's prayers in Ephesians 1:15–23 and 1 Corinthians 1:4–9 focus on believers recognizing and experiencing their end-time blessings more fully, while they await their future, consummate restoration.

Chapter 9: Missions: *Extending God's Eschatological Presence to the Ends of the Earth*

Our final chapter highlights a central concern of God's story—the establishment of the people of God, who dwell intimately with God in his kingdom in the new heavens and earth. Though Noah, Israel, and Solomon failed to fulfill the original eschatological, Adamic commission, God remained profoundly committed to seeing the fulfillment of his commission to Adam. God promised to establish his latter-day rule over creation through his human vice-regents and fill the earth with his glorious presence. Jesus succeeds where Adam, Israel, and all who have gone before failed. Through Jesus's sacrificial death on the cross, he pays the penalty that Adam, Israel, and all humanity deserved for their sinful rebellion against God. By his resurrection as a new creation, Jesus attains the glorified state that Adam, Israel, and all of humanity failed to attain. The church now, as God's end-time people, is the vehicle by which God continues to fulfill his original end-time mission introduced in Genesis 1–2.

A Plea to Pastors, Elders, and Church Leaders

It is a task in and of itself to explain the end-time, already–not yet framework of the nature of the church, the Christian life, pastoral leadership, and the various aspects of ministry such as worship, prayer, and missions. But without the intentional effort of its leadership, the church will not live as citizens of God's inaugurated, latter-day kingdom in a manner worthy of the gospel of Jesus Christ. We realize that implementing these ideas may prove challenging. Pastors and the church leadership must be proactive, even creative at times, to flesh out these principles. The leadership of the church must grasp the already–not yet at a conceptual level and then begin the task of putting it into practice. This will require a coordinated effort that spreads from the leadership out to the rest of the congregation. But do you not want your church to be an outpost of God's new-creational kingdom here on earth? Do you not want to see God's people bearing the fruit of the eschatological Spirit as they participate in God's mission to fill the earth with his glory? When pastors and congregations grasp God's plan of redemption as it relates to the already–not yet, the message of the NT will be illuminated, lives will be changed, and God will be glorified.

Bibliography

Alexander, T. Desmond. *From Eden to the New Jerusalem: An Introduction to Biblical Theology.* Grand Rapids: Kregel, 2008.

Alexander, T. Desmond, and Brian S. Rosner, eds. *New Dictionary of Biblical Theology.* Downers Grove, IL: IVP Academic, 2000.

Allison, Dale C., Jr. "Eschatology." *DJG* 206–9.

Aune, David E. "Early Christian Eschatology." *ABD* 2:594–609.

Banks, Robert. "Matthew's Understanding of the Law: Authenticity and Interpretation in Matthew 5:17–20." *JBL* 93 (1974): 226–42.

Bauckham, Richard. "Colossians 1:24 Again: The Apocalyptic Motif." *EvQ* 47 (1975): 168–70.

———. *The Theology of the Book of Revelation.* NTT. Cambridge: Cambridge University Press, 1993.

Beale, G. K. *The Book of Revelation: A Commentary on the Greek Text.* NIGTC. Grand Rapids: Eerdmans, 1999.

———. "The Descent of the Eschatological Temple in the Form of the Spirit at Pentecost, Part 1: The Clearest Evidence." *TynBul* 56.1 (2005): 73–102.

———. "The Descent of the Eschatological Temple in the Form of the Spirit at Pentecost, Part 2: Corroborating Evidence." *TynBul* 56.2 (2005): 63–90.

———. "The Eschatological Conception of New Testament Theology." In *"The Reader Must Understand": Eschatology in the Bible and Theology,* edited by K. E. Brower and M. W. Elliott, 11–52. Leicester, UK: Apollos, 1997.

———. "The Eschatological Hour in 1 John 2:18 in the Light of Its Daniel Background." *Bib* 92 (2011): 231–54.

———. "Eschatology." *DLNT* 330–45.

———. *1–2 Thessalonians*. IVPNT. Downers Grove, IL: InterVarsity, 2003.

———. *Handbook on the New Testament Use of the Old Testament: Exegesis and Interpretation*. Grand Rapids: Baker Academic, 2012.

———. *A New Testament Biblical Theology: The Unfolding of the Old Testament in the New*. Grand Rapids: Baker Academic, 2011.

———. "The Old Testament Background of Reconciliation in 2 Corinthians 5–7 and Its Bearing on the Literary Problem of 2 Corinthians 6.14–7.1." *NTS* 35 (1989): 550–81.

———. "The Old Testament Background of Rev 3.14." *NTS* 42 (1996): 133–52.

———. "Peace and Mercy upon the Israel of God." *Bib* 80 (1999): 204–23.

———. *The Temple and the Church's Mission: A Biblical Theology of the Dwelling Place of God*. NSBT 17. Downers Grove, IL: InterVarsity, 2004.

———. *The Use of Daniel in Jewish Apocalyptic Literature and in the Revelation of St. John*. Lanham, MD: University Press of America, 1984.

———. "The Use of Hosea 11:1 in Matthew 2:15: One More Time." *JETS* 55 (2012): 697–715.

———. *We Become What We Worship: A Biblical Theology of Idolatry*. Downers Grove, IL: InterVarsity, 2008.

Beale, G. K., and D. A. Carson, eds. *Commentary on the New Testament Use of the Old Testament*. Grand Rapids: Baker Academic, 2007.

Beale, G. K., and Benjamin L. Gladd. *Hidden but Now Revealed: A Biblical Theology of Mystery*. Downers Grove, IL: InterVarsity, 2014.

Beasley-Murray, G. R. *Jesus and the Kingdom of God*. Grand Rapids: Eerdmans, 1986.

Bennett, Arthur, ed. *The Valley of Vision: A Collection of Puritan Prayers & Devotions*. Carlisle, PA: Banner of Truth, 2002.

Blaising, Craig A., and Darrell L. Bock. *Progressive Dispensationalism*. Wheaton: BridgePoint, 1993. Reprint, Grand Rapids: Baker Books, 2000.

Block, Daniel I. *The Book of Ezekiel*. 2 vols. NICOT. Grand Rapids: Eerdmans, 1997.

Blomberg, Craig L. *1 Corinthians*. NIVAC. Grand Rapids: Zondervan, 1994.

———. *Neither Poverty nor Riches: A Biblical Theology of Possessions*. NSBT. Downers Grove, IL: InterVarsity, 1999.

Bock, Darrell L., Walter C. Kaiser, and Craig A. Blaising. *Dispensationalism, Israel and the Church: The Search for Definition*. Grand Rapids: Zondervan, 1992.

Brower, K. E., and M. W. Elliott, eds. *"The Reader Must Understand": Eschatology in the Bible and Theology*. Leicester, UK: Apollos, 1997.

Bruce, F. F. *1 & 2 Thessalonians*. WBC 45. Dallas: Word, 1982.

Cabaniss, Allen. "Note on the Liturgy of the Apocalypse." *Int* 7 (1953): 78–86.

Carson, D. A. *The Gospel according to John*. PNTC. Grand Rapids: Eerdmans, 1991.

———. *Jesus' Sermon on the Mount and His Confrontation with the World: An Exposition of Matthew 5–10*. Grand Rapids: Baker, 1999.

———. "Matthew." In *The Expositor's Bible Commentary*, edited by F. E. Gaebelein, 8:1–599. Grand Rapids: Zondervan, 1984.

———. *Praying with Paul: A Call to Spiritual Reformation*. 2nd ed. Grand Rapids: Baker Academic, 2014.

Chapell, Bryan. *Christ-Centered Preaching: Redeeming the Expository Sermon*. 2nd ed. Grand Rapids: Baker Academic, 2005.

Chesterton, G. K. *Orthodoxy*. New York: John Lane, 1908. Reprint, San Francisco: Ignatius, 1995.

Ciampa, Roy E., and Brian S. Rosner. *The First Letter to the Corinthians*. PNTC. Grand Rapids: Eerdmans, 2010.

Collins, Raymond. *First Corinthians*. SP 7. Collegeville, MN: Liturgical Press, 1999.

Cullmann, Oscar. *Christ and Time*. Philadelphia: Westminster, 1950.

DeSilva, David A. *An Introduction to the New Testament: Contexts, Methods & Ministry Formation*. Downers Grove, IL: InterVarsity, 2004.

Dever, Mark, and Paul Alexander. *The Deliberate Church: Building Your Ministry on the Gospel*. Wheaton: Crossway, 2005.

DeYoung, Kevin, and Greg Gilbert. *What Is the Mission of the Church? Making Sense of Social Justice, Shalom, and the Great Commission*. Wheaton: Crossway, 2011.

Dumbrell, William J. *The Search for Order: Biblical Eschatology in Focus*. Grand Rapids: Baker, 1994.

Dunn, J. D. G. *The Christ and the Spirit: Christology*. 2 vols. Grand Rapids: Eerdmans, 1998.

Edwards, Jonathan. *The Sermons of Jonathan Edwards: A Reader*. New Haven: Yale University Press, 1999.

Fee, Gordon D. *The First Epistle to the Corinthians*. NICNT. Grand Rapids: Eerdmans, 1987.

———. *God's Empowering Presence: The Holy Spirit in the Letters of Paul*. Peabody, MA: Hendrickson, 1994.

France, R. T. *The Gospel of Matthew*. NICNT. Grand Rapids: Eerdmans, 2007.

Furfey, P. H. "The Mystery of Lawlessness." *CBQ* 8 (1946): 179–91.

García Martínez, F., and Eibert J. C. Tigchelaar, eds. *The Dead Sea Scrolls Study Edition*. 2 vols. Leiden: Brill, 2000.

Gentry, Peter J., and Stephen J. Wellum. *Kingdom through Covenant: A Biblical-Theological Understanding of the Covenants.* Wheaton: Crossway, 2012.

Gibson, David, and Jonathan Gibson, eds. *From Heaven He Came and Sought Her: Definite Atonement in Historical, Biblical, Theological, and Pastoral Perspective.* Wheaton: Crossway, 2013.

Gladd, Benjamin L. "The Last Adam as the 'Life-Giving Spirit' Revisited: A Possible Old Testament Background of One of Paul's Most Perplexing Phrases." *WTJ* 71 (2009): 297–309.

———. *Revealing the* Mysterion: *The Use of* Mystery *in Daniel and Second Temple Judaism with Its Bearing on First Corinthians.* BZNW 160. Berlin: de Gruyter, 2009.

Greidanus, Sidney. *Preaching Christ from the Old Testament: A Contemporary Hermeneutical Method.* Grand Rapids: Eerdmans, 1999.

Grudem, Wayne A. *Systematic Theology: An Introduction to Biblical Doctrine.* Grand Rapids: Zondervan, 1994.

Gundry, Stanley N., ed. *Five Views on Law and Gospel.* Grand Rapids: Zondervan, 1996.

Hamilton, James M. *Revelation: The Spirit Speaks to the Churches.* Preaching the Word. Wheaton: Crossway, 2011.

Harmon, Matthew S. "Allegory, Typology, or Something Else? Revisiting Galatians 4:21–5:1." In *Studies in the Pauline Epistles: Essays in Honor of Douglas J. Moo,* edited by Matthew S. Harmon and Jay E. Smith, 144–58. Grand Rapids: Zondervan, 2014.

———. "For the Glory of the Father and the Salvation of His People: Definite Atonement in the Synoptics and Johannine Literature." In *From Heaven He Came and Sought Her: Definite Atonement in Historical, Biblical, Theological, and Pastoral Perspective,* edited by David Gibson and Jonathan Gibson, 267–88. Wheaton: Crossway, 2013.

———. "Letter Carriers and Paul's Use of Scripture." *JSPL* 4 (2014): 25–44.

———. *Philippians.* Mentor Commentary. Fearn, Ross-shire, Scotland: Christian Focus, 2015.

———. *She Must and Shall Go Free: Paul's Isaianic Gospel in Galatians.* BZNW 168. Berlin: de Gruyter, 2010.

Harmon, Matthew S., and Jay E. Smith, eds. *Studies in the Pauline Epistles: Essays in Honor of Douglas J. Moo.* Grand Rapids: Zondervan, 2014.

Hays, Richard B. *The Conversion of the Imagination: Paul as Interpreter of Israel's Scripture.* Grand Rapids: Eerdmans, 2005.

———. *The Moral Vision of the New Testament: Community, Cross, New Creation; A Contemporary Introduction to New Testament Ethics.* San Francisco: Harper-SanFrancisco, 1996.

Hendriksen, William. *More than Conquerors: An Interpretation of the Book of Revelation.* 1939. Reprint, Grand Rapids: Baker, 1998.

Hoehner, Harold W. *Ephesians: An Exegetical Commentary.* Grand Rapids: Baker Academic, 2002.

Hoekema, Anthony A. *The Bible and the Future.* Grand Rapids: Eerdmans, 1979.

———. *Created in God's Image.* Grand Rapids: Eerdmans, 1986.

Jeremias, Joachim. *The Prayers of Jesus.* SBT 6. Naperville, IL: Allenson, 1967.

Johnson, Alan F. *1 Corinthians.* IVPNT. Downers Grove, IL: InterVarsity, 2004.

Johnson, Dennis E. *Triumph of the Lamb: A Commentary on Revelation.* Phillipsburg, NJ: P&R, 2001.

Johnson, Philip S. *Shades of Sheol: Death and Afterlife in the Old Testament.* Downers Grove, IL: InterVarsity, 2002.

Keener, Craig S. *A Commentary on the Gospel of Matthew: A Socio-Rhetorical Commentary.* Grand Rapids: Eerdmans, 2009.

———. *The Gospel of John: A Commentary.* 2 vols. Peabody, MA: Hendrickson, 2003.

Keller, Timothy. *Prayer: Experiencing Awe and Intimacy with God.* New York: Dutton, 2014.

Kodell, Jerome. "The Word of God Grew: The Ecclesial Tendency of Logos in Acts 6,7; 12,24; 19,20." *Bib* 55 (1974): 505–19.

Kreitzer, Larry J. "Eschatology." *DPL* 253–69.

Ladd, George Eldon. *The Presence of the Future: The Eschatology of Biblical Realism.* Grand Rapids: Eerdmans, 1974.

LaRondelle, H. K. *The Israel of God in Prophecy.* Berrien Springs, MI: Andrews University Press, 1983.

Lietaert Peerbolte, L. J. *The Antecedents of Antichrist: A Traditio-Historical Study of the Earliest Christian Views on Eschatological Opponents.* JSJSup 49. Leiden: Brill, 1996.

Lundbom, Jack R. *Jeremiah 21–36.* AB 21B. New York: Doubleday, 2004.

Luther, Martin. *Luther's Works.* Vol. 54. Edited and translated by Theodore G. Tappert. Philadelphia: Fortress, 1967.

Manson, William. "Eschatology in the New Testament." In *Eschatology: Four Papers Read to the Society for the Study of Theology.* SJTOP 2. Edinburgh: Oliver & Boyd, 1953.

Marshall, I. H. *1 and 2 Thessalonians*. NCBC. Grand Rapids: Eerdmans, 1983.

Mathison, Keith A. *From Age to Age: The Unfolding of Biblical Eschatology*. Phillipsburg: P&R, 2009.

Mihalios, Stefanos. *The Danielic Eschatological Hour in the Johannine Literature*. LNTS 436. New York: T&T Clark, 2011.

Moo, Douglas J. *Galatians*. BECNT. Grand Rapids: Baker Academic, 2013.

———. "Jesus and the Authority of the Mosaic Law." *JSNT* 20 (1984): 3–49.

Moore, Russell. *Tempted and Tried: Temptation and the Triumph of Christ*. Wheaton: Crossway, 2011.

O'Brien, Peter T. *Colossians, Philemon*. WBC 44. Waco: Word, 1982.

———. *The Letter to the Ephesians*. PNTC. Grand Rapids: Eerdmans, 1999.

Pao, David W. *Acts and the Isaianic New Exodus*. Grand Rapids: Baker Academic, 2002.

———. *Colossians & Philemon*. ZECNT 12. Grand Rapids: Zondervan, 2012.

Pennington, Jonathan T. *Heaven and Earth in the Gospel of Matthew*. NovTSup 126. Leiden: Brill, 2007. Reprint, Grand Rapids: Baker Academic, 2009.

Peterson, David. *The Acts of the Apostles*. PNTC. Grand Rapids: Eerdmans, 2009.

Piper, John. *The Supremacy of God in Preaching*. Rev. ed. Grand Rapids: Baker Books, 2015.

Pitre, Brant. *Jesus, the Tribulation, and the End of the Exile: Restoration Eschatology and the Origin of the Atonement*. WUNT 204. Tübingen: Mohr Siebeck, 2005.

Poythress, Vern. *The Shadow of Christ in the Law of Moses*. Brentwood, TN: Wolgemuth & Hyatt, 1991.

Prigent, Pierre. *Apocalypse et liturgie*. CahT 52. Neuchâtel, Switzerland: Delachaux & Niestlé, 1964.

Ross, Allen P. *Recalling the Hope of Glory: Biblical Worship from the Garden to the New Creation*. Grand Rapids: Kregel, 2006.

Schmidt, K. L. "ἐκκλησία." *TDNT* 3:501–36.

Schnabel, Eckhard J. *Acts*. ZECNT. Grand Rapids: Zondervan, 2012.

Seebass, H. "אַחֲרִית *'achªrîth*." *TDOT* 1:207–12.

Smit, Joop F. M. "'What Is Apollos? What Is Paul?': In Search for the Coherence of First Corinthians 1:10–4:21." *NovT* 44 (2002): 231–51.

Thielman, Frank. *Theology of the New Testament: A Canonical and Synthetic Approach*. Grand Rapids: Zondervan, 2005.

Thiselton, Anthony C. *The First Epistle to the Corinthians: A Commentary on the Greek Text*. NIGTC. Grand Rapids: Eerdmans, 2000.

Thompson, Alan J. *The Acts of the Risen Lord Jesus: Luke's Account of God's Unfolding Plan*. NSBT 27. Downers Grove, IL: InterVarsity, 2011.

Wells, David F. *The Courage to Be Protestant: Truth-Lovers, Marketers, and Emergents in the Postmodern World*. Grand Rapids: Eerdmans, 2008.

Willis, John T. "The Expression *be'acharith hayyamim* in the Old Testament." *ResQ* 22 (1979): 54–71.

Witherington, Ben, III. *Conflict and Community in Corinth: A Socio-Rhetorical Commentary on 1 and 2 Corinthians*. Grand Rapids: Eerdmans, 1995.

Wright, N. T. *Jesus and the Victory of God*. Minneapolis: Fortress, 1996.

———. *The Resurrection of the Son of God*. Minneapolis: Fortress, 2003.

Author Index

Alexander, P. 130n22, 132
Alexander, T. D. 6n5, 77, 77n30
Allison, D. C., Jr. 3n1
Allison, G. 98
Aune, D. E. 3n1

Banks, R. 40n7, 40–41n8
Bauckham, R. F. 70n20, 102, 102n4
Beale, G. K. xii, xiiin1, 3n1, 5n4, 6n6, 6n7, 8n9,
    10n17, 21–22n5, 23n7, 23n8, 23n9, 24n10,
    24n11, 24n12, 24n13, 24–25n14, 25n16,
    26n17, 29n25, 33n29, 34, 41, 42n11, 44,
    45n15, 45n16, 47n20, 49n24, 50n27, 53n30,
    58, 62n1, 62n2, 63n4, 63n5, 64n7, 67n15,
    71n22, 79n1, 82n3, 87n9, 89n13, 91n15,
    94n18, 100n1, 101n3, 104n5, 117n1, 119n4,
    122n8, 123n9, 124n12, 125n13, 126n15,
    127n17, 128, 128n18, 128n19, 141n13, 154,
    154n4, 154n5, 154n6, 155n7, 156n8, 159n9,
    160n11, 161n12, 167n22, 168n24, 170
Bennett, A. 150n25, 151
Blaising, C. A. xiiin2
Block, D. I. 21n4
Blomberg, C. L. 42n12, 107n8
Bock, D. L. xiiin2
Brower, K. E. 3 unnumbered note
Bruce, F. F. 82n4

Cabaniss, A. 128n20
Carson, D. A. xiiin1, 40n7, 47n19, 48n23, 58,
    64n7, 67n15, 77, 77n30, 113, 136, 136n3,
    136n4, 137, 137n5, 137n6, 138n7, 139n9,
    140n10, 140n12, 147n22, 151
Chapell, B. 74–75n28, 78, 132

Chesterton, G. K. 100, 100n2
Ciampa, R. E. 67n15, 69n19, 144n17, 144–
    45n18, 145n20
Clowney, E. P. 35, 78
Collins, R. 107n8, 108n11
Cullmann, O. 9n14

deSilva, D. A. 66n11
Dever, M. 35, 130n22, 132
DeYoung, K. 168, 168n23, 169n25, 170
Dumbrell, W. J. 47n19
Dunn, J. D. G. 43n13

Edwards, J. 120, 120n6
Elliott, M. W. 3 unnumbered note

Fee, G. D. 72, 72n26, 73n27, 92n15, 108n11,
    145n19
Ferguson, E. 98
France, R. T. 41, 41n9, 140n12
Furfey, P. H. 87n10

Gentry, P. J. xiiin2, 20n3
Gilbert, G. 168, 168n23, 169n25, 170
Gladd, B. L. 33n29, 45n15, 49n24, 53n29,
    67n16, 79n1, 101n3, 105
Greidanus, S. 74n28, 78
Gundry, S. N. 40n6

Hamilton, J. M. 126n16
Harmon, M. S. 27n19, 28n22, 29n23, 57n32,
    63n5, 70n21, 71n24, 147n23, 148n24,
    162n14, 165n20, 166n21
Hays, R. B. 41n10, 56, 56n31, 67n13, 67n14

187

Scripture and Ancient Sources Index